Mometrix
TEST PREPARATION

ABCTE

Biology Exam

Secrets Study Guide

Dear Future Exam Success Story

First of all, **THANK YOU** for purchasing Mometrix study materials!

Second, congratulations! You are one of the few determined test-takers who are committed to doing whatever it takes to excel on your exam. **You have come to the right place.** We developed these study materials with one goal in mind: to deliver you the information you need in a format that's concise and easy to use.

In addition to optimizing your guide for the content of the test, we've outlined our recommended steps for breaking down the preparation process into small, attainable goals so you can make sure you stay on track.

We've also analyzed the entire test-taking process, identifying the most common pitfalls and showing how you can overcome them and be ready for any curveball the test throws you.

Standardized testing is one of the biggest obstacles on your road to success, which only increases the importance of doing well in the high-pressure, high-stakes environment of test day. Your results on this test could have a significant impact on your future, and this guide provides the information and practical advice to help you achieve your full potential on test day.

Your success is our success

We would love to hear from you! If you would like to share the story of your exam success or if you have any questions or comments in regard to our products, please contact us at **800-673-8175** or **support@mometrix.com**.

Thanks again for your business and we wish you continued success!

Sincerely,
The Mometrix Test Preparation Team

Need more help? Check out our flashcards at:
http://MometrixFlashcards.com/ABCTE

TABLE OF CONTENTS

Introduction

Thank you for purchasing this resource! You have made the choice to prepare yourself for a test that could have a huge impact on your future, and this guide is designed to help you be fully ready for test day. Obviously, it's important to have a solid understanding of the test material, but you also need to be prepared for the unique environment and stressors of the test, so that you can perform to the best of your abilities.

For this purpose, the first section that appears in this guide is the **Secret Keys**. We've devoted countless hours to meticulously researching what works and what doesn't, and we've boiled down our findings to the five most impactful steps you can take to improve your performance on the test. We start at the beginning with study planning and move through the preparation process, all the way to the testing strategies that will help you get the most out of what you know when you're finally sitting in front of the test.

We recommend that you start preparing for your test as far in advance as possible. However, if you've bought this guide as a last-minute study resource and only have a few days before your test, we recommend that you skip over the first two Secret Keys since they address a long-term study plan.

If you struggle with **test anxiety**, we strongly encourage you to check out our recommendations for how you can overcome it. Test anxiety is a formidable foe, but it can be beaten, and we want to make sure you have the tools you need to defeat it.

Secret Key #1 – Plan Big, Study Small

There's a lot riding on your performance. If you want to ace this test, you're going to need to keep your skills sharp and the material fresh in your mind. You need a plan that lets you review everything you need to know while still fitting in your schedule. We'll break this strategy down into three categories.

Information Organization

Start with the information you already have: the official test outline. From this, you can make a complete list of all the concepts you need to cover before the test. Organize these concepts into groups that can be studied together, and create a list of any related vocabulary you need to learn so you can brush up on any difficult terms. You'll want to keep this vocabulary list handy once you actually start studying since you may need to add to it along the way.

Time Management

Once you have your set of study concepts, decide how to spread them out over the time you have left before the test. Break your study plan into small, clear goals so you have a manageable task for each day and know exactly what you're doing. Then just focus on one small step at a time. When you manage your time this way, you don't need to spend hours at a time studying. Studying a small block of content for a short period each day helps you retain information better and avoid stressing over how much you have left to do. You can relax knowing that you have a plan to cover everything in time. In order for this strategy to be effective though, you have to start studying early and stick to your schedule. Avoid the exhaustion and futility that comes from last-minute cramming!

Study Environment

The environment you study in has a big impact on your learning. Studying in a coffee shop, while probably more enjoyable, is not likely to be as fruitful as studying in a quiet room. It's important to keep distractions to a minimum. You're only planning to study for a short block of time, so make the most of it. Don't pause to check your phone or get up to find a snack. It's also important to **avoid multitasking**. Research has consistently shown that multitasking will make your studying dramatically less effective. Your study area should also be comfortable and well-lit so you don't have the distraction of straining your eyes or sitting on an uncomfortable chair.

The time of day you study is also important. You want to be rested and alert. Don't wait until just before bedtime. Study when you'll be most likely to comprehend and remember. Even better, if you know what time of day your test will be, set that time aside for study. That way your brain will be used to working on that subject at that specific time and you'll have a better chance of recalling information.

Finally, it can be helpful to team up with others who are studying for the same test. Your actual studying should be done in as isolated an environment as possible, but the work of organizing the information and setting up the study plan can be divided up. In between study sessions, you can discuss with your teammates the concepts that you're all studying and quiz each other on the details. Just be sure that your teammates are as serious about the test as you are. If you find that your study time is being replaced with social time, you might need to find a new team.

Secret Key #2 – Make Your Studying Count

You're devoting a lot of time and effort to preparing for this test, so you want to be absolutely certain it will pay off. This means doing more than just reading the content and hoping you can remember it on test day. It's important to make every minute of study count. There are two main areas you can focus on to make your studying count.

Retention

It doesn't matter how much time you study if you can't remember the material. You need to make sure you are retaining the concepts. To check your retention of the information you're learning, try recalling it at later times with minimal prompting. Try carrying around flashcards and glance at one or two from time to time or ask a friend who's also studying for the test to quiz you.

To enhance your retention, look for ways to put the information into practice so that you can apply it rather than simply recalling it. If you're using the information in practical ways, it will be much easier to remember. Similarly, it helps to solidify a concept in your mind if you're not only reading it to yourself but also explaining it to someone else. Ask a friend to let you teach them about a concept you're a little shaky on (or speak aloud to an imaginary audience if necessary). As you try to summarize, define, give examples, and answer your friend's questions, you'll understand the concepts better and they will stay with you longer. Finally, step back for a big picture view and ask yourself how each piece of information fits with the whole subject. When you link the different concepts together and see them working together as a whole, it's easier to remember the individual components.

Finally, practice showing your work on any multi-step problems, even if you're just studying. Writing out each step you take to solve a problem will help solidify the process in your mind, and you'll be more likely to remember it during the test.

Modality

Modality simply refers to the means or method by which you study. Choosing a study modality that fits your own individual learning style is crucial. No two people learn best in exactly the same way, so it's important to know your strengths and use them to your advantage.

For example, if you learn best by visualization, focus on visualizing a concept in your mind and draw an image or a diagram. Try color-coding your notes, illustrating them, or creating symbols that will trigger your mind to recall a learned concept. If you learn best by hearing or discussing information, find a study partner who learns the same way or read aloud to yourself. Think about how to put the information in your own words. Imagine that you are giving a lecture on the topic and record yourself so you can listen to it later.

For any learning style, flashcards can be helpful. Organize the information so you can take advantage of spare moments to review. Underline key words or phrases. Use different colors for different categories. Mnemonic devices (such as creating a short list in which every item starts with the same letter) can also help with retention. Find what works best for you and use it to store the information in your mind most effectively and easily.

Secret Key #3 – Practice the Right Way

Your success on test day depends not only on how many hours you put into preparing, but also on whether you prepared the right way. It's good to check along the way to see if your studying is paying off. One of the most effective ways to do this is by taking practice tests to evaluate your progress. Practice tests are useful because they show exactly where you need to improve. Every time you take a practice test, pay special attention to these three groups of questions:

- The questions you got wrong
- The questions you had to guess on, even if you guessed right
- The questions you found difficult or slow to work through

This will show you exactly what your weak areas are, and where you need to devote more study time. Ask yourself why each of these questions gave you trouble. Was it because you didn't understand the material? Was it because you didn't remember the vocabulary? Do you need more repetitions on this type of question to build speed and confidence? Dig into those questions and figure out how you can strengthen your weak areas as you go back to review the material.

Additionally, many practice tests have a section explaining the answer choices. It can be tempting to read the explanation and think that you now have a good understanding of the concept. However, an explanation likely only covers part of the question's broader context. Even if the explanation makes perfect sense, **go back and investigate** every concept related to the question until you're positive you have a thorough understanding.

As you go along, keep in mind that the practice test is just that: practice. Memorizing these questions and answers will not be very helpful on the actual test because it is unlikely to have any of the same exact questions. If you only know the right answers to the sample questions, you won't be prepared for the real thing. **Study the concepts** until you understand them fully, and then you'll be able to answer any question that shows up on the test.

It's important to wait on the practice tests until you're ready. If you take a test on your first day of study, you may be overwhelmed by the amount of material covered and how much you need to learn. Work up to it gradually.

On test day, you'll need to be prepared for answering questions, managing your time, and using the test-taking strategies you've learned. It's a lot to balance, like a mental marathon that will have a big impact on your future. Like training for a marathon, you'll need to start slowly and work your way up. When test day arrives, you'll be ready.

Start with the strategies you've read in the first two Secret Keys—plan your course and study in the way that works best for you. If you have time, consider using multiple study resources to get different approaches to the same concepts. It can be helpful to see difficult concepts from more than one angle. Then find a good source for practice tests. Many times, the test website will suggest potential study resources or provide sample tests.

Practice Test Strategy

If you're able to find at least three practice tests, we recommend this strategy:

Untimed and Open-Book Practice

Take the first test with no time constraints and with your notes and study guide handy. Take your time and focus on applying the strategies you've learned.

Timed and Open-Book Practice

Take the second practice test open-book as well, but set a timer and practice pacing yourself to finish in time.

Timed and Closed-Book Practice

Take any other practice tests as if it were test day. Set a timer and put away your study materials. Sit at a table or desk in a quiet room, imagine yourself at the testing center, and answer questions as quickly and accurately as possible.

Keep repeating timed and closed-book tests on a regular basis until you run out of practice tests or it's time for the actual test. Your mind will be ready for the schedule and stress of test day, and you'll be able to focus on recalling the material you've learned.

Secret Key #4 – Pace Yourself

Once you're fully prepared for the material on the test, your biggest challenge on test day will be managing your time. Just knowing that the clock is ticking can make you panic even if you have plenty of time left. Work on pacing yourself so you can build confidence against the time constraints of the exam. Pacing is a difficult skill to master, especially in a high-pressure environment, so **practice is vital**.

Set time expectations for your pace based on how much time is available. For example, if a section has 60 questions and the time limit is 30 minutes, you know you have to average 30 seconds or less per question in order to answer them all. Although 30 seconds is the hard limit, set 25 seconds per question as your goal, so you reserve extra time to spend on harder questions. When you budget extra time for the harder questions, you no longer have any reason to stress when those questions take longer to answer.

Don't let this time expectation distract you from working through the test at a calm, steady pace, but keep it in mind so you don't spend too much time on any one question. Recognize that taking extra time on one question you don't understand may keep you from answering two that you do understand later in the test. If your time limit for a question is up and you're still not sure of the answer, mark it and move on, and come back to it later if the time and the test format allow. If the testing format doesn't allow you to return to earlier questions, just make an educated guess; then put it out of your mind and move on.

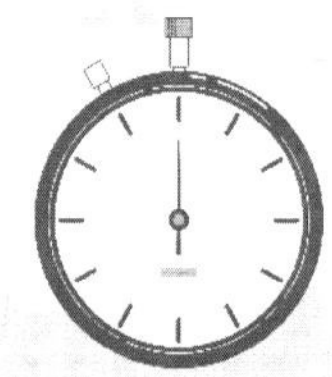

On the easier questions, be careful not to rush. It may seem wise to hurry through them so you have more time for the challenging ones, but it's not worth missing one if you know the concept and just didn't take the time to read the question fully. Work efficiently but make sure you understand the question and have looked at all of the answer choices, since more than one may seem right at first.

Even if you're paying attention to the time, you may find yourself a little behind at some point. You should speed up to get back on track, but do so wisely. Don't panic; just take a few seconds less on each question until you're caught up. Don't guess without thinking, but do look through the answer choices and eliminate any you know are wrong. If you can get down to two choices, it is often worthwhile to guess from those. Once you've chosen an answer, move on and don't dwell on any that you skipped or had to hurry through. If a question was taking too long, chances are it was one of the harder ones, so you weren't as likely to get it right anyway.

On the other hand, if you find yourself getting ahead of schedule, it may be beneficial to slow down a little. The more quickly you work, the more likely you are to make a careless mistake that will affect your score. You've budgeted time for each question, so don't be afraid to spend that time. Practice an efficient but careful pace to get the most out of the time you have.

Secret Key #5 – Have a Plan for Guessing

When you're taking the test, you may find yourself stuck on a question. Some of the answer choices seem better than others, but you don't see the one answer choice that is obviously correct. What do you do?

The scenario described above is very common, yet most test takers have not effectively prepared for it. Developing and practicing a plan for guessing may be one of the single most effective uses of your time as you get ready for the exam.

In developing your plan for guessing, there are three questions to address:

- When should you start the guessing process?
- How should you narrow down the choices?
- Which answer should you choose?

When to Start the Guessing Process

Unless your plan for guessing is to select C every time (which, despite its merits, is not what we recommend), you need to leave yourself enough time to apply your answer elimination strategies. Since you have a limited amount of time for each question, that means that if you're going to give yourself the best shot at guessing correctly, you have to decide quickly whether or not you will guess.

Of course, the best-case scenario is that you don't have to guess at all, so first, see if you can answer the question based on your knowledge of the subject and basic reasoning skills. Focus on the key words in the question and try to jog your memory of related topics. Give yourself a chance to bring the knowledge to mind, but once you realize that you don't have (or you can't access) the knowledge you need to answer the question, it's time to start the guessing process.

It's almost always better to start the guessing process too early than too late. It only takes a few seconds to remember something and answer the question from knowledge. Carefully eliminating wrong answer choices takes longer. Plus, going through the process of eliminating answer choices can actually help jog your memory.

Summary: Start the guessing process as soon as you decide that you can't answer the question based on your knowledge.

How to Narrow Down the Choices

The next chapter in this book (**Test-Taking Strategies**) includes a wide range of strategies for how to approach questions and how to look for answer choices to eliminate. You will definitely want to read those carefully, practice them, and figure out which ones work best for you. Here though, we're going to address a mindset rather than a particular strategy.

Your odds of guessing an answer correctly depend on how many options you are choosing from.

Number of options left	5	4	3	2	1
Odds of guessing correctly	20%	25%	33%	50%	100%

You can see from this chart just how valuable it is to be able to eliminate incorrect answers and make an educated guess, but there are two things that many test takers do that cause them to miss out on the benefits of guessing:

- Accidentally eliminating the correct answer
- Selecting an answer based on an impression

We'll look at the first one here, and the second one in the next section.

To avoid accidentally eliminating the correct answer, we recommend a thought exercise called **the $5 challenge**. In this challenge, you only eliminate an answer choice from contention if you are willing to bet $5 on it being wrong. Why $5? Five dollars is a small but not insignificant amount of money. It's an amount you could afford to lose but wouldn't want to throw away. And while losing $5 once might not hurt too much, doing it twenty times will set you back $100. In the same way, each small decision you make—eliminating a choice here, guessing on a question there—won't by itself impact your score very much, but when you put them all together, they can make a big difference. By holding each answer choice elimination decision to a higher standard, you can reduce the risk of accidentally eliminating the correct answer.

The $5 challenge can also be applied in a positive sense: If you are willing to bet $5 that an answer choice *is* correct, go ahead and mark it as correct.

Summary: Only eliminate an answer choice if you are willing to bet $5 that it is wrong.

Which Answer to Choose

You're taking the test. You've run into a hard question and decided you'll have to guess. You've eliminated all the answer choices you're willing to bet $5 on. Now you have to pick an answer. Why do we even need to talk about this? Why can't you just pick whichever one you feel like when the time comes?

The answer to these questions is that if you don't come into the test with a plan, you'll rely on your impression to select an answer choice, and if you do that, you risk falling into a trap. The test writers know that everyone who takes their test will be guessing on some of the questions, so they intentionally write wrong answer choices to seem plausible. You still have to pick an answer though, and if the wrong answer choices are designed to look right, how can you ever be sure that you're not falling for their trap? The best solution we've found to this dilemma is to take the decision out of your hands entirely. Here is the process we recommend:

Once you've eliminated any choices that you are confident (willing to bet $5) are wrong, select the first remaining choice as your answer.

Whether you choose to select the first remaining choice, the second, or the last, the important thing is that you use some preselected standard. Using this approach guarantees that you will not be enticed into selecting an answer choice that looks right, because you are not basing your decision on how the answer choices look.

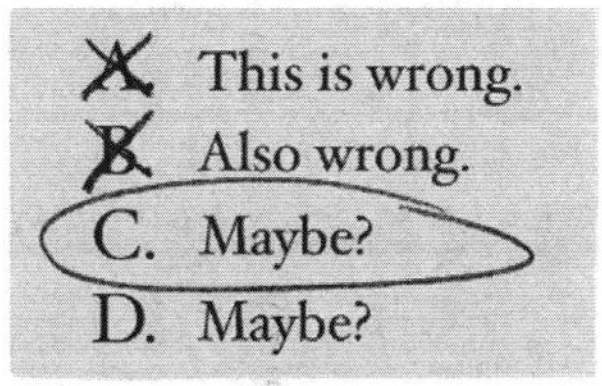

This is not meant to make you question your knowledge. Instead, it is to help you recognize the difference between your knowledge and your impressions. There's a huge difference between thinking an answer is right because of what you know, and thinking an answer is right because it looks or sounds like it should be right.

Summary: To ensure that your selection is appropriately random, make a predetermined selection from among all answer choices you have not eliminated.

Test-Taking Strategies

This section contains a list of test-taking strategies that you may find helpful as you work through the test. By taking what you know and applying logical thought, you can maximize your chances of answering any question correctly!

It is very important to realize that every question is different and every person is different: no single strategy will work on every question, and no single strategy will work for every person. That's why we've included all of them here, so you can try them out and determine which ones work best for different types of questions and which ones work best for you.

Question Strategies

☑ Read Carefully

Read the question and the answer choices carefully. Don't miss the question because you misread the terms. You have plenty of time to read each question thoroughly and make sure you understand what is being asked. Yet a happy medium must be attained, so don't waste too much time. You must read carefully and efficiently.

☑ Contextual Clues

Look for contextual clues. If the question includes a word you are not familiar with, look at the immediate context for some indication of what the word might mean. Contextual clues can often give you all the information you need to decipher the meaning of an unfamiliar word. Even if you can't determine the meaning, you may be able to narrow down the possibilities enough to make a solid guess at the answer to the question.

☑ Prefixes

If you're having trouble with a word in the question or answer choices, try dissecting it. Take advantage of every clue that the word might include. Prefixes can be a huge help. Usually, they allow you to determine a basic meaning. *Pre-* means before, *post-* means after, *pro-* is positive, *de-* is negative. From prefixes, you can get an idea of the general meaning of the word and try to put it into context.

☑ Hedge Words

Watch out for critical hedge words, such as *likely, may, can, often, almost, mostly, usually, generally, rarely,* and *sometimes.* Question writers insert these hedge phrases to cover every possibility. Often an answer choice will be wrong simply because it leaves no room for exception. Be on guard for answer choices that have definitive words such as *exactly* and *always.*

☑ Switchback Words

Stay alert for *switchbacks.* These are the words and phrases frequently used to alert you to shifts in thought. The most common switchback words are *but, although,* and *however.* Others include *nevertheless, on the other hand, even though, while, in spite of, despite,* and *regardless of.* Switchback words are important to catch because they can change the direction of the question or an answer choice.

☑ Face Value

When in doubt, use common sense. Accept the situation in the problem at face value. Don't read too much into it. These problems will not require you to make wild assumptions. If you have to go beyond creativity and warp time or space in order to have an answer choice fit the question, then you should move on and consider the other answer choices. These are normal problems rooted in reality. The applicable relationship or explanation may not be readily apparent, but it is there for you to figure out. Use your common sense to interpret anything that isn't clear.

Answer Choice Strategies

ANSWER SELECTION

The most thorough way to pick an answer choice is to identify and eliminate wrong answers until only one is left, then confirm it is the correct answer. Sometimes an answer choice may immediately seem right, but be careful. The test writers will usually put more than one reasonable answer choice on each question, so take a second to read all of them and make sure that the other choices are not equally obvious. As long as you have time left, it is better to read every answer choice than to pick the first one that looks right without checking the others.

ANSWER CHOICE FAMILIES

An answer choice family consists of two (in rare cases, three) answer choices that are very similar in construction and cannot all be true at the same time. If you see two answer choices that are direct opposites or parallels, one of them is usually the correct answer. For instance, if one answer choice says that quantity *x* increases and another either says that quantity *x* decreases (opposite) or says that quantity *y* increases (parallel), then those answer choices would fall into the same family. An answer choice that doesn't match the construction of the answer choice family is more likely to be incorrect. Most questions will not have answer choice families, but when they do appear, you should be prepared to recognize them.

ELIMINATE ANSWERS

Eliminate answer choices as soon as you realize they are wrong, but make sure you consider all possibilities. If you are eliminating answer choices and realize that the last one you are left with is also wrong, don't panic. Start over and consider each choice again. There may be something you missed the first time that you will realize on the second pass.

AVOID FACT TRAPS

Don't be distracted by an answer choice that is factually true but doesn't answer the question. You are looking for the choice that answers the question. Stay focused on what the question is asking for so you don't accidentally pick an answer that is true but incorrect. Always go back to the question and make sure the answer choice you've selected actually answers the question and is not merely a true statement.

EXTREME STATEMENTS

In general, you should avoid answers that put forth extreme actions as standard practice or proclaim controversial ideas as established fact. An answer choice that states the "process should be used in certain situations, if..." is much more likely to be correct than one that states the "process should be discontinued completely." The first is a calm rational statement and doesn't even make a definitive, uncompromising stance, using a hedge word *if* to provide wiggle room, whereas the second choice is far more extreme.

BENCHMARK

As you read through the answer choices and you come across one that seems to answer the question well, mentally select that answer choice. This is not your final answer, but it's the one that will help you evaluate the other answer choices. The one that you selected is your benchmark or standard for judging each of the other answer choices. Every other answer choice must be compared to your benchmark. That choice is correct until proven otherwise by another answer choice beating it. If you find a better answer, then that one becomes your new benchmark. Once you've decided that no other choice answers the question as well as your benchmark, you have your final answer.

✓ PREDICT THE ANSWER

Before you even start looking at the answer choices, it is often best to try to predict the answer. When you come up with the answer on your own, it is easier to avoid distractions and traps because you will know exactly what to look for. The right answer choice is unlikely to be word-for-word what you came up with, but it should be a close match. Even if you are confident that you have the right answer, you should still take the time to read each option before moving on.

General Strategies

✓ TOUGH QUESTIONS

If you are stumped on a problem or it appears too hard or too difficult, don't waste time. Move on! Remember though, if you can quickly check for obviously incorrect answer choices, your chances of guessing correctly are greatly improved. Before you completely give up, at least try to knock out a couple of possible answers. Eliminate what you can and then guess at the remaining answer choices before moving on.

✓ CHECK YOUR WORK

Since you will probably not know every term listed and the answer to every question, it is important that you get credit for the ones that you do know. Don't miss any questions through careless mistakes. If at all possible, try to take a second to look back over your answer selection and make sure you've selected the correct answer choice and haven't made a costly careless mistake (such as marking an answer choice that you didn't mean to mark). This quick double check should more than pay for itself in caught mistakes for the time it costs.

✓ PACE YOURSELF

It's easy to be overwhelmed when you're looking at a page full of questions; your mind is confused and full of random thoughts, and the clock is ticking down faster than you would like. Calm down and maintain the pace that you have set for yourself. Especially as you get down to the last few minutes of the test, don't let the small numbers on the clock make you panic. As long as you are on track by monitoring your pace, you are guaranteed to have time for each question.

✓ DON'T RUSH

It is very easy to make errors when you are in a hurry. Maintaining a fast pace in answering questions is pointless if it makes you miss questions that you would have gotten right otherwise. Test writers like to include distracting information and wrong answers that seem right. Taking a little extra time to avoid careless mistakes can make all the difference in your test score. Find a pace that allows you to be confident in the answers that you select.

✓ KEEP MOVING

Panicking will not help you pass the test, so do your best to stay calm and keep moving. Taking deep breaths and going through the answer elimination steps you practiced can help to break through a stress barrier and keep your pace.

Final Notes

The combination of a solid foundation of content knowledge and the confidence that comes from practicing your plan for applying that knowledge is the key to maximizing your performance on test day. As your foundation of content knowledge is built up and strengthened, you'll find that the strategies included in this chapter become more and more effective in helping you quickly sift through the distractions and traps of the test to isolate the correct answer.

Now that you're preparing to move forward into the test content chapters of this book, be sure to keep your goal in mind. As you read, think about how you will be able to apply this information on the test. If you've already seen sample questions for the test and you have an idea of the question format and style, try to come up with questions of your own that you can answer based on what you're reading. This will give you valuable practice applying your knowledge in the same ways you can expect to on test day.

Good luck and good studying!

General Science Knowledge

Physics

Laws of Thermodynamics

The **laws of thermodynamics** are generalized principles dealing with energy and heat.

- The **zeroth law** of thermodynamics states that two objects in thermodynamic equilibrium with a third object are also in equilibrium with each other. Being in thermodynamic equilibrium basically means that different objects are at the same temperature.
- The **first law** deals with conservation of energy. It states that neither mass nor energy can be destroyed; only converted from one form to another.
- The **second law** states that the entropy (the amount of energy in a system that is no longer available for work or the amount of disorder in a system) of an isolated system can only increase. The second law also states that heat is not transferred from a lower-temperature system to a higher-temperature one unless additional work is done.
- The **third law** of thermodynamics states that as temperature approaches absolute zero, entropy approaches a constant minimum. It also states that a system cannot be cooled to absolute zero.

Review Video: Laws of Thermodynamics
Visit mometrix.com/academy and enter code: 253607

Heat and Temperature

Heat is energy transfer (other than direct work) from one body or system to another due to thermal contact. Everything tends to become less organized and less orderly over time (**entropy**). In all energy transfers, therefore, the overall result is that the energy is spread out uniformly. This transfer of heat energy from hotter to cooler objects is accomplished by conduction, radiation, or convection. **Temperature** is a measurement of an object's stored heat energy. More specifically, temperature is the average kinetic energy of an object's particles. When the temperature of an object increases and its atoms move faster, kinetic energy also increases. Temperature is not energy since it changes and is not conserved. Thermometers are used to measure temperature.

Review Video: What is the Difference between Heat and Temperature?
Visit mometrix.com/academy and enter code: 879095

Mass, Weight, Volume, Density, and Specific Gravity

- **Mass** — Mass is a measure of the amount of substance in an object.
- **Weight** — Weight is a measure of the gravitational pull of Earth on an object.
- **Volume** — Volume is a measure of the amount of space occupied. There are many formulas to determine volume. For example, the volume of a cube is the length of one side cubed (a^3) and the volume of a rectangular prism is length times width times height ($l \times w \times h$). The volume of an irregular shape can be determined by how much water it displaces.
- **Density** — Density is a measure of the amount of mass per unit volume. The formula to find density is mass divided by volume (D = m/V). It is expressed in terms of mass per cubic unit (e.g., grams per cubic centimeter $\frac{g}{cm^3}$).
- **Specific gravity** — This is a measure of the ratio of a substance's density compared to the density of water.

Review Video: Mass, Weight, Volume, Density, and Specific Gravity
Visit mometrix.com/academy and enter code: 920570

THERMAL CONTACT

Thermal contact refers to energy transferred to a body by a means other than work. A system in thermal contact with another can exchange energy with it through the process of heat transfer. Thermal contact does not necessarily involve direct physical contact. **Heat** is energy that can be transferred from one body or system to another without work being done. Everything tends to become less organized and less useful over time (entropy). In all energy transfers, therefore, the overall result is that the heat is spread out so that objects are in thermodynamic equilibrium and the heat can no longer be transferred without additional work.

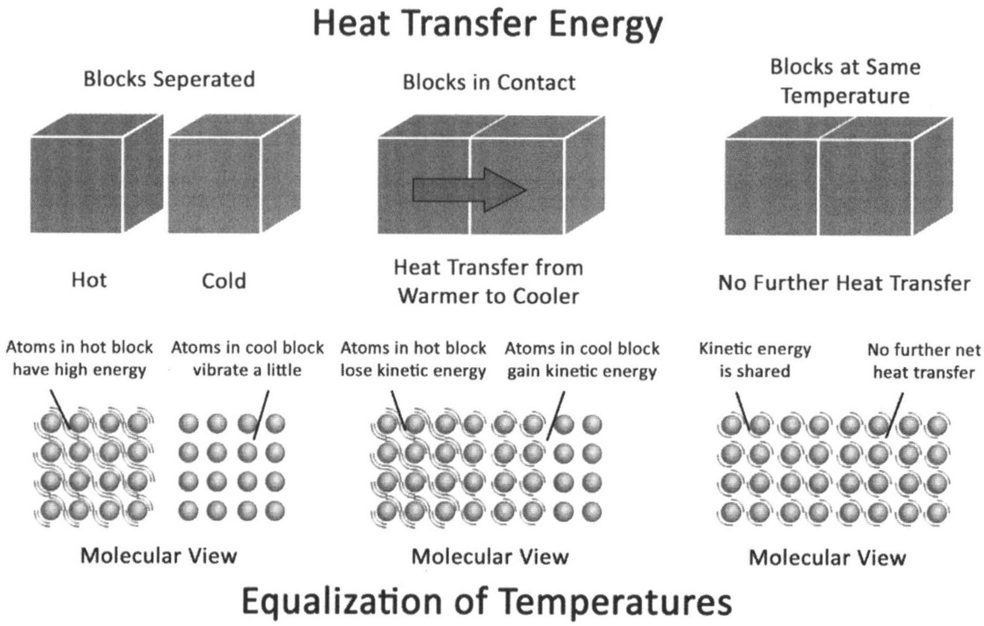

MODELS FOR FLOW OF ELECTRIC CHARGE

Models that can be used to explain the **flow of electric current, potential, and circuits** include water, gravity, and roller coasters. For example, just as a mass can have a potential for energy based on its location, so can a charge within an electrical field. Just as a force is required to move an object uphill, a force is also required to move a charge from a low to high potential. Another example is water. Water does not flow when it is level. If it is lifted to a point and then placed on a downward path, it will flow. A roller coaster car requires work to be performed to transport it to a point where it has potential energy (the top of a hill). Once there, gravity provides the force for it to flow (move) downward. If either path is broken, the flow or movement stops or is not completed.

ATOMIC STRUCTURES

MAGNETIC FIELDS

The motions of subatomic structures (nuclei and electrons) produce a **magnetic field**. It is the direction of the spin and orbit that indicates the direction of the field. The strength of a magnetic field is known as the **magnetic moment**. As electrons spin and orbit a nucleus, they produce a magnetic field. Pairs of electrons that spin and orbit in opposite directions cancel each other out, creating a net magnetic field of zero. Materials that have an unpaired electron are magnetic. Those with a weak attractive force are referred to as paramagnetic materials, while ferromagnetic materials have a strong attractive force. A diamagnetic material has electrons that are paired and, therefore, does not typically have a magnetic moment. There are, however, some diamagnetic materials that have a weak magnetic field.

Electric Charges

The attractive force between the electrons and the nucleus is called the **electric force.** A positive (+) charge or a negative (−) charge creates a field of sorts in the empty space around it, which is known as an **electric field**. The direction of a positive charge is away from the electric field and the direction of a negative charge is towards it. An electron within the force of the field is pulled towards a positive charge because an electron has a negative charge. A particle with a positive charge is pushed away, or repelled, by another positive charge. Like charges repel each other and opposite charges attract. Lines of force show the paths of charges. The **electric force** between two objects is directly proportional to the product of the charge magnitudes and inversely proportional to the square of the distance between the two objects. **Electric charge** is measured with the unit Coulomb (C). It is the amount of charge moved in one second by a steady current of one ampere ($1C = 1A \times 1s$).

> **Review Video: Electric Charge**
> Visit mometrix.com/academy and enter code: 323587

Electric Current Movement Through Circuits

Electric current is the sustained flow of electric charge along a path in a circuit. This differs from a static electric charge, which is a constant non-moving charge rather than a continuous flow. The **rate of flow of electric charge** is expressed using the ampere (amp or A) and can be measured using an ammeter. A current of 1 ampere means that 1 coulomb of charge passes through a given area every second. Electric charges typically only move from areas of high electric potential to areas of low electric potential. To get charges to flow into a high potential area, you must connect it to an area of higher potential by introducing a battery or other voltage source.

Simple Circuits

Movement of electric charge along a path between areas of high electric potential and low electric potential, with a resistor or load device between them, is the definition of a **simple circuit**. It is a closed conducting path between the high and low potential points, such as the positive and negative terminals on a battery. One example of a circuit is the flow from one terminal of a car battery to the other. The electrolyte solution of water and sulfuric acid provides work in chemical form to start the flow. A frequently used classroom example of circuits involves using a D cell (1.5 V) battery, a small light bulb, and a piece of copper wire to create a circuit to light the bulb.

> **Review Video: Resistance of Electric Currents**
> Visit mometrix.com/academy and enter code: 668423

Magnets

A **magnet** is any object or material, such as iron, steel, or magnetite (lodestone), that can affect another substance within its **field of force** that has like characteristics. Magnets can either attract or repel other substances. Magnets have two **poles**: north and south. Like poles repel and opposite poles (pairs of north and south) attract. The magnetic field is a set of invisible lines representing the paths of attraction and repulsion. Magnetism can occur naturally, or ferromagnetic materials can be magnetized. Certain matter that is magnetized can retain its magnetic properties indefinitely and become a permanent magnet. Other matter can lose its magnetic properties. For example, an iron nail can be temporarily magnetized by stroking it repeatedly in the same direction using one pole of another magnet. Once magnetized, it can attract or repel other magnetically inclined materials, such as paper clips. Dropping the nail repeatedly will cause it to lose its charge.

> **Review Video: Magnets**
> Visit mometrix.com/academy and enter code: 570803

Magnetic Fields, Current, and Magnetic Domains

A **magnetic field** can be formed not only by a magnetic material, but also by electric current flowing through a wire. When a coiled wire is attached to the two ends of a battery, for example, an electromagnet can be formed by inserting a ferromagnetic material such as an iron bar within the coil. When electric current flows through the wire, the bar becomes a magnet. If there is no current, the magnetism is lost. A **magnetic domain** occurs when the magnetic fields of atoms are grouped and aligned. These groups form what can be thought of as miniature magnets within a material. This is what happens when an object like an iron nail is temporarily magnetized. Prior to magnetization, the organization of atoms and their various polarities are somewhat random with respect to where the north and south poles are pointing. After magnetization, a significant percentage of the poles are lined up in one direction, which is what causes the magnetic force exerted by the material.

Motion and Displacement

Motion is a change in the location of an object and is the result of an unbalanced net force acting on the object. Understanding motion requires an understanding of three basic quantities: displacement, velocity, and acceleration.

When something moves from one place to another, it has undergone **displacement**. Displacement along a straight line is a very simple example of a vector quantity. If an object travels from position $x = -5$ cm to $x = 5$ cm, it has undergone a displacement of 10 cm. If it traverses the same path in the opposite direction, its displacement is -10 cm. A vector that spans the object's displacement in the direction of travel is known as a displacement vector.

Review Video: Displacement, Velocity, and Acceleration
Visit mometrix.com/academy and enter code: 671849

Review Video: Displacement in Physics
Visit mometrix.com/academy and enter code: 236197

Gravitational Force

Gravitational force is a universal force that causes every object to exert a force on every other object. The gravitational force between two objects can be described by the formula, $F = Gm_1m_2/r^2$, where m_1 and m_2 are the masses of two objects, r is the distance between them, and G is the gravitational constant, $G = 6.672 \times 10^{-11}\ \text{N m}^2/\text{kg}^2$. In order for this force to have a noticeable effect, one or both of the objects must be extremely large, so the equation is generally only used in problems involving planetary bodies. For problems involving objects on the earth being affected by earth's gravitational pull, the force of gravity is simply calculated as $F = mg$, where g is 9.81 m/s^2 toward the ground.

Review Video: Newton's Law of Gravitation
Visit mometrix.com/academy and enter code: 709086

Newton's First Two Laws of Motion

Newton's First Law

An object at rest or in motion will remain at rest or in motion unless acted upon by an external force.

This phenomenon is commonly referred to as **inertia**, the tendency of a body to remain in its present state of motion. In order for the body's state of motion to change, it must be acted on by an unbalanced force.

Review Video: Newton's First Law of Motion
Visit mometrix.com/academy and enter code: 590367

Newton's Second Law

An object's acceleration is **directly proportional** to the net force acting on the object and **inversely proportional** to the object's mass.

This law is generally written in equation form $F = ma$, where F is the net force acting on a body, m is the mass of the body, and a is its acceleration. Note that since the mass is always a positive quantity, the acceleration is always in the same direction as the force.

Review Video: Newton's Second Law of Motion
Visit mometrix.com/academy and enter code: 737975

Simple Machines

Simple machines include the inclined plane, lever, wheel and axle, and pulley. These simple machines have no internal source of energy. More complex or compound machines can be formed from them. Simple machines provide a mechanical advantage to make it easier to accomplish a task. The **inclined plane** enables a force less than the object's weight to be used to push an object to a greater height. A **lever** enables a multiplication of force. The wheel and axle allows for movement with less resistance. Single or double **pulleys** allow for easier direction of force. The wedge and screw are forms of the inclined plane. A **wedge** turns a smaller force working over a greater distance into a larger force. The **screw** is similar to an incline that is wrapped around a shaft.

Review Video: Simple Machines
Visit mometrix.com/academy and enter code: 950789

Review Video: Simple Machines - Wheel and Axle
Visit mometrix.com/academy and enter code: 574045

Friction

Friction is a force that arises as a **resistance to motion** where two surfaces are in contact. The maximum magnitude of the frictional force (f) can be calculated as $f = F_c\mu$, where F_c is the contact force between the two objects and μ is a coefficient of friction based on the surfaces' material composition. Two types of friction are static and kinetic. To illustrate these concepts, imagine a book resting on a table. The force of its weight (W) is equal and opposite to the force of the table on the book, or the normal force (N). If we exert a small force (F) on the book, attempting to push it to one side, a frictional force (f) would arise, equal and opposite to our force. At this point, it is a **static frictional force** because the book is not moving. If we increase our force on the book, we will eventually cause it to move. At this point, the frictional force opposing us will be a **kinetic frictional force**. Generally, the kinetic frictional force is lower than static frictional force (because the frictional coefficient for static friction is larger), which means that the amount of force needed to maintain the movement of the book will be less than what was needed to start it moving.

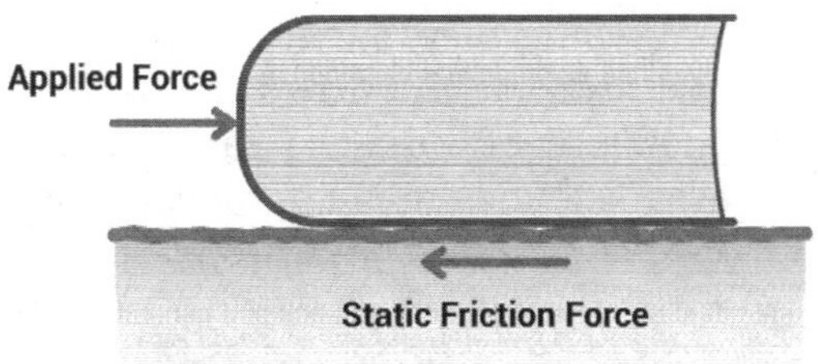

Review Video: Friction
Visit mometrix.com/academy and enter code: 716782

Review Video: Push and Pull Forces
Visit mometrix.com/academy and enter code: 104731

SOUND

Sound is a pressure disturbance that moves through a medium in the form of mechanical waves, which transfer energy from one particle to the next. Sound requires a medium to travel through, such as air, water, or other matter since it is the chain reaction of collisions that transfers energy to adjacent particles, not the actual movement of particles over a great distance. Sound is transferred through the movement of particles, which can be atoms or molecules. Waves of sound energy move outward in all directions from the source. Sound waves consist of compressions (particles are forced together) and rarefactions (particles move farther apart and their density decreases). A wavelength consists of one compression and one rarefaction. Different sounds have different wavelengths. Sound is a form of kinetic energy.

Review Video: Sound
Visit mometrix.com/academy and enter code: 562378

PITCH, LOUDNESS, SOUND INTENSITY, TIMBRE, AND OSCILLATION

Pitch — Pitch is the quality of sound determined by frequency. For example, a musical note can be tuned to a specific frequency. A, for instance, has a frequency of 440 Hz, which is a higher frequency than middle C. Humans can detect frequencies between about 20 Hz to 20,000 Hz.

Loudness — Loudness is a human's perception of sound intensity.

Sound intensity — Sound intensity is measured as the sound power per unit area and can be expressed in decibels.

Timbre — This is a human's perception of the type or quality of sound.

Oscillation — This is a measurement, usually of time, against a basic value, equilibrium, or rest point.

DOPPLER EFFECT

The **Doppler effect** refers to the effect the relative motion of the source of the wave and the location of the observer has on waves. The Doppler effect is easily observable in sound waves. What a person hears when a train approaches or a car honking its horn passes by are examples of the Doppler effect. The pitch of the sound is different not because the *emitted frequency* has changed, but because the *received frequency* has changed. The frequency is higher (as is the pitch) as the train approaches, the same as emitted just as it passes, and lower as the train moves away. This is because the wavelength changes. The Doppler effect can occur when an observer is stationary, and can also occur when two trains approach and pass each other. **Electromagnetic waves** are also affected in this manner. The motion of the medium can also affect the wave. For waves that do not travel in a medium, such as light waves, it is the difference in velocity that determines the outcome.

WAVES

Waves have energy and can transfer energy when they interact with matter. Although waves transfer energy, they do not transport matter. The two basic categories of waves are mechanical and electromagnetic. Mechanical waves are a disturbance of matter that transfers energy from one particle to an adjacent particle. There are many types of mechanical waves, including sound, seismic, and water. **Electromagnetic waves can transmit energy through a vacuum like visible light, microwaves, and radio waves**. A **transverse wave** provides a good illustration of the features of a wave, which include crests, troughs, amplitude, and wavelength.

ELECTROMAGNETIC SPECTRUM

The electromagnetic spectrum is defined by frequency (f) and wavelength (λ). Frequency is typically measured in hertz and wavelength is usually measured in meters. Because light travels at a fairly constant speed, frequency is inversely proportional to wavelength, a relationship expressed by the formula $f = c/\lambda$, where c is the speed of light (about 3.0×10^8 m/s). Frequency multiplied by wavelength equals the speed of the wave; for electromagnetic waves, this is the speed of light, with some variance for the medium in which it is traveling. Electromagnetic waves include (from largest to smallest wavelength) radio waves, microwaves, infrared radiation (radiant heat), visible light, ultraviolet radiation, x-rays, and gamma rays. The energy of electromagnetic waves is carried in packets that have a magnitude inversely proportional to the wavelength. Radio waves have a range of wavelengths, from about 10^{-3} to 10^5 meters, while their frequencies range from 10^3 to about 10^{11} Hz.

Review Video: Electromagnetic Spectrum
Visit mometrix.com/academy and enter code: 771761

Visible Light

Visible light is defined as the portion of the electromagnetic spectrum that stimulates the human retina. It is absorbed and emitted by electrons, atoms, and molecules that move from one energy level to another. Visible light interacts with matter through molecular electron excitation (which occurs in the human retina) and through plasma oscillations (which occur in metals). Visible light is between ultraviolet and infrared light on the spectrum. The wavelengths of visible light cover a range from 380 nm (violet) to 760 nm (red). Different wavelengths correspond to different colors.

Review Video: Light
Visit mometrix.com/academy and enter code: 900556

Reflection and Refraction

Reflection is the rebounding of a light wave from a surface back toward the medium from where it came. A light wave that hits a reflecting surface at a 90-degree angle retraces its original path back to its source. Striking the surface at any other angle results in reflection of the wave at an angle in the opposite direction. Reflectance is the amount of light a material reflects; metals have high reflectance. The smoother a surface, the higher its reflectance. **Refraction is the change in the direction of a light wave as it passes between transparent mediums with different optical densities**. This results in a change in the wave's velocity. The ratio of the sine of the angle of the incoming ray to the sine of the angle of refraction is equal to the ratio of the speed of light in the original medium to the speed of light in the refracting medium.

$$\frac{\sin\theta_{in}}{\sin\theta_{ref}} = \frac{v_{in}}{v_{ref}}$$

Review Video: Reflection, Transmission, and Absorption of Light
Visit mometrix.com/academy and enter code: 109410

Chemistry

Past Atomic Models and Theories

There have been many revisions to theories regarding the structure of **atoms** and their **particles**. Part of the challenge in developing an understanding of matter is that atoms and their particles are too small to be seen. It is believed that the first conceptualization of the atom was developed by **Democritus** in 400 B.C. Some of the more notable models are the solid sphere or billiard ball model postulated by John Dalton, the plum pudding or raisin bun model by J.J. Thomson, the planetary or nuclear model by Ernest Rutherford, the Bohr or orbit model by Niels Bohr, and the electron cloud or quantum mechanical model by Louis de Broglie and Erwin Schrodinger. Rutherford directed the alpha scattering experiment that discounted the plum pudding model. The shortcoming of the Bohr model was the belief that electrons orbited in fixed rather than changing ecliptic orbits.

Review Video: Atomic Models
Visit mometrix.com/academy and enter code: 434851

Models of Atoms

Atoms are extremely small. A hydrogen atom is about 5×10^{-8} mm in diameter. According to some estimates, five trillion hydrogen atoms could fit on the head of a pin. **Atomic radius** refers to the average distance between the nucleus and the outermost electron. Models of atoms that include the proton, nucleus, and electrons typically show the electrons very close to the nucleus and revolving around it, similar to how the Earth orbits the sun. However, another model relates the Earth as the nucleus and its atmosphere as electrons, which is the basis of the term "**electron cloud.**" Another description is that electrons swarm around the nucleus. It should be noted that these atomic models are not to scale. A more accurate representation would be a nucleus with a diameter of about 2 cm in a stadium. The electrons would be in the bleachers. This model is similar to the not-to-scale solar system model. In reference to the periodic table, atomic radius increases as energy levels are added and decreases as more protons are added (because they pull the electrons closer to the nucleus). Essentially, atomic radius increases toward the left and toward the bottom of the periodic table.

Structure of Atoms

All matter consists of **atoms**. Atoms consist of a nucleus and electrons. The **nucleus** consists of protons and neutrons. The properties of these are measurable; they have mass and an electrical charge. The nucleus is positively charged due to the presence of protons. **Electrons** are negatively charged and orbit the nucleus. The nucleus has considerably more mass than the surrounding electrons. Atoms can bond together to make

molecules. Atoms that have an equal number of protons and electrons are electrically neutral. If the number of protons and electrons in an atom is not equal, the atom has a positive or negative charge and is an ion.

Review Video: Structure of Atoms
Visit mometrix.com/academy and enter code: 905932

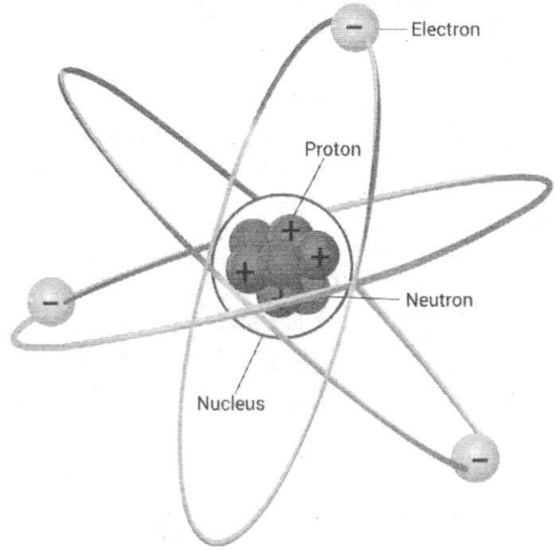

Atomic Number, Neutrons, Nucleon, and Element

- **Atomic number** (proton number) — The atomic number of an element refers to the number of protons in the nucleus of an atom. It is a unique identifier. It can be represented as Z. Atoms with a neutral charge have an atomic number that is equal to the number of electrons.
- **Neutrons** — Neutrons are the uncharged atomic particles contained within the nucleus. The number of neutrons in a nucleus can be represented as "N."
- **Nucleon** — This refers collectively to both neutrons and protons.
- **Element** — An element is matter with one particular type of atom. It can be identified by its atomic number or the number of protons in its nucleus. There are approximately 118 elements currently known, 94 of which occur naturally on Earth. Elements from the periodic table include hydrogen, carbon, iron, helium, mercury, and oxygen.

Molecules

Electrons in an atom can orbit different levels around the nucleus. They can absorb or release energy, which can change the location of their orbit or even allow them to break free from the atom. The outermost layer is the **valence layer**, which contains the valence electrons. The valence layer tends to have or share eight electrons. **Molecules** are formed by a chemical bond between atoms, a bond that occurs at the valence level. Two basic types of bonds are covalent and ionic. A **covalent bond** is formed when atoms share electrons. An **ionic bond** is formed when an atom transfers an electron to another atom. A cation or positive ion is formed when an atom loses one or more electrons. An anion or negative ion is formed when an atom gains one or more electrons. A **hydrogen bond** is a weak bond between a hydrogen atom of one molecule and an electronegative atom (such as nitrogen, oxygen, or fluorine) of another molecule. The **Van der Waals force** is a weak force between molecules. This type of force is much weaker than actual chemical bonds between atoms.

Review Video: Molecules
Visit mometrix.com/academy and enter code: 349910

Review Video: Anion, Cation, and Octet Rule
Visit mometrix.com/academy and enter code: 303525

Review Video: Ionic Bonding
Visit mometrix.com/academy and enter code: 116546

Interaction of Atoms to Form Compounds

Atoms interact by **transferring** or sharing the electrons furthest from the nucleus. Known as the outer or **valence electrons**, they are responsible for the chemical properties of an element. **Bonds** between atoms are created when electrons are paired up by being transferred or shared. If electrons are transferred from one atom to another, the bond is ionic. If electrons are shared, the bond is covalent. Atoms of the same element may bond together to form molecules or crystalline solids. When two or more different types of atoms bind together chemically, a compound is made. The physical properties of compounds reflect the nature of the interactions among their molecules. These interactions are determined by the structure of the molecule, including the atoms they consist of and the distances and angles between them.

Matter

Matter refers to substances that have mass and occupy space (or volume). The traditional definition of matter describes it as having three states: solid, liquid, and gas. These different states are caused by differences in the distances and angles between molecules or atoms, which result in differences in the energy that binds them. **Solid** structures are rigid or nearly rigid and have strong bonds. Molecules or atoms of **liquids** move around and have weak bonds, although they are not weak enough to readily break. Molecules or atoms of **gases** move almost independently of each other, are typically far apart, and do not form bonds. The current definition of matter describes it as having four states. The fourth is **plasma**, which is an ionized gas that has some electrons that are described as free because they are not bound to an atom or molecule.

Review Video: States of Matter
Visit mometrix.com/academy and enter code: 742449

Most Abundant Elements in the Universe and on Earth

Aside from dark energy and dark matter, which are thought to account for all but four percent of the universe, the two most abundant elements in the universe are **hydrogen** (H) and **helium** (He). After hydrogen and helium, the most abundant elements are oxygen, neon, nitrogen, carbon, silicon, and magnesium. The most abundant isotopes in the solar system are hydrogen-1 and helium-4. Measurements of the masses of elements in the Earth's crust indicate that oxygen (O), silicon (Si), and aluminum (Al) are the most abundant on Earth. Hydrogen in its plasma state is the most abundant chemical element in stars in their main sequences but is relatively rare on planet Earth.

Energy Transformations

The following are some examples of energy transformations:

- **Electric to mechanical**: Ceiling fan
- **Chemical to heat**: A familiar example of a chemical to heat energy transformation is the internal combustion engine, which transforms the chemical energy (a type of potential energy) of gas and oxygen into heat. This heat is transformed into propulsive energy, which is kinetic. Lighting a match and burning coal are also examples of chemical to heat energy transformations.

- **Chemical to light**: Phosphorescence and luminescence (which allow objects to glow in the dark) occur because energy is absorbed by a substance (charged) and light is re-emitted comparatively slowly. This process is different from the one involved with glow sticks. They glow due to chemiluminescence, in which an excited state is created by a chemical reaction and transferred to another molecule.
- **Heat to electricity**: Examples include thermoelectric, geothermal, and ocean thermal.
- **Nuclear to heat**: Examples include nuclear reactors and power plants.
- **Mechanical to sound**: Playing a violin or almost any instrument
- **Sound to electric**: Microphone
- **Light to electric**: Solar panels
- **Electric to light**: Light bulbs

Relationship Between Conservation of Matter and Atomic Theory

Atomic theory is concerned with the characteristics and properties of atoms that make up matter. It deals with matter on a *microscopic level* as opposed to a *macroscopic level.* Atomic theory, for instance, discusses the kinetic motion of atoms in order to explain the properties of macroscopic quantities of matter. John Dalton (1766-1844) is credited with making many contributions to the field of atomic theory that are still considered valid. This includes the notion that all matter consists of atoms and that atoms are indestructible. In other words, atoms can be neither created nor destroyed. This is also the theory behind the conservation of matter, which explains why chemical reactions do not result in any detectable gains or losses in matter. This holds true for chemical reactions and smaller-scale processes. When dealing with large amounts of energy, however, atoms can be destroyed by nuclear reactions. This can happen in particle colliders or atom smashers.

Review Video: John Dalton
Visit mometrix.com/academy and enter code: 565627

Difference Between Atoms and Molecules

Elements from the periodic table such as hydrogen, carbon, iron, helium, mercury, and oxygen are **atoms**. Atoms combine to form molecules. For example, two atoms of hydrogen (H) and one atom of oxygen (O) combine to form one molecule of water (H_2O).

Chemical and Physical Properties

Matter has both physical and chemical properties. **Physical properties** can be seen or observed without changing the identity or composition of matter. For example, the mass, volume, and density of a substance can be determined without permanently changing the sample. Other physical properties include color, boiling point, freezing point, solubility, odor, hardness, electrical conductivity, thermal conductivity, ductility, and malleability. **Chemical properties** cannot be measured without changing the identity or composition of matter. Chemical properties describe how a substance reacts or changes to form a new substance. Examples of chemical properties include flammability, corrosivity, oxidation states, enthalpy of formation, and reactivity with other chemicals.

Chemical and Physical Changes

Physical changes do not produce new substances. The atoms or molecules may be rearranged, but no new substances are formed. Phase changes or changes of state such as melting, freezing, and sublimation are physical changes. For example, physical changes include the melting of ice, the boiling of water, sugar dissolving into water, and the crushing of a piece of chalk into a fine powder. **Chemical changes** involve a chemical reaction and do produce new substances. When iron rusts, iron oxide is formed, indicating a chemical change. Other examples of chemical changes include baking a cake, burning wood, digesting a cracker, and mixing an acid and a base.

Physical and Chemical Properties and Changes

Both physical changes and chemical reactions are everyday occurrences. **Physical changes** do not result in different substances. For example, when water becomes ice it has undergone a physical change, but not a chemical change. It has changed its form, but not its composition. It is still H_2O. **Chemical properties** are concerned with the constituent particles that make up the physicality of a substance. Chemical properties are apparent when **chemical changes** occur. The chemical properties of a substance are influenced by its electron configuration, which is determined in part by the number of protons in the nucleus (the atomic number). Carbon, for example, has 6 protons and 6 electrons. It is an element's outermost valence electrons that mainly determine its chemical properties. Chemical reactions may release or consume energy.

Review Video: Chemical and Physical Properties of Matter
Visit mometrix.com/academy and enter code: 717349

Elements, Compounds, Solutions, and Mixtures

- **Elements** — These are substances that consist of only one type of atom.
- **Compounds** — These are substances containing two or more elements. Compounds are formed by chemical reactions and frequently have different properties than the original elements. Compounds are decomposed by a chemical reaction rather than separated by a physical one.
- **Solutions** — These are homogeneous mixtures composed of two or more substances that have become one.
- **Mixtures** — Mixtures contain two or more substances that are combined but have not reacted chemically with each other. Mixtures can be separated using physical methods, while compounds cannot.

Review Video: Pure Substances and Mixtures
Visit mometrix.com/academy and enter code: 100384

Heat, Energy, Work, and Thermal Energy

- **Heat** — Heat is the transfer of energy from a body or system as a result of thermal contact. Heat consists of random motion and the vibration of atoms, molecules, and ions. The higher the temperature is, the greater the atomic or molecular motion will be.
- **Energy** — Energy is the capacity to do work.
- **Work** — Work is the quantity of energy transferred by one system to another due to changes in a system that is the result of external forces, or macroscopic variables. Another way to put this is that work is the amount of energy that must be transferred to overcome a force. Lifting an object in the air is an example of work. The opposing force that must be overcome is gravity. Work is measured in joules (J). The rate at which work is performed is known as power.
- **Thermal energy** — Thermal energy is the energy present in a system due to temperature.

Types of Energy

Some discussions of energy consider only two types of energy: **kinetic energy** (the energy of motion) and **potential energy** (which depends on relative position or orientation). There are, however, other types of energy. **Electromagnetic waves**, for example, are a type of energy contained by a field. Another type of potential energy is electrical energy, which is the energy it takes to pull apart positive and negative electrical charges. **Chemical energy** refers to the manner in which atoms form into molecules, and this energy can be released or absorbed when molecules regroup. **Solar energy** comes in the form of visible light and non-visible light, such as infrared and ultraviolet rays. **Sound energy** refers to the energy in sound waves.

Review Video: Potential and Kinetic Energy
Visit mometrix.com/academy and enter code: 491502

Chemical Reactions

Chemical reactions measured in human time can take place quickly or slowly. They can take fractions of a second or billions of years. The rates of chemical reactions are determined by how frequently reacting atoms and molecules interact. Rates are also influenced by the temperature and various properties (such as shape) of the reacting materials. **Catalysts** accelerate chemical reactions, while inhibitors decrease reaction rates. Some types of reactions release energy in the form of heat and light. Some types of reactions involve the transfer of either electrons or hydrogen ions between reacting ions, molecules, or atoms. In other reactions, chemical bonds are broken down by heat or light to form reactive radicals with electrons that will readily form new bonds. Processes such as the formation of ozone and greenhouse gases in the atmosphere and the burning and processing of fossil fuels are controlled by radical reactions.

> **Review Video: Understanding Chemical Reactions**
> Visit mometrix.com/academy and enter code: 579876
>
> **Review Video: Catalysts**
> Visit mometrix.com/academy and enter code: 288189

Reading Chemical Equations

Chemical equations describe chemical reactions. The reactants are on the left side before the arrow. The products are on the right side after the arrow. The arrow is the mark that points to the reaction or change. The coefficient is the number before the element. This gives the ratio of reactants to products in terms of moles.

The equation for making water from hydrogen and oxygen is $2H_{2(g)} + O_{2(g)} \rightarrow 2H_2O_{(l)}$. The number 2 before hydrogen and water is the coefficient. This means that there are 2 moles of hydrogen and 2 of water. There is 1 mole of oxygen. This does not need to have the number 1 before the symbol for the element. For additional information, the following subscripts are often included to indicate the state of the substance: (g) stands for gas, (l) stands for liquid, (s) stands for solid, and (aq) stands for aqueous. Aqueous means the substance is dissolved in water. Charges are shown by superscript for individual ions, not for ionic compounds. Polyatomic ions are separated by parentheses. This is done so the kind of ion will not be confused with the number of ions.

> **Review Video: The Process of a Reaction**
> Visit mometrix.com/academy and enter code: 808039

Balancing Equations

An **unbalanced equation** is one that does not follow the **law of conservation of mass**, which states that matter can only be changed, not created or destroyed. If an equation is unbalanced, the numbers of atoms indicated by the stoichiometric coefficients on each side of the arrow will not be equal. Start by writing the formulas for each species in the reaction. Count the atoms on each side and determine if the number is equal. Coefficients must be whole numbers. Fractional amounts, such as half a molecule, are not possible. Equations can be balanced by adjusting the coefficients of each part of the equation to the smallest possible whole number coefficient. $H_2 + O_2 \rightarrow H_2O$ is an example of an unbalanced equation. The balanced equation is $2H_2 + O_2 \rightarrow 2H_2O$, which indicates that it takes two moles of hydrogen and one of oxygen to produce two moles of water.

> **Review Video: Balancing Chemical Equations**
> Visit mometrix.com/academy and enter code: 341228

Periodic Table

The **periodic table** groups elements with similar chemical properties together. The grouping of elements is based on **atomic structure**. It shows periodic trends of physical and chemical properties and identifies families of elements with similar properties. It is a common model for organizing and understanding elements.

In the periodic table, each element has its own cell that includes varying amounts of information presented in symbol form about the properties of the element. Cells in the table are arranged in **rows** (periods) and **columns** (groups or families). At minimum, a cell includes the symbol for the element and its atomic number. The cell for hydrogen, for example, which appears first in the upper left corner, includes an "H" and a "1" above the letter. Elements are ordered by atomic number, left to right, top to bottom.

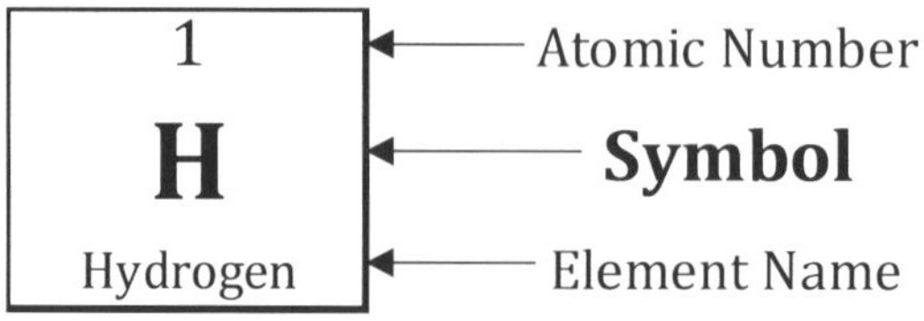

Review Video: The Periodic Table
Visit mometrix.com/academy and enter code: 154828

Solutions

A solution is a homogeneous mixture, meaning that it is uniform in composition. Solutions consist of a solute (the substance that is dissolved) and a solvent (the substance that does the dissolving). For example, in sugar water the solvent is the water and the solute is the sugar. The intermolecular attraction between the solvent and the solute is called solvation. **Hydration** refers to solutions in which water is the solvent. Solutions are formed when the forces between the molecules of the solute and the solvent are as strong as the forces holding the solute together. An example is that salt (NaCl) dissolves in water to create a solution. The Na^+ and the Cl^- ions in salt interact with the molecules of water and vice versa to overcome the intramolecular forces of the solute.

Review Video: Solutions
Visit mometrix.com/academy and enter code: 995937

Review Video: Volume Percent of a Solution
Visit mometrix.com/academy and enter code: 400152

Mixtures, Suspensions, Colloids, Emulsions, and Foams

A **mixture** is a combination of two or more substances that are not bonded. **Suspensions** are mixtures of heterogeneous materials. Particles in suspensions are usually larger than those found in true solutions. Dirt mixed vigorously with water is an example of a suspension. The dirt is temporarily suspended in water, but it settles to the bottom of the container once the mixing is ceased. A mixture of large (1 nm to 500 nm) particles is called a **colloidal suspension**. The particles are termed dispersants and the dispersing medium is similar to the solvent in a solution. Sol refers to a liquid or a solid that also has solids dispersed through it, such as milk or gelatin. An aerosol spray is a colloid suspension of gas and the solid or liquid being dispersed. An **emulsion** refers to a liquid or a solid that has small droplets of another liquid dispersed through it. A **foam** is a liquid that has gas dispersed through it.

pH

The **potential of hydrogen** (pH) is a measurement of the concentration of hydrogen ions in a substance in terms of the number of moles of H^+ per liter of solution. All substances fall between 0 and 14 on the pH scale. A lower pH indicates a higher H^+ concentration, while a higher pH indicates a lower H^+ concentration. Pure water has a neutral pH, which is 7. Anything with a pH lower than water (<7) is considered acidic. Anything with a pH higher than water (>7) is a base. Drain cleaner, soap, baking soda, ammonia, egg whites, and sea water are common bases. Urine, stomach acid, citric acid, vinegar, hydrochloric acid, and battery acid are acids.

A pH indicator is a substance that acts as a detector of hydrogen or hydronium ions. It is halochromic, meaning it changes color to indicate that hydrogen or hydronium ions have been detected.

Review Video: Overview of pH Levels
Visit mometrix.com/academy and enter code: 187395

Properties of Acids

When they are dissolved in aqueous solutions, some properties of **acids** are that they conduct electricity, change blue litmus paper to red, have a sour taste, react with bases to neutralize them, and react with active metals to free hydrogen. A **weak acid** is one that does not donate all of its protons or disassociate completely. **Strong acids** include hydrochloric, hydriodic, hydrobromic, perchloric, nitric, and sulfuric. They ionize completely. **Superacids** are those that are stronger than 100 percent sulfuric acid. They include fluoroantimonic, magic, and perchloric acids. Acids can be used in pickling, a process used to remove rust and corrosion from metals. They are also used as catalysts in the processing of minerals and the production of salts and fertilizers. Phosphoric acid (H_3PO_4) is added to sodas and other acids are added to foods as preservatives or to add taste.

Review Video: Properties of Acids and Bases
Visit mometrix.com/academy and enter code: 645283

Properties of Bases

When they are dissolved in aqueous solutions, some properties of **bases** are that they conduct electricity, change red litmus paper to blue, feel slippery, and react with acids to neutralize their properties. A **weak base** is one that does not completely ionize in an aqueous solution, and usually has a low pH. **Strong bases** can free protons in very weak acids. Examples of strong bases are hydroxide compounds such as potassium, barium, and lithium hydroxides. Most are in the first and second groups of the periodic table. A **superbase** is extremely strong compared to sodium hydroxide and cannot be kept in an aqueous solution. Superbases are organized into organic, organometallic, and inorganic classes. Bases are used as insoluble catalysts in heterogeneous reactions and as catalysts in hydrogenation.

Properties of Salts

Some properties of **salts** are that they are formed from acid base reactions, are ionic compounds consisting of metallic and nonmetallic ions, dissociate in water, and are comprised of tightly bonded ions. Some common salts are sodium chloride ($NaCl$), sodium bisulfate ($NaHSO_4$), potassium dichromate ($K_2Cr_2O_7$), and calcium chloride ($CaCl_2$). Calcium chloride is used as a drying agent, and may be used to absorb moisture when freezing mixtures. Potassium nitrate (KNO_3) is used to make fertilizer and in the manufacturing of explosives. Sodium nitrate ($NaNO_3$) is also used in the making of fertilizer. Baking soda [sodium bicarbonate ($NaHCO_3$)] is a salt, as are Epsom salts [magnesium sulfate ($MgSO_4$)]. Salt and water can react to form a base and an acid. This is called a **hydrolysis reaction**.

Unique Properties of Water

The important properties of water (H_2O) are high polarity, hydrogen bonding, cohesiveness, adhesiveness, high specific heat, high latent heat, and high heat of vaporization. Water is vital to life as we know it. The reason is that water is one of the main parts of many living things.

Water is a liquid at room temperature. The high specific heat of water means that it does not easily break its hydrogen bonds. Also, it resists heat and motion. This is why it has a high boiling point and high vaporization point.

Most substances are denser in their solid forms. However, water is different because its solid-state floats in its liquid state. Water is cohesive. This means that it is drawn to itself. It is also adhesive. This means that it draws in other molecules. If water will attach to another substance, the substance is said to be hydrophilic. Because of its cohesive and adhesive properties, water makes a good solvent. Substances with polar ions and molecules easily dissolve in water.

Review Video: Properties of Water
Visit mometrix.com/academy and enter code: 279526

Kinetic Theory of Gases

The **kinetic theory of gases** assumes that gas molecules are small compared to the distances between them and that they are in constant random motion. The attractive and repulsive forces between gas molecules are negligible. Their kinetic energy does not change with time as long as the temperature remains the same. The higher the temperature is, the greater the motion will be. As the temperature of a gas increases, so does the kinetic energy of the molecules. In other words, gas will occupy a greater volume as the temperature is increased and a lesser volume as the temperature is decreased. In addition, the same amount of gas will occupy a greater volume as the temperature increases, but pressure remains constant. At any given temperature, gas molecules have the same average kinetic energy. The **ideal gas law** is derived from the kinetic theory of gases.

Review Video: Ideal Gas vs. Real Gas
Visit mometrix.com/academy and enter code: 619477

Organic Compounds

Two of the main characteristics of organic compounds are that they generally include carbon and are formed by covalent bonds. Carbon can form long chains, double and triple bonds, and rings. While inorganic compounds tend to have high melting points, organic compounds tend to melt at temperatures below 300° C. They also tend to boil, sublimate, and decompose below this temperature. Unlike inorganic compounds, they are not very water-soluble. Organic molecules are organized into functional groups based on their specific atoms, which helps determine how they will react chemically. A few groups are alkanes, nitro, alkenes, sulfides, amines, and carbolic acids. The hydroxyl group (−OH) consists of alcohols. These molecules are polar, which increases their solubility. By some estimates, there are more than 16 million organic compounds.

Review Video: Organic Compounds
Visit mometrix.com/academy and enter code: 264922

Hydrogen Bonds

Hydrogen bonds are weaker than covalent and ionic bonds and refer to the type of attraction in an electronegative atom such as oxygen, fluorine, or nitrogen. Hydrogen bonds can form within a single molecule or between molecules. A water molecule is **polar**, meaning it is partially positively charged on one end (the hydrogen end) and partially negatively charged on the other (the oxygen end). This is because the hydrogen atoms are arranged around the oxygen atom in a close tetrahedron. Hydrogen is **oxidized** (its number of electrons is reduced) when it bonds with oxygen to form water. Hydrogen bonds tend not only to be weak but also short-lived. They also tend to be numerous. Hydrogen bonds give water many of its important properties, including its high specific heat and high heat of vaporization, its solvent qualities, its adhesiveness and cohesiveness, its hydrophilic qualities, and its ability to float in its solid form. Hydrogen bonds are also an important component of proteins, nucleic acids, and DNA.

Inorganic Compounds

The main trait of inorganic compounds is that they generally lack carbon. Inorganic compounds include mineral salts, alloys, non-metallic compounds such as phosphate, and metal complexes. A metal complex has a central atom (or ion) bonded to surrounding ligands (molecules or anions). The ligands sacrifice the donor atoms (in the form of at least one pair of electrons) to the central atom. Many inorganic compounds are ionic, meaning they form ionic bonds rather than share electrons. They may have high melting points because of this. They may also be colorful, but this is not an absolute identifier of an inorganic compound. Salts, which are inorganic compounds, are an example of inorganic bonding of cations and anions. Some examples of salts are magnesium chloride ($MgCl_2$) and sodium oxide (Na_2O). Oxides, carbonates, sulfates, and halides are classes of inorganic compounds. They are typically poor conductors, are very water soluble, and crystallize easily. Minerals and silicates are also inorganic compounds.

Geology

Earth System Science

The complex and interconnected dynamics of the continents, atmosphere, oceans, ice, and life forms are the subject of Earth system science. These interconnected dynamics require an interdisciplinary approach that includes chemistry, physics, biology, mathematics, and applied sciences in order to study the Earth as an integrated system and determine (while considering human impact and interaction) the past, present, and future states of the Earth. Scientific inquiry in this field includes exploration of:

- Extreme weather events as they pertain to a changing climate
- Earthquakes and volcanic eruptions as they pertain to tectonic shifts
- Losses in biodiversity in relation to the changes in the Earth's ecosystems
- Causes and effects in the environment
- The Sun's solar variability in relation to the Earth's climate
- The atmosphere's increasing concentrations of carbon dioxide and aerosols
- Trends in the Earth's systems in terms of changes and their consequences

Traditional Earth Science Disciplines

Modern science is approaching the study of the Earth in an integrated fashion that sees the Earth as an interconnected system that is impacted by humankind and, therefore, must include social dimensions. Traditionally, though, the following were the Earth science disciplines:

- **Geology** – This is the study of the origin and structure of the Earth and of the changes it has undergone and is in the process of undergoing. Geologists work from the crust inward.
- **Meteorology** – This is the study of the atmosphere, including atmospheric pressure, temperature, clouds, winds, precipitation, etc. It is also concerned with describing and explaining weather.
- **Oceanography** – This is the study of the oceans, which includes studying their extent and depth, the physics and chemistry of ocean waters, and the exploitation of their resources.
- **Ecology** – This is the study of living organisms in relation to their environment and to other living things. It is the study of the interrelations between the different components of the ecosystem.

Geological Eras

Geologists divide the history of the Earth into units of time called eons, which are divided into **eras**, then into **periods**, then into **epochs** and finally into **ages**. Dates are approximate of course, and there may be variations of a few million years. (Million years ago is abbreviated as Ma.) Some of the most commonly known time periods are:

- **Hadean Eon** – About 4.5 to 3.8 billion years ago
- **Archaean Eon** – 3.8 to 2.5 billion years ago
- **Proterozoic Eon** – 2.5 billion to 542 Ma
- **Phanerozoic Eon** – 542 Ma to the present
  - **Paleozoic Era** – 542 Ma to 251 Ma
    - **Cambrian Period** – 542 to 488 Ma
    - **Ordovician Period** – 488 to 443 Ma
    - **Silurian Period** – 443 to 416 Ma
    - **Devonian Period** – 416 to 359 Ma

    - **Carboniferous Period** – 359 to 290 Ma
    - **Permian Period** – 290 to 252 Ma
  - **Mesozoic Era** – 252 to 65 Ma
    - **Triassic Period** – 252 to 200 Ma
    - **Jurassic Period** – 200 to 150 Ma
    - **Cretaceous Period** – 150 to 65 Ma
  - **Cenozoic Era** – 65 Ma to the present
    - **Paleogene Period** – 65 to 28 Ma
    - **Neogene Period** – 28 to 2 Ma
    - **Quaternary Period** – about 2 Ma to the present

Development of Life on Earth According to Time Periods

The evolution of life on Earth is believed to have occurred as follows:

- Igneous rocks formed. (Hadean Eon)
- The continents formed. (Archaean Eon)
- The first multi-cellular creatures such as hydras, jellyfish, and sponges appeared about 600 Ma.
- Flatworms, roundworms, and segmented worms appeared about 550 Ma.
- Moss, arthropods, octopus, and eels appeared. (Cambrian Period)
- Mushrooms, fungi, and other primitive plants appeared; sea animals began to use calcium to build bones and shells. (Ordovician Period)
- Fish with jaws appeared. (Silurian Period)
- Fish developed lungs and legs (frogs) and went on land; ferns appeared. (Devonian period)
- Reptiles developed the ability to lay eggs on land and pine trees appeared. (Carboniferous Period)
- Dinosaurs dominated the land during the Triassic and Jurassic Periods.
- Flying insects, birds, and the first flowering plants appeared; dinosaurs died out. (Cretaceous Period)
- Mammals evolved and dominated; grasses became widespread. (50 Ma)
- Hominids appeared more than 2 Ma.

Hydrosphere and Hydrologic Cycle

The **hydrosphere** is anything on Earth that is related to water, whether it is in the air, on land, or in a plant or animal system. A water molecule consists of only two atoms of hydrogen and one of oxygen, yet it is what makes life possible. Unlike any other planets that have been discovered, Earth is able to sustain water in a liquid state most of the time. Water vapor and ice are of no use to living organisms. The **hydrologic cycle** is the journey water takes as it proceeds through different forms. Liquid surface water evaporates to form the gaseous state of a cloud, and then becomes liquid again in the form of rain. This process takes about 10 days.

This cycle is for surface water only: rivers, lakes, groundwater, ocean surface, etc. Water in the deep ocean and in the heart of glaciers is typically sequestered from the cycle for many thousands of years.

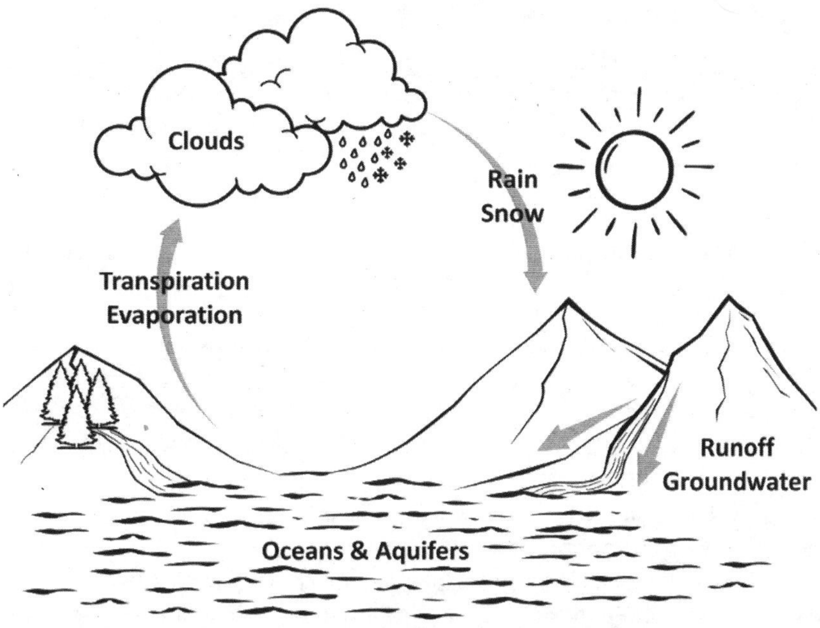

Review Video: Hydrologic Cycle
Visit mometrix.com/academy and enter code: 426578

AQUIFERS

An **aquifer** is an underground water reservoir formed from groundwater that has infiltrated from the surface by passing through the soil and permeable rock layers to whereever the rock layer is impermeable. The section of permeable layers with water present is called the zone of saturation, and the area above that (with no water) is the zone of aeration. There are two types of aquifers. In one, the water is under pressure (**confined**) as the supply builds up between layers of impermeable rocks and has to move back towards the surface, resulting in a spring or artesian well. The second type of aquifer is called "**unconfined**" because it has room to expand and contract, and the water has to be pumped out. The highest level of the aquifer is called the water table. If water is pumped out of the aquifer such that the water table dips in a specific area, that area is called a cone of depression.

BIOSPHERE

Biosphere is the term used by physical geographers to describe the living world of trees, bugs, and animals. It refers to any place where life exists on Earth, and is the intersection of the hydrosphere, the atmosphere, the land, and the energy that comes from space. The biosphere includes the upper areas of the atmosphere where birds and insects can travel, areas deep inside caves, and hydrothermal vents at the bottom of the ocean.

Factors that affect the biosphere include:

- The **distance and tilt** between the Earth and the Sun – This produces temperatures that are conducive to life and causes the seasons.
- **Climate, daily weather, and erosion** – These change the land and the organisms on and in it.
- Earthquakes, tornadoes, volcanoes, tsunamis, and other **natural phenomena** – These all change the land.
- **Chemical erosion** – This changes the composition of rocks and organic materials.

- **Biological erosion** – This is bacteria and single-celled organisms breaking down organic and inorganic materials.

Ecological System and Biome

An **ecological system**, or ecosystem, is the community of all the living organisms in a specific area interacting with non-living factors such as temperature, sunlight, atmospheric pressure, weather patterns, wind, types of nutrients, etc. An ecosystem's development depends on the energy that passes in and out of it. The boundaries of an ecosystem depend on the use of the term, whether it refers to an ecosystem under a rock or in a valley, pond, or ocean.

A **biome** is a general ecosystem type defined by the plants and animals that live there and the local climate patterns. Examples include tropical rainforests or savannas, deserts, grasslands, deciduous forests, tundra, woodlands, and ice caps. There can be more than one type of biome within a larger climate zone. The transition area between two biomes is an ecotone, which may have characteristics of both biomes.

Erosion

Erosion is the process that breaks down matter, whether it is a rock that is broken into pebbles or mountains that are blown by wind and rained on until they become hills. The erosion of land by weather or breaking waves is called **denudation**. **Mass wasting** is the movement of masses of dirt and rock from one place to another. This can occur in two ways: **mechanical** (such as breaking a rock with a hammer) or **chemical** (such as pouring acid on a rock to dissolve it). If the material changes color, it indicates that a break down was chemical in nature. Whatever is broken down must go somewhere, so erosion eventually builds something up. For example, an eroded mountain ends up in a river that carries the sediment towards the ocean, where it builds up and creates a wetland or delta at the mouth of the river.

Climates

Scientists have determined the following different types of **climates**:

- Polar (ice caps)
- Polar (tundra)
- Subtropical (dry summer)
- Subtropical (dry winter)
- Subtropical (humid)
- Subtropical (marine west coast)
- Subtropical (Mediterranean)
- Subtropical (wet)
- Tropical (monsoon)
- Tropical (savannah/grasslands)
- Tropical (wet)

Several factors make up and affect climates. These include:

- Temperature
- Atmospheric pressure
- The number of clouds and the amount of dust or smog
- Humidity
- Winds

The moistest and warmest of all the climates is that of the tropical rainforest. It has daily convection thunderstorms caused by the surface daytime heat and the high humidity, which combine to form thunderclouds.

Review Video: Climates
Visit mometrix.com/academy and enter code: 991320

LAYERS OF THE EARTH

The Earth has several distinct layers, each with its own properties:

- **Crust** – This is the outermost layer of the Earth that is comprised of the continents and the ocean basins. It has a variable thickness (35-70 km in the continents and 5-10 km in the ocean basins) and is composed mostly of alumino-silicates.
- **Mantle** – This is about 2900 km thick, and is made up mostly of ferro-magnesium silicates. It is divided into an upper and lower mantle. Most of the internal heat of the Earth is located in the mantle. Large convective cells circulate heat, and may cause plate tectonic movement.
- **Core** – This is separated into the liquid outer core and the solid inner core. The outer core is 2300 km thick (composed mostly of nickel-iron alloy), and the inner core (almost entirely iron) is 12 km thick. The Earth's magnetic field is thought to be controlled by the liquid outer core.

Layers of the Earth

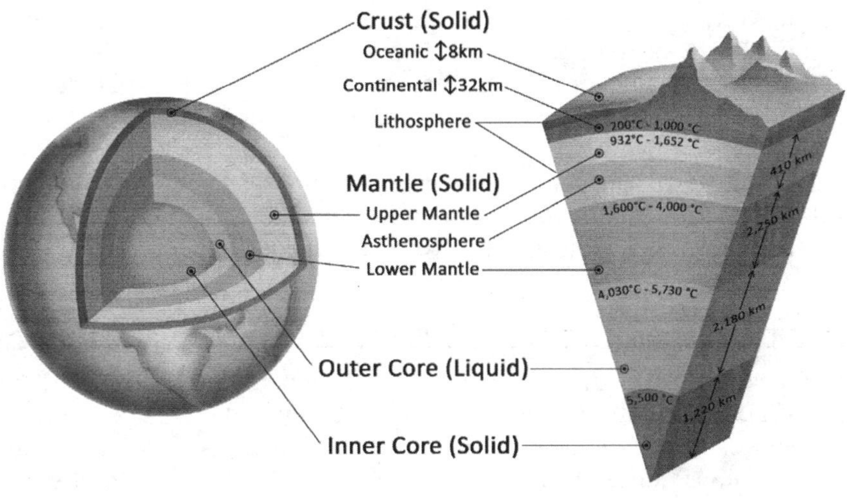

COMPOSITION OF EARTH'S ATMOSPHERE

The Earth's atmosphere is 79% nitrogen, 20% oxygen, and 1% other gases. The oxygen was originally produced almost entirely by algae-type plants. The atmosphere has four layers:

- **Troposphere** – This is the layer closest to the Earth where all weather takes place. It is the region that contains rising and falling packets of air. Air pressure at sea level is 0.1 atmospheres, but the top of the troposphere is about 10% of that amount.
- **Stratosphere** – In this layer, air flow is mainly horizontal. The upper portion has a thin layer of concentrated ozone (a reactive form of oxygen) that is largely responsible for absorbing the Sun's ultraviolet rays.
- **Mesosphere** – This is the coldest layer. Temperatures drop to -100°C at the top.

- **Thermosphere** – This is divided into the lower ionosphere and the higher exosphere. This layer is very thin and has many ionized atoms with a net electrical charge. The aurora and Van Allen Belts are here. This layer also absorbs the most energetic photons from the Sun and reflects radio waves, enabling long distance radio communication.

Review Video: Earth's Atmosphere
Visit mometrix.com/academy and enter code: 417614

PALEONTOLOGY

Paleontology is the study of prehistoric plant and animal life through the analysis of **fossil remains**. These fossils reveal the ecologies of the past and the path of evolution for both extinct and living organisms. A historical science, paleontology seeks information about the identity, origin, environment, and evolution of past organisms and what they can reveal about the past of the Earth as a whole. Paleontologists seek to explain causes rather than conduct experiments to observe effects. It is related to the fields of biology, geology, and archaeology, and is divided into several sub-disciplines concerned with the types of fossils studied, the process of fossilization, and the ecology and climate of the past. Paleontologists also help identify the composition of the Earth's rock layers by the fossils that are found, thus identifying potential sites for oil, mineral, and water extraction.

THE ROCK RECORD

The **Law of Superposition** logically assumes that the bottom layer of a series of sedimentary layers is the oldest, unless it has been overturned or older rock has been pushed over it. In addition, igneous intrusions can cut through or flow above already present rocks (e.g., lava flows). This is a further indication that the lower rock layers are older. Another guideline for the rock record is that **rock layers** are older than the folds and faults in them because the rocks must exist before they can be folded or faulted. If a rock contains **atomic nuclei**, reference tables of the half-lives of commonly used radio isotopes can be used to match the decay rate of known substances to the nuclei in a rock, and thereby determine its age. Ages of rocks can also be determined from **contact metamorphism**, the re-crystallization of pre-existing rocks due to changes in physical and chemical conditions, such as heat, pressure, and chemically active fluids that might be present in lava or polluted waters.

MATCHING ROCKS AND GEOLOGIC EVENTS IN ONE PLACE WITH THOSE OF ANOTHER

Geologists physically follow rock layers from one location to another by a process called "walking the outcrop." Geologists walk along the outcropping to see where it goes and what the differences and similarities of the neighboring locations they cross are. Similar rock **types** or **patterns** of rock layers that are similar in terms of thickness, color, composition, and fossil remains tell geologists that two locations have a similar geologic history. Fossils are found all over the Earth, but are from a relatively **small time period** in Earth's history. Therefore, fossil evidence helps date a rock layer, regardless of where it occurs. **Volcanic ash** is a good time indicator since ash is deposited quickly over a widespread area. Matching the date of an eruption to the ash allows for a precise identification of time. Similarly, the **meteor impact** at the intersection of the Cretaceous and Tertiary Periods left a time marker. Wherever the meteor's iridium content is found, geologists are able to date rock layers.

SEQUENCING THE EARTH'S GEOLOGIC HISTORY FROM THE FOSSIL AND ROCK RECORD

Reference tables are used to match specimens and time periods. For example, the fossil record has been divided into time units of the Earth's history. Rocks can therefore be dated by the fossils found with them. There are also reference tables for dating plate motions and mountain building events in geologic history. Since humans have been around for a relatively short period of time, **fossilized human remains** help to affix a date to a location. Some areas have missing **geologic layers** because of erosion or other factors, but reference tables specific to a region will list what is complete or missing. The theory of **uniformitarianism** assumes that geologic processes have been the same throughout history. Therefore, the way erosion or volcanic eruptions happen today is the same as the way these events happened millions of years ago because there is no reason for them to have changed. Therefore, knowledge about current events can be applied to the past to make judgments about events in the rock record.

Revealing Changes in Earth's History by the Fossil and Rock Records

Fossils can show how animal and plant life have changed or remained the same over time. For example, fossils have provided evidence of the existence of dinosaurs even though they no longer roam the Earth, and have also been used to prove that certain insects have been around for hundreds of millions of years. Fossils have been used to identify four basic eras: **Proterozoic**, the age of primitive life; **Paleozoic**, the age of fishes; **Mesozoic**, the age of dinosaurs; and **Cenozoic**, the age of mammals. Most ancient forms of life have disappeared, and there are reference tables that list when this occurred. Fossil records also show the evolution of certain life forms, such as the horse from the eohippus. However, the majority of changes do not involve evolution from simple to complex forms, but rather an increase in the variety of forms.

Mountains

A **mountain** is a portion of the Earth that has been raised above its surroundings by volcanic action or tectonic plate movement. Mountains can be made of any type of rock and most lie along active plate boundaries. There are two major mountain systems. The **Circum-Pacific** encircles the entire Pacific Ocean, from New Guinea up across Japan and the Aleutians and down to southern South America. The **Alpine-Himalaya** stretches from northern Africa across the Alps and to the Himalayas and Indonesia. **Orogeny** is the term for the process of natural mountain formation. Therefore, physical mountains are orogens. **Folded mountains** are created through the folding of rock layers when two crustal plates come together. The Alps and Himalayas are folded mountains. The latter was formed by the collision of India with Asia. **Fault-block mountains** are created from the tension forces of plate movements. These produce faults that vertically displace one section to form a mountain. **Dome mountains** are created from magma pushing up through the Earth's crust.

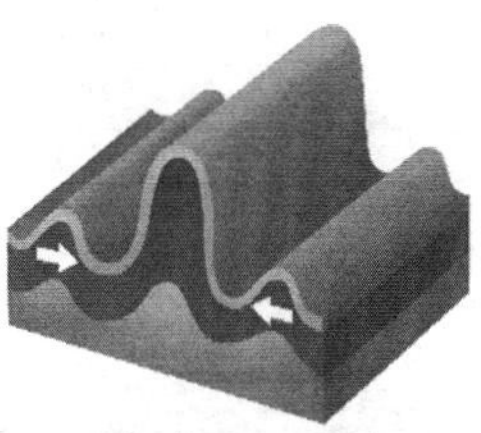

Folded Mountains
Formed when continental plates collide

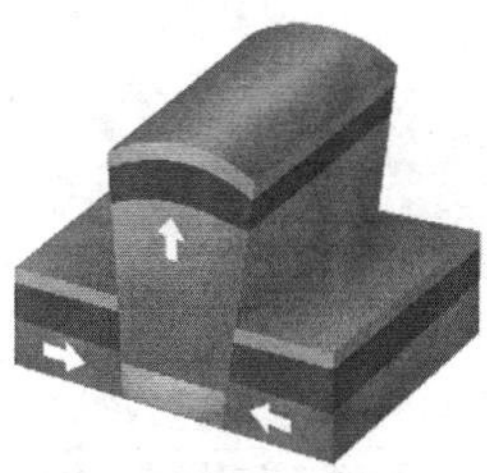

Dome Mountains
Formed when rock rises up and pushes layers of rock up

Fault-Block Mountains
Formed when block of rocks drops drown compared to other blocks

Volcanic Mountains
Formed when magma spills and hardens on the Earth's crust

Volcanoes and Volcanic Mountains

Volcanoes are classified according to their activity level. An **active** volcano is in the process of erupting or building to an eruption; a dormant volcano has erupted before and may erupt again someday, but is not currently active; and an **extinct** volcano has died out volcanically and will not erupt ever again. Active volcanoes endanger plant and animal life, but lava and ash add enriching minerals to the soil. There are three types of volcanic mountains:

- **Shield volcanoes** are the largest volcanic mountains because of a repeated, viscous lava flow from small eruptions over a long period of time that cause the mountain to grow.
- **Cinder cone volcanoes**, or linear volcanoes, are small in size, but have massive explosions through linear shafts that spread cinders and ash around the vent. This results in a cone-shaped hill.
- **Composite volcanoes** get their name from the mix of lava and ash layers that build the mountain.

Cinder Cone Volcanoes

Composite Volcanoes

Shield Volcanoes

Subdivisions of Rock

The three major subdivisions of rock are:

- **Igneous** (magmatites) – This type is formed from the cooling of liquid magma. In the process, minerals crystallize and amalgamate. If solidification occurs deep in the Earth (plutonic rock), the cooling process is slow. This allows for the formation of large crystals, giving rock a coarse-grained texture (granite). Quickly cooled magma has a glassy texture (obsidian).
- **Metamorphic** – Under conditions of high temperature and pressure within the Earth's crust, rock material melts and changes structure, transitioning or metamorphosing into a new type of rock with different minerals. If the minerals appear in bands, the rock is foliated. Examples include marble (unfoliated) and slate (foliated).
- **Sedimentary** – This is the most common type of rock on Earth. It is formed by sedimentation, compaction, and then cementation of many small particles of mineral, animal, or plant material. There are three types of sedimentary rocks: clastic, clay, and sand that came from disintegrated rocks; chemical (rock salt and gypsum), formed by evaporation of aqueous solutions; and biogenic (coal), formed from animal or plant remnants.

Review Video: Igneous, Sedimentary, and Metamorphic Rocks
Visit mometrix.com/academy and enter code: 689294

Glaciers

Glaciers start high in the mountains, where snow and ice accumulate inside a cirque (a small semicircular depression). The snow becomes firmly packed into masses of coarse-grained ice that are slowly pulled down a slope by gravity. Glaciers grow with large amounts of snowfall and retreat (diminish) if warm weather melts more ice than can be replaced. Glaciers once covered large areas of both the northern and southern hemispheres with mile-thick ice that carved out valleys, fjords, and other land formations. They also moved plants, animals, and rocks from one area to another. There were two types of glaciers: **valley**, which produced U-shaped erosion and sharp-peaked mountains; and **continental**, which moved over and rounded mountain tops and ridges. These glaciers existed during the ice ages, the last of which occurred from 2.5 million years ago to 12,000 years ago.

Earth Science and Weather

Layers Above the Surface of Earth

The **ozone layer**, although contained within the stratosphere, is determined by ozone (O_3) concentrations. It absorbs the majority of ultraviolet light from the Sun. The ionosphere is part of both the exosphere and the thermosphere. It is characterized by the fact that it is a plasma, a partially ionized gas in which free electrons and positive ions are attracted to each other, but are too energetic to remain fixed as a molecule. It starts at about 50 km above Earth's surface and goes to 1,000 km. It affects radio wave transmission and auroras. The ionosphere pushes against the inner edge of the Earth's magnetosphere, which is the highly magnetized, non-spherical region around the Earth. The homosphere encompasses the troposphere, stratosphere, and mesosphere. Gases in the homosphere are considered well mixed. In the heterosphere, the distance that particles can move without colliding is large. As a result, gases are stratified according to their molecular weights. Heavier gases such as oxygen and nitrogen occur near the bottom of the heterosphere, while hydrogen, the lightest element, is found at the top.

Review Video: Earth's Atmosphere
Visit mometrix.com/academy and enter code: 417614

Tropospheric Circulation

Most weather takes place in the **troposphere**. Air circulates in the atmosphere by convection and in various types of "cells." Air near the equator is warmed by the Sun and rises. Cool air rushes under it, and the higher, warmer air flows toward Earth's poles. At the poles, it cools and descends to the surface. It is now under the hot air, and flows back to the equator. Air currents coupled with ocean currents move heat around the planet, creating winds, weather, and climate. Winds can change direction with the seasons. For example, in Southeast Asia and India, summer monsoons are caused by air being heated by the Sun. This air rises, draws moisture from the ocean, and causes daily rains. In winter, the air cools, sinks, pushes the moist air away, and creates dry weather.

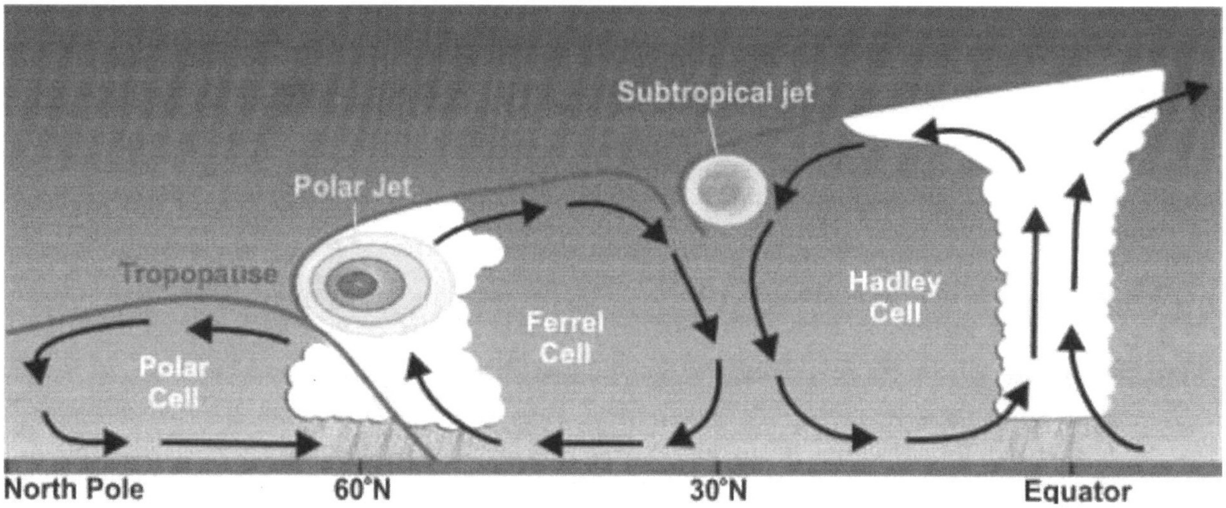

Common Weather Phenomena and Equipment to Measure Them

Common **atmospheric conditions** that are frequently measured are temperature, precipitation, wind, and humidity. These weather conditions are often measured at permanently fixed **weather stations** so weather data can be collected and compared over time and by region. Measurements may also be taken by ships, buoys, and underwater instruments. Measurements may also be taken under special circumstances. Common instruments used and measurements taken include:

- A **thermometer** for measuring temperature
- A **barometer** for measuring barometric/air pressure
- A **hygrometer** for measuring humidity
- An **anemometer** for measuring wind speed
- A **weather vane** for measuring wind direction
- A **rain gauge** for measuring precipitation

Weather, Climate, and Meteorology

Meteorology is the study of the atmosphere, particularly as it pertains to forecasting the weather and understanding its processes. **Weather** is the condition of the atmosphere at any given moment. Most weather occurs in the troposphere and includes changing events such as clouds, storms, and temperature, as well as more extreme events such as tornadoes, hurricanes, and blizzards. **Climate** refers to the average weather for a particular area over time, typically at least 30 years. Latitude is an indicator of climate. Changes in climate occur over long time periods.

Winds and Global Wind Belts

Winds are the result of air moving by convection. Masses of warm air rise, and cold air sweeps into their place. The warm air also moves, cools, and sinks. The term "prevailing wind" refers to the wind that usually blows in an area in a single direction. **Dominant winds** are the winds with the highest speeds. Belts or bands that run latitudinally and blow in a specific direction are associated with **convection cells. Hadley cells** are formed directly north and south of the equator. The **Farrell cell*s*** occur at about 30° to 60°. The jet stream runs between the Farrell cells and the polar cells. At the higher and lower latitudes, the direction is easterly. At mid latitudes, the direction is westerly. From the North Pole to the south, the surface winds are Polar High Easterlies, Subpolar Low Westerlies, Subtropical High or Horse Latitudes, North-East Trade winds, Equatorial

Low or Doldrums, South-East Trades, Subtropical High or Horse Latitudes, Subpolar Low Easterlies, and Polar High.

Review Video: Source of Wind
Visit mometrix.com/academy and enter code: 451712

Relative Humidity, Absolute Humidity, and Dew Point Temperature

Humidity refers to water vapor contained in the air. The amount of moisture contained in air depends upon its temperature. The higher the air temperature, the more moisture it can hold. These higher levels of moisture are associated with higher humidity. **Absolute humidity** refers to the total amount of moisture air is capable of holding at a certain temperature. **Relative humidity** is the ratio of water vapor in the air compared to the amount the air is capable of holding at its current temperature. As temperature decreases, absolute humidity stays the same and relative humidity increases. A hygrometer is a device used to measure humidity. The **dew point** is the temperature at which water vapor condenses into water at a particular humidity.

Precipitation

After clouds reach the dew point, **precipitation** occurs. Precipitation can take the form of a liquid or a solid. It is known by many names, including rain, snow, ice, dew, and frost. **Liquid** forms of precipitation include rain and drizzle. Rain or drizzle that freezes on contact is known as freezing rain or freezing drizzle. **Solid or frozen** forms of precipitation include snow, ice needles or diamond dust, sleet or ice pellets, hail, and graupel or snow pellets. Virga is a form of precipitation that evaporates before reaching the ground. It usually looks like sheets or shafts falling from a cloud. The amount of rainfall is measured with a rain gauge. Intensity can be measured according to how fast precipitation is falling or by how severely it limits visibility. Precipitation plays a major role in the water cycle since it is responsible for depositing much of the Earth's fresh water.

Clouds

Clouds form when air cools and warm air is forced to give up some of its water vapor because it can no longer hold it. This vapor condenses and forms tiny droplets of water or ice crystals called clouds. Particles, or aerosols, are needed for water vapor to form water droplets. These are called **condensation nuclei**. Clouds are created by surface heating, mountains and terrain, rising air masses, and weather fronts. Clouds precipitate, returning the water they contain to Earth. Clouds can also create atmospheric optics. They can scatter light, creating colorful phenomena such as rainbows, colorful sunsets, and the green flash phenomenon.

Review Video: Types of Clouds
Visit mometrix.com/academy and enter code: 803166

High, Middle, and Low Cloud Types

Most clouds can be classified according to the altitude of their base above Earth's surface. **High clouds** occur at altitudes between 5,000 and 13,000 meters. **Middle clouds** occur at altitudes between 2,000 and 7,000 meters. **Low clouds** occur from the Earth's surface to altitudes of 2,000 meters. Types of high clouds include cirrus (Ci), thin wispy mare's tails that consist of ice; cirrocumulus (Cc), small, pillow-like puffs that often appear in rows; and cirrostratus (Cs), thin, sheet-like clouds that often cover the entire sky. Types of middle clouds include altocumulus (Ac), gray-white clouds that consist of liquid water; and altostratus (As), grayish or blue-gray clouds that span the sky. Types of low clouds include stratus (St), gray and fog-like clouds consisting of water droplets that take up the whole sky; stratocumulus (Sc), low-lying, lumpy gray clouds; and nimbostratus (Ns), dark gray clouds with uneven bases that indicate rain or snow. Two types of clouds, cumulus (Cu) and cumulonimbus (Cb), are capable of great vertical growth. They can start at a wide range of altitudes, from the Earth's surface to altitudes of 13,000 meters.

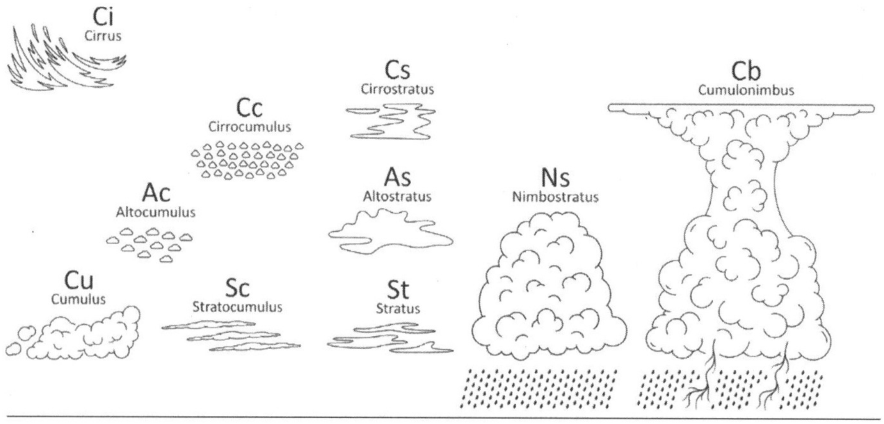

Air Masses

Air masses are large volumes of air in the troposphere of the Earth. They are categorized by their temperature and by the amount of water vapor they contain:

- **Arctic** and **Antarctic** air masses are cold
- **Polar** air masses are cool
- **Tropical** and **equatorial** air masses are hot
- **Maritime** and **monsoon** air masses are moist and unstable
- **Continental** and **superior** air masses are dry

Weather Fronts and Weather Maps

A **weather front** is the area between two differing masses of air that affects weather. Movement of a front is influenced by the jet stream and other high winds as well as the type of front; cold fronts move up to twice as fast as warm ones. It is in the turbulent frontal area that weather events take place, both commonplace and dramatic. This area also creates temperature changes. Weather phenomena include rain, thunderstorms, high winds, tornadoes, cloudiness, clear skies, and hurricanes. Different fronts can be plotted on weather maps using a set of designated symbols. Surface weather maps can also include symbols representing clouds, rain, temperature, air pressure, and fair weather.

Space Science

Astronomy

Astronomy is the scientific study of celestial objects and their positions, movements, and structures. *Celestial* does not refer to the Earth by itself, but does include its movement through space. Other celestial objects include the Sun, the Moon, planets, satellites, asteroids, meteors, comets, stars, galaxies, the universe, and other space phenomena. The term astronomy has its roots in the Greek words *astro* and *nomos*, which means "laws of the stars."

Review Video: Astronomy
Visit mometrix.com/academy and enter code: 640556

Universe

Origin

The **universe** can be said to consist of everything and nothing. The universe contains all of space, matter, energy, and time. There are likely still phenomena that have yet to be discovered. The universe can also be thought of as nothing, since a vast portion of the known universe is empty space. It is believed that the universe is expanding. The **Big Bang** is a core part of a theory developed to explain the origin of the universe. It is widely accepted among astronomers, though there are other theories regarding the origin of the universe, such as the **Steady-State theory** and the **Creationist theory**. According to the Big Bang model, all the matter in the universe was once in one place. This matter underwent a huge explosion that spread it into space. Galaxies formed from, this material and the universe is still expanding.

Structure

What can be seen of the universe is believed to be at least 93 billion light years across. To put this into perspective, the Milky Way galaxy is about 100,000 light years across. Our view of matter in the universe is that it forms into clumps which become stars, galaxies, clusters of galaxies, superclusters, and the Great Wall of galaxies. **Galaxies** consist of stars, some with planetary systems. Some estimates state that the universe is about 13 billion years old. It is not considered dense and is believed to consist of 73% dark energy, 23% cold dark matter, and 4% regular matter. Cosmology is the study of the universe. Interstellar medium (ISM) is the gas and dust in the interstellar space between a galaxy's stars.

Review Video: Dark Matter
Visit mometrix.com/academy and enter code: 251909

Galaxies

Galaxies consist of stars, stellar remnants, and dark matter. **Dwarf galaxies** contain as few as 10 million stars, while giant galaxies contain as many as 1 trillion stars. Galaxies are gravitationally bound, meaning that stars, star systems, other gases, and dust orbit the galaxy's center. The Earth exists in the **Milky Way galaxy** and the nearest galaxy to ours is the **Andromeda galaxy**. Galaxies can be classified by their visual shape into elliptical, spiral, irregular, and starburst galaxies. It is estimated that there are more than 100 billion galaxies in the universe ranging from 1,000 to 100,000 parsecs in diameter. Galaxies can be megaparsecs apart. Intergalactic space consists of a gas with an average density of less than one atom per cubic meter. Galaxies are organized into clusters which form superclusters. Dark matter may account for up to 90% of the mass of galaxies. Dark matter is still not well understood.

Review Video: What is a Galaxy?
Visit mometrix.com/academy and enter code: 226539

Planets

In order of their distance from the Sun (closest to furthest away), the **planets** are: Mercury, Venus, Earth, Mars, Jupiter, Saturn, Uranus, and Neptune (Pluto is now considered to be a dwarf planet). All the planets revolve around the Sun, which is an average-sized star in the spiral Milky Way galaxy. They revolve in the same direction in nearly circular orbits. If the planets were viewed by looking down from the Sun, they would rotate in a counter-clockwise direction. All the planets are in, or near, the same plane, called the ecliptic, and their axis of rotation is nearly perpendicular to the ecliptic. The only exception is Uranus, which is tipped on its side.

Terrestrial Planets, Jovian Planets, and Mass of Planets

The **Terrestrial Planets** are: Mercury, Venus, Earth, and Mars. These are the four planets closest to the Sun. They are called terrestrial because they all have a compact, rocky surface similar to the Earth's. Venus, Earth, and Mars have significant atmospheres, but Mercury has almost no atmosphere.

The **Jovian Planets** are: Jupiter (the largest planet), Saturn, Uranus, and Neptune. They are called Jovian (Jupiter-like) because of their huge sizes in relation to that of the Earth, and because they all have a gaseous nature like Jupiter. Although gas giants, some or all of the Jovian Planets may have small, solid cores.

The Sun represents 99.85% of all the matter in our solar system. Combined, the planets make up only 0.135% of the mass of the solar system, with Jupiter having twice the mass of all the other planets combined. The remaining 0.015% of the mass comes from comets, planetary satellites, asteroids, meteoroids, and interplanetary medium.

Review Video: Terrestrial Planets
Visit mometrix.com/academy and enter code: 100346

Definition of Planet

On August 24, 2006, the International Astronomical Union redefined the criteria a body must meet to be classified as a planet, stating that the following conditions must be met:

- "A planet orbits around a star and is neither a star nor a moon."
- "Its shape is spherical due to its gravity."
- "It has 'cleared' the space of its orbit."

A **dwarf planet** such as Pluto does not meet the third condition. Small solar system bodies such as asteroids and comets meet only the first condition.

Solar System

The **solar system** developed about 4.6 billion years ago out of an enormous cloud of dust and gas circling around the Sun. Four rocky planets orbit relatively close to the Sun. Their inside orbits are separated from the outside orbits of the four, larger gaseous planets by an asteroid belt. Pluto, some comets, and several small objects circle in the Kuiper belt outside Neptune's orbit. The Oort cloud, composed of icy space objects, encloses the planetary system like a shell.

Review Video: The Solar System
Visit mometrix.com/academy and enter code: 273231

Earth's Moon

The Moon is the closest celestial body to Earth. Its proximity has allowed it to be studied since the invention of the telescope. As a result, its landforms have been named after astronomers, philosophers, and other scholars. Its surface has many craters created by asteroids since it has no protective atmosphere. These dark lowlands looked like seas to early astronomers, so many have been given names like the Sea of Tranquility, even though there is virtually no water on the Moon except possibly in its polar regions. These impact craters and depressions actually contain solidified lava flows. The bright highlands were thought to be continents, and were named terrae. The rocks of the Moon have been pounded by asteroids so often that there is a layer of rubble and dust called the regolith. Also, because there is no protective atmosphere, temperatures on the Moon vary widely, from 265°F to -255°F.

Earth's Sun and Other Stars

A **star** begins as a cloud of hydrogen and some heavier elements drawn together by their own mass. As the matter coalesces due to its own gravity, it begins to rotate. Once there is sufficient mass, the core heats up to several million degrees Fahrenheit, which causes the hydrogen atoms to lose their shells and their nuclei to fuse. This releases enormous amounts of energy, generates an outward pressure that is balanced by the pull of gravity, and enables the star to become stable. At this point the star is in a stage called the **main sequence**. This is the stage our Sun is in, and it will remain in this stage until its supply of hydrogen fuel runs out. Stars are not always alone like our Sun, and may exist in pairs or groups. The hottest stars shine blue-white;

medium-hot stars like our Sun glow yellow; and cooler stars appear orange. The Sun is an **average star** in terms of mass, light production, and size. All stars, including our Sun, have a **core** where fusion happens; a **photosphere** (surface) that produces sunspots (cool, dark areas); a red **chromosphere** that emits solar (bright) flares and shooting gases; and a **corona**, the transparent area only seen during an eclipse.

Review Video: The Sun
Visit mometrix.com/academy and enter code: 699233

Comets, Asteroids, and Meteoroids

Comets are celestial bodies composed of dust, rock, frozen gases, and ice. Invisible until they near the Sun, comets emit volatile components in jets of gas and dust when exposed to the Sun's heat. The **coma** is the comet's fog-like envelope that glows as it reflects sunlight and releases radiation. **Solar winds** blow a comet away from the Sun and give it a tail of dust or electrically charged molecules. Each orbit of a comet causes it to lose matter until it breaks up or vaporizes into the Sun.

Asteroids are irregularly-shaped boulders, usually less than 60 miles in diameter, that orbit the Sun. Most are made of graphite; about 25% are silicates, or iron and nickel. Collisions or gravitational forces can cause them to fly off and possibly hit a planet.

Meteoroids are fragments of asteroids of various sizes. If they come through Earth's atmosphere, they are called meteors or shooting stars. If they land on Earth, they are called meteorites, and create craters on impact (the Barringer Crater in Arizona).

Review Video: Comets, Asteroids, and Meteoroids
Visit mometrix.com/academy and enter code: 100347

The Role of Pedagogy and Scientific Inquiry in Science Education

Developing Scientific Understanding

Scientific understanding involves not merely the knowledge of scientific theories and equations, but a comprehension of how science is done, how we come to know these theories (and how confident we are in them), and how the different domains of science fit together. Students are unlikely to develop a good scientific understanding merely by being presented with isolated facts. Rather, research suggests that a scientific understanding is best fostered by **inquiry** and by **problem-based learning** approaches, which help students develop their own critical thinking and reasoning skills. In these methods, students are not just provided with facts and theories to memorize but are led to "discover" principles on their own, through experimentation and analogy. The instructor must still provide guidance in the process; if students are completely left to their own devices they may be confused or arrive at incorrect conclusions that may do more harm than good. Furthermore, assessments used in the classroom should promote **higher-order learning**, focusing not just on repetition of facts but on reasoning and evaluation of claims. It is critical that students understand that science is a process and a way of knowing, not a collection of facts.

Prior Knowledge

Students vary in their prior knowledge and capabilities, and science instruction is not a one-size-fits-all process. Sometimes prior knowledge helps student, in that they already have some knowledge about the subject in question, but sometimes prior knowledge may seem to conflict with the new information being taught—a dilemma sometimes called the "**paradox of continuity**." Learning therefore can require a **conceptual change**, in a way that allows the students to reformulate their understanding to fit new information.

Students' experience and developmental characteristics can also affect their science learning. Some students learn more effectively through different **learning styles**, or modalities: some learn best from what they see (**visual learners**), others from what they hear (**auditory learners**), still others from handling objects (**tactile learners**), and others from active participation (**kinesthetic learners**). **Abstract thinking** develops during adolescence and may develop more rapidly in some students than others; students who have not fully developed this capability may benefit from more structured teaching methods. Adolescents tend to be at a stage in their social development in which they learn well in cooperative group activities.

Planning Activities

Instructors should be aware of and sensitive to students' different preferred styles of learning and prepare lessons that engage all these styles. The instructor should also try to tie lessons to students' individual interests in order to promote active engagement. A **positive learning environment** is one that adapts to students' individual needs and that often involves students working cooperatively.

In science in particular it's important for instructors not to exclude women and minorities, since they have been excluded so much in the past that it's easy to do so unconsciously. The instructor should make an effort to mention scientists of different ethnicities and genders and make it clear that women and minorities can be and are capable scientists.

Students currently learning English have their own needs that must be addressed. The instructor can help English learners, for instance, by speaking slowly and clearly, by writing down and providing definitions of key terms, by using visual aids and graphic organizers (which also may help visual learners who are not English language learners), and by giving access to translating devices if necessary. English learners can also benefit from working in groups with capable English speakers who can help explain instructions and procedures they don't understand.

Motivation and Engagement

Regardless of how clearly and accurately an instructor explains the topic, the students may not learn if they're unengaged and not paying attention. Therefore, it's important for the teacher to engage the students' interest and keep their attention. One of the advantages of inquiry-based learning is that it actively involves the students and keeps them more engaged by relating the topic to their interests and goals and finding ways to tie the topics in to the students' own experiences, prior knowledge, and daily lives. This requires the teacher to get to know the students and their interests, but this has other benefits as well: the students are also more engaged when there is a good relationship between the teachers and students.

Students also tend to be more engaged by collaborative group activities than by working on their own. Adolescents are at a stage in their social development in which they are increasingly driven to form social attachments with their peers. They are comfortable working in groups and benefit from collaborative learning environments.

Texts Used in the Classroom

Science instruction often involves the students acquiring information from textbooks and handouts, but not all students may be able to effectively use these texts without guidance. Most textbooks have various features designed to make it easier to locate information: an **index**, a **table of contents**, and often a **glossary** and/or a list of important variables and formulas. An instructor can explain how to use these features at the beginning of the year and perhaps even assign an activity that involves making use of them.

It may also be helpful to teach **active reading** techniques. One such technique is **pre-reading**—skimming and reading the headings before reading the text in depth, making predictions and building background knowledge. The instructor can also encourage active reading techniques through providing graphic organizers or techniques like **SQ3R**—a method that involves the student first Surveying the chapter, then formulating Questions about each section, then Reading the section, Reciting the main ideas (putting them in their own words), and Reviewing the material.

In the modern classroom, textbooks aren't the only kind of text that students can take advantage of. An effective teacher can also show students how to find information online, through web searches and reference sites.

Total School Program

While the science teachers plan the curriculum for their classes, they must also be aware of the **total school program**—the overall objectives for the students' learning in all subjects. The science teacher must be aware of school-wide objectives, and make sure that they are being adequately met in his or her class. The science instructor may also have a role in *setting* those objectives, in conjunction with other teachers and administrators; the science instructor in this case should work cooperatively with the rest of the team and ensure that any issues unique or important to the science classroom are properly addressed and incorporated into the objectives.

The science teacher must also be mindful of the statewide objectives. State standards lay out the curriculum requirements for the course and specify topics that must be covered. Students must master these topics to be ready not only for standardized exams, but to ensure that no gaps in understanding exist prior to advancing to the next grade-level.

Supportive Learning Environment

Creating a learning environment that supports student inquiries involves both setting certain procedures and expectations in the class and providing resources that lend themselves to inquiry-based learning. To encourage inquiry-based learning, the instructor should encourage students to ask questions, but try to guide them toward finding answers for themselves rather than giving direct answers to their questions. The instructor should pose questions that require higher-order thinking rather than rote recall or yes or no answers and include a time for reflection in each lesson. Lessons in inquiry-based classrooms are centered around projects and experiments rather than lectures—in fact, one increasingly popular technique is to "**flip the classroom**," having the students read the lesson or watch video lectures you provide as their homework and freeing up class time for discussion and analysis.

An inquiry-centered classroom environment should put a priority on student collaboration. The instructor should give the students assignments that involve their working together as much as practical. It is helpful to have some online resources that facilitate collaboration and sharing of information, such as a class website, and perhaps a class blog and wiki. Many online resources allow students to share documents and work on them together.

Participation in Scientific Investigation

Scientific investigations are an important part of science teaching, and it is vital that all students are given the opportunity to participate. Ideally, there will be enough space and equipment for the students to work in small groups on an experiment, but in practice this may not be possible. In this case, one solution is to have rotating stations in the classroom, where for one day or for part of the period one group works on one experiment, while another group works on a different activity that uses different equipment; as they rotate through the different stations, all the students will have the opportunity to do every activity, just not in the same order.

Another important part of making it possible for all students to participate in scientific investigations is to ensure that they all have the means to understand and carry out the instructions. Going over the procedure in a lecture may not be enough; it may be better to have a written handout and/or a screencast that the students can watch and refer back to as needed. Students with special needs must also be accommodated; for instance, English language learners can be given definitions of key terms.

Active Learning, Inquiry, and Reflection

Active learning and inquiry-based learning are two related pedagogical techniques that have been shown by research to be effective in teaching science. **Active learning** refers to teaching by making the student an active participant in the learning process. A class in which the instructor lectures, the students take notes, and the students later demonstrate their learning of the topic by taking a written exam is *not* engaged in active learning, and is not likely to be as effective. Active learning can include experiments that the students perform, interactive online simulations of processes that they can't physically experience in the classroom, and having the students create presentations and projects rather than have exams and worksheets as the main assessments.

Inquiry-based learning is a form of teaching by asking questions, having discussions, and helping students do their own research rather than just presenting them with lists of facts and formulas to be learned. Inquiry-based learning is effective not only because it involves the students directly, but because allowing them to formulate their own questions engages their curiosity and critical thinking. **Reflection** is also an important part of inquiry-based learning, having students think back on what they learned and how they learned it.

Modeling Scientific Thought

Modeling, in a pedagogical context, refers to *showing* the students what they should do, rather than telling them. This doesn't mean just demonstrating an activity at the front of the classroom while the students watch passively; effective modeling also involves the students as active participants. The important thing is that the teacher sets an example of the principles he or she wants to convey.

To model scientific attitudes, therefore, means to demonstrate and embody those attitudes. To instill curiosity and skepticism in students, the teacher should display those attributes. If the teacher doesn't know the answer to a question, the teacher should not be afraid to say "I don't know"—but should follow that by trying to find the answer, by looking it up online or by performing an experiment. When discussing a topic and coming up with questions about it, the instructor should come up with questions as well—ideally questions the instructor honestly doesn't know the answer to. On the other hand, the instructor should not be too quick to accept answers—not, for instance, immediately latching onto the first answer found online, but looking for multiple sources of information and analyzing their credibility.

Inquiry-Based Scientific Investigation

An **inquiry-based scientific investigation** is one that follows the **scientific method**. While the scientific method is often formalized in different ways, there are some essential aspects. The investigator formulates a specific **question** that the investigation will answer. Usually this question is based on an **observation** that the investigation is intended to explain. The investigator then does some background **research**, reviewing previously published information on the subject in question. For a professional scientist, this will usually involve reading articles in scientific journals; in a classroom setting, a web search may suffice. The investigator may formulate a **hypothesis**—a proposed possible answer to the question.

The investigator decides how to **gather evidence** to find an answer to the question and prove or disprove the hypothesis, designing an **experiment** that will test the hypothesis, and selecting the proper tools to carry it out. The investigator makes **predictions** as to what will happen in the experiment if the hypothesis is true or if it is not. The investigator then carries out the experiment, gathers data, and analyzes the results, drawing **conclusions** based on the data.

There remain other important steps: **communication** of the results to others, defending the results, and possibly formulating further questions.

Formulating Scientific Questions

Formulating scientific questions is an important part of an inquiry-based investigation; an investigation starts with a specific question, and then an experiment is designed to answer that question. The question usually is based on an observation: the student observes a phenomenon and then formulates a question about what was observed. The question should be as concrete, objective, quantitative, and measurable as possible. "Why did this object move?" is a vague and abstract question that cannot be easily answered. "Did this object move because of this force?" is more concrete. "What is the relationship between this force and the motion of this object?" is a good quantitative question that can potentially be answered by experiment.

To help the student to formulate a question, the instructor can first guide students through an observation, encouraging the students to think of anything about the observation they're curious about or that they don't understand. The instructor can then help the students come up with questions addressing the subject of their curiosity, and then gradually guide the students into making the questions more specific and measurable.

Hypotheses

The **hypothesis** is an educated guess as to the answer to the central question of a scientific investigation. It is an important part of the investigation because it helps guide the inquiry and suggest specific lines of investigation that can prove or disprove the hypothesis: the experiment at the heart of the investigation should be designed such that it will have different results depending on whether or not the hypothesis is correct.

It is important that the hypothesis is an *educated* guess; the student may not know the answer to the question, but there should be some basis for choosing the hypothesis—by extrapolation from known cases, or by analogy with similar scenarios. If the student has trouble coming up with a hypothesis, the instructor might prompt the student to think of similar situations the student understands better, or to research such situations that have been investigated before, and then to consider what those situations imply about the present question. Even a very loose analogy can be enough to make a hypothesis—for the purposes of the investigation, it doesn't matter that the student chooses a hypothesis that turns out to be *right*, only that it relates to the question.

Scientific Results

There are many methods that can be used to analyze and evaluate scientific results. Often **graphs** help investigators and readers visualize data better. If one variable is plotted against another and the points seem to form a straight line, that is evidence that a linear relationship may exist between these variables; if they form a parabola, they may have a quadratic relationship; and so on. In more advanced classes, **statistical methods** may be useful, from methods as simple as taking the **mean** of multiple measurements and comparing the means of sets of data rather than the individual points, to methods as complex as calculating **standard deviations** and **correlation coefficients**. All of these methods help show the relationships between quantities and can help to evaluate possible explanations of a result.

Error analysis is another important part of evaluating results. Students should have an idea of what possible sources of error exist in the experiment, and whether they are **random** or **systematic**. Random error can be identified by taking repeated measurements and seeing how close they are; identifying systematic error involves a more thoughtful consideration of what could lead results to be off in one direction or the other.

Higher-Level Thinking Skills

Students should be encouraged to engage in not just rote memorization and learning of procedures, but in higher-order thinking as well that involves putting together what they've learned in constructive ways. The most commonly used model of different levels of thinking in education is **Bloom's taxonomy**, which divides cognitive processes into six categories or levels. The lowest level, **Remember**, involves simple recall of data. The next, **Understand**, requires students to be able to explain or discuss concepts in their own words. Then come **Apply**, using the concepts in practice; **Analyze**, drawing connections and comparisons between ideas; **Evaluate**, judging and justifying ideas; and **Create**, synthesizing something new from the concepts.

It's easy to design activities that utilize the lower levels of Bloom's Taxonomy. Engaging the higher orders of thinking is more difficult, but it is important for developing a more thorough understanding of a topic. Some verbs commonly associated with each level of Bloom's Taxonomy give clues as to how to promote them. "Create", for example, is associated with the verbs "construct," "plan," and "design" (among others)—certainly designing an experiment to answer a specific question fits here. "Evaluate" is associated with "appraise," "argue," and "justify"—students could be asked to assess a scientific claim and argue for or against it.

Systematic Observations and Measurements

In a scientific investigation, observations are not haphazard; there are certain systematic principles that must be followed for useful observations. As far as possible, the observations should be **quantitative**; there should be some measured value recorded, and not simply a qualitative observation such as "it is longer". Measurements should be taken by a consistent method and recorded with proper units—and with an estimate of their **uncertainty**. A measurement taken with a meter stick with markings every millimeter, for instance, has an uncertainty of ±0.5 mm.

It is also important when making observations to vary only one quantity at a time. If you want to measure how a plant's growth is affected by temperature and by amount of light, it isn't useful to change both factors for each measurement—that would make it impossible to see how much of the effect was produced by each change. Rather, it is better to do at least one set of measurements in which the temperature is held constant and the amount of light is changed, and another where the reverse is true, so that the effects of each factor can be isolated. In many cases, an **experimental control** is also desirable.

Students' Prior Knowledge

Prior knowledge refers to the knowledge the student has about the subject matter before it's covered in class. This may come from previous classes, from books and television, from peers or parents, from experience, or from other sources. It's useful to know what prior knowledge students possess before the lesson begins, and there are a number of ways of finding out. One way is through **formative assessments**, assessments that are designed not to test what the student has learned but to test what the students already know in order to guide lesson planning. Another popular way of testing prior knowledge is a **K-W-L chart**, in which students write down what they *know* about the topic, what they *want* to know, and, after the lesson, what they *learned.*

The instructor can use the students' prior knowledge as a starting point for the lesson; having the students share what they already know can help introduce the topic. Prior knowledge may also guide the instructor's approach to the topic, since it may carry some assumptions or preconceptions that will affect the way the student might react to different presentations. In some cases, prior knowledge may even lead to misconceptions that must be overcome.

Performance in Inquiry-Based Investigations

The stereotypical classroom assessment may be a multiple-choice quiz, but this is not generally the most effective way of assessing student learning in an inquiry-based classroom. There may be a place for written exams as summative assessments, but more effective assessment methods will engage students' higher-order thinking processes and may involve collaboration and active participation.

For example, in a science class, a lab report can be a useful assessment; after performing an experiment, students may be asked to turn in a written account of the procedure and results. Along similar lines, a laboratory journal that students keep during an experiment can also be used for assessment, or a field journal for longer-term projects. The instructor may require students to compile all their work in a portfolio, to be turned in at the end of the semester or at shorter intervals; this can serve as a summative assessment in lieu of or in addition to a traditional exam. To assess the student's participation in a classroom activity as objectively as possible, rather than make a subjective judgment call the instructor can use checklists or a detailed rubric prepared ahead of time.

Assessment and Instruction

An **assessment** is an activity designed to measure students' knowledge, learning, or abilities, such as an exam. Assessments are not limited to testing how much the student has learned after a lesson; there are also formative assessments used before or during a lesson to test the student's prior knowledge and how well they are learning the topic.

There are important relationships between assessment and instruction, and the two must be designed together. Formative assessments guide instruction, since the instructor should take into account students' prior knowledge in planning a lesson, and if a formative assessment shows that students are not learning what the instructor expects, the instructor should use that information to try a different pedagogical approach. As for summative assessments, they should be designed to match the learning objectives; the instructor should make sure that the summative assessment is designed to test that the students have met the specific instructional goals of the lessons.

Ongoing Assessment

Ongoing assessment is vital in science instruction for several reasons. For one thing, formative assessments are important so that the instructor can be informed of the students' prior knowledge and plan the lesson accordingly. If the instructor learns from a formative assessment that the students lack some prior knowledge necessary to the lesson, then the instructor will have to be sure to cover that first; if the instructor learns that the students have a significant misconception about the topic, then the instructor may have to plan for a conceptual change. During the lesson, further formative assessments can monitor students' learning and inform the instructor whether the students are absorbing the information and methodologies that the instructor intends them to absorb, or whether the pace of the lesson should be changed or different pedagogical methods adopted.

Ongoing assessments can also benefit the students by reinforcing the subject matter. The assessments give the students another opportunity to put what they have learned to use, and may help them better retain it. They also give the students an idea of how well they are learning, and what topics they might need to review or about which they should ask more questions.

Types of Assessments

Assessments are divided into two main categories: **summative assessments** that measure how well students have learned the subject matter at the end of a unit, and **formative assessments** that are used before or during a lesson to test the student's prior knowledge and how well they are learning the topic. Both these types of assessment are important, and both can be carried out in a number of ways. Assessments can also be **formal**—data-driven, standardized assessments the results of which can be compared against preset benchmarks—or **informal**—less structured assessments based around performance and content. An effective science classroom utilizes a variety of different assessment methods.

For example, a **performance assessment** is an assessment that requires the student to demonstrate skills by completing a task, rather than by selecting a pre-set answer or filling in a blank. A **self-assessment** is an activity in which the student assesses his or her own work, perhaps using a rubric provided by the instructor; these are often not graded and serve to inform the student of his or her own learning. A **peer assessment** is an activity in which the student's work is assessed not by the instructor, but by a fellow student.

Review Video: Formative and Summative Assessments
Visit mometrix.com/academy and enter code: 804991

Combatting Misconceptions

One of the reasons it's important to gauge students' prior knowledge of a topic is because some of that prior knowledge may be incorrect or misleading, and the student may have misconceptions about the topic that must be overcome. Simply telling the students that their prior beliefs were incorrect is unlikely to be effective, and it may in fact be counterproductive, leading to their misconceptions being reinforced instead of removed. Rather, a better goal is to bring about a **conceptual change**, a gradual revision and rearrangement of prior knowledge to accommodate new ideas, in which the student is an active participant.

There are several research-based methods of bringing about conceptual change. One method is to promote **cognitive conflict**: presenting data or demonstrations that contradict the students' prior conceptions, and guiding the students into finding a resolution to the conflict. Another is the use of **refutational texts** that discuss and refute various views on the topic. Other methods include **collaborative argumentation**, in which students are encouraged to discuss, defend, and evaluate their positions; and **persuasive pedagogy**, applying methods of persuasion such as response shaping and reinforcing.

Reliability and Validity

Two measurements of the soundness of an assessment are reliability and validity. An assessment is **reliable** if it yields consistent results; students' scores on the assessment should not depend on external circumstances and should be similar for different questions that test the same skill. An assessment is **valid** if it measures what it is meant to measure. These two qualities can vary independently; it is possible for an exam to have a high reliability but a low validity, or vice versa.

The reliability of an assessment can be affected by many factors. Longer tests tend to be more reliable; tests with a short time limit so that many students cannot complete all the questions, or must rush to do so, tend to be less reliable. Reliability is also affected by difficulty; a test is most reliable when the questions are not so easy that almost every student answers the questions correctly, but not so hard that almost none do. It requires finding a suitable middle ground of difficulty. An assessment will tend to be more valid if it is designed to cover all the material that it is supposed to cover, but only that material. It will be less valid if it has hidden biases against certain categories of student.

Assessment as a Learning Experience

Though an obvious purpose of assessments is to allow the instructor to assign students a grade in the class, the assessments themselves can provide learning experiences. For one thing, as the students see what questions on the assessment they are unable to answer, or do not answer correctly, this helps them see what topics they have not fully learned and may need to further review. On the other hand, the questions that the students got right will help build their confidence and perhaps help them better remember in the future what they learned about those topics. Assessments also give students further practice with the methods and concepts they are testing, which may further work to reinforce them. They may also help students to learn new problem-solving strategies; as students go over the assessment after the fact and discuss how they were supposed to solve a particular problem, the answer might give them information about a strategy they were previously unaware of or underutilizing.

Equitable Use of Assessments

One important consideration that must be kept in mind in designing assessments is that they must be **equitable**—they must not be biased toward or against any part of the student population. Every student must have an adequate opportunity to demonstrate his or her skills and knowledge. There are many biases that may carelessly enter into assessments: cultural biases, language biases, biases against students with special needs.

There are a number of steps that instructors can take to ensure that assessments are equitable. Questions should not rely on "common knowledge" that may not be common to students of different cultures. Students with special needs must be provided with adequate accommodations. English language learners should be given definitions or paraphrases of difficult words and sentences. Other steps that can be taken toward making assessments more equitable include clearly laying out learning outcomes and grading rubrics, using many different methods of assessment that allow students to show their accomplishments in different ways, and ensuring that the subject matter covered in assessments is closely matched to what the instructor teaches in class.

Sharing Criteria and Results

It's important to share the evaluation criteria of assessments with students so that the students will know what to expect from the assessments and prepare accordingly, and so that during the assessment they will know where to best focus their time and attention. If the students have no idea how an assessment will be graded, then the assessment is not fair or equitable; students will not know what aspects of the assessment they should focus on the most and doing well on the assessment may be largely a matter of luck. Sharing the rubric for the assessment ahead of time makes the instructor's expectations clear and ensures that the students know what specifically they will be tested on and can prepare accordingly.

It is also important to share the results of assessments with the students. If the students know the results of their assessments, they can gauge their own progress and learning, and decide where they need to focus in the future and what topics they may need to revisit. Knowing their assessment results may also help students evaluate their study strategies and judge whether or not they are working and how or if they might need to be revised.

Scientific Inquiry Skills for Elementary Students

The six abilities that **grades K-4 students** should acquire are as follows:

- They should be able to ask questions about objects, organisms, and events in the environment.
- They should be able to devise a simple investigation to answer a question.
- They should be able to use tools such as magnifying glasses, rulers, and balances to gather data and make observations.
- They should be able to use the gathered data and observations to provide an explanation.
- They should be able to talk about, draw pictures, or use another method to communicate the results of an investigation and what they learned.
- With respect to the nature of scientific inquiry and scientists, students should understand that investigations involve formulating questions and answers, using different methods of discovering and disclosing answers, using basic tools, observing, sharing answers, and looking at and understanding others' work.

Scientific Inquiry Skills for Middle Grade Students

The five abilities that **grades 5–8 students** should acquire are as follows:

- They should be able to reformulate and clarify questions until they can be answered through scientific investigation.
- They should be able to create and carry out a scientific investigation, interpret the data to provide explanations, and use further data to revise explanations.
- They should be able to identify the tools necessary to gather and analyze data. They should be able to use computer hardware and software to store, organize, and gather data.
- They should be able to provide descriptions and explanations, create models, and make predictions based on the body of knowledge they possess.
- They should be able to explain cause and effect relationships using explanations and data from experiments.

Scientific Inquiry Skills for Older Students

The six abilities that **grades 9–12 students** should acquire are as follows:

- They should be able to identify questions and concepts that guide scientific investigation. In other words, they should be able to create a hypothesis and an appropriate experiment to test that hypothesis.
- They should be able to design and conduct a scientific investigation from start to finish. This includes being able to guide the inquiry by choosing the proper technologies and methods, determining variables, selecting an appropriate method for presenting data, and conducting peer review.
- They should be able to use technology and mathematics in investigations.
- They should be able to formulate and revise scientific explanations and models.

- They should be able to recognize and analyze alternative explanations. In other words, they should be able to devise other possibilities based on the current body of knowledge.
- They should be able to communicate and defend a scientific argument in both written and oral form.

Chapter Quiz

Ready to see how well you retained what you just read? Scan the QR code to go directly to the chapter quiz interface for this study guide. If you're using a computer, simply visit the online resources page at **mometrix.com/resources719/abctebio** and click the Chapter Quizzes link.

Scientific Investigation

Safety and Equipment

Laboratory Accidents

Any spills or accidents should be **reported** to the teacher so that the teacher can determine the safest clean-up method. The student should start to wash off a **chemical** spilled on the skin while reporting the incident. Some spills may require removal of contaminated clothing and use of the **safety shower**. Broken glass should be disposed of in a designated container. If someone's clothing catches fire they should walk to the safety shower and use it to extinguish the flames. A fire blanket may be used to smother a **lab fire**. A fire extinguisher, phone, spill neutralizers, and a first aid box are other types of **safety equipment** found in the lab. Students should be familiar with **routes** out of the room and the building in case of fire. Students should use the **eye wash station** if a chemical gets in the eyes.

Safety Procedures

Students should wear a **lab apron** and **safety goggles**. Loose or dangling clothing and jewelry, necklaces, and earrings should not be worn. Those with long hair should tie it back. Care should always be taken not to splash chemicals. Open-toed shoes such as sandals and flip-flops should not be worn, nor should wrist watches. Glasses are preferable to contact lenses since the latter carry a risk of chemicals getting caught between the lens and the eye. Students should always be supervised. The area where the experiment is taking place and the surrounding floor should be free of clutter. Only the lab book and the items necessary for the experiment should be present. Smoking, eating, and chewing gum are not permitted in the lab. Cords should not be allowed to dangle from work stations. There should be no rough-housing in the lab. Hands should be washed after the lab is complete.

Fume Hoods

Because of the potential safety hazards associated with chemistry lab experiments, such as fire from vapors and the inhalation of toxic fumes, a **fume hood** should be used in many instances. A fume hood carries away vapors from reagents or reactions. Equipment or reactions are placed as far back in the hood as practical to help enhance the collection of the fumes. The **glass safety shield** automatically closes to the appropriate height, and it should be low enough to protect the face and body. The safety shield should only be raised to move equipment in and out of the hood. One should not climb inside a hood or stick one's head inside. All spills should be wiped up immediately, and the glass should be cleaned if a splash occurs.

Common Safety Hazards

Some specific safety hazards possible in a chemistry lab include:

- **Fire**: Fire can be caused by volatile solvents such as ether, acetone, or benzene being kept in an open beaker or Erlenmeyer flask. Vapors can creep along the table and ignite if they reach a flame or spark. Solvents should be heated in a hood with a steam bath, not on a hot plate.
- **Explosion**: Heating or creating a reaction in a closed system can cause an explosion, resulting in flying glass and chemical splashes. The system should be vented to prevent this.
- **Chemical and thermal burns**: Many chemicals are corrosive to the skin and eyes.
- **Inhalation of toxic fumes**: Some compounds severely irritate membranes in the eyes, nose, throat, and lungs.
- **Absorption** of toxic chemicals such as dimethyl sulfoxide (DMSO) and nitrobenzene through the skin.
- **Ingestion** of toxic chemicals.

Safety Gloves

There are many types of **gloves** available to help protect the skin from cuts, burns, and chemical splashes. There are many considerations when choosing a glove. For example, gloves that are highly protective may limit dexterity. Some gloves may not offer appropriate protection against a specific chemical. Other considerations include degradation rating, which indicates how effective a glove is when exposed to chemicals; breakthrough time, which indicates how quickly a chemical can break through the surface of the glove; and permeation rate, which indicates how quickly chemicals seep through after the initial breakthrough. Disposable latex, vinyl, or nitrile gloves are usually appropriate for most circumstances, and offer protection from incidental splashes and contact. Other types of gloves include butyl, neoprene, PVC, PVA, Viton, Silver Shield, and natural rubber. Each offers its own type of protection but may have drawbacks as well.

Proper Handling and Storage of Chemicals

Students should take care when **carrying chemicals** from one place to another. Chemicals should never be taken from the room, tasted, or touched with bare hands. **Safety gloves** should be worn when appropriate and glove/chemical interactions and glove deterioration should be considered. Hands should always be **washed** thoroughly after a lab. Potentially hazardous materials intended for use in chemistry, biology, or other science labs should be secured in a safe area where relevant **Safety Data Sheets (SDS)** can be accessed. Chemicals and solutions should be used as directed and labels should be read before handling solutions and chemicals. Extra chemicals should not be returned to their original containers, but should be disposed of as directed by the school district's rules or local ordinances. Local municipalities often have hazardous waste disposal programs. Acids should be stored separately from other chemicals. Flammable liquids should be stored away from acids, bases, and oxidizers.

Bunsen Burners

When using a **Bunsen burner**, loose clothing should be tucked in, long hair should be tied back, and safety goggles and aprons should be worn. Students should know what to do in case of a fire or accident. When lighting the burner, strikers should always be used instead of matches. Do not touch the hot barrel. Tongs (never fingers) should be used to hold the material in the flame. To heat liquid, a flask may be set upon wire gauze on a tripod and secured with an iron ring or clamp on a stand. The flame is extinguished by turning off the gas at the source.

Safety Procedures Related to Animals

Animals to be used for **dissections** should be obtained from a company that provides animals for this purpose. Road kill or decaying animals that a student brings in should not be used. It is possible that such an animal may have a pathogen or a virus, such as rabies, which can be transmitted via the saliva of even a dead animal. Students should use gloves and should not participate if they have open sores or moral objections to dissections. It is generally accepted that biological experiments may be performed on lower-order life forms and invertebrates, but not on mammalian vertebrates and birds. No animals should be harmed physiologically. Experimental animals should be kept, cared for, and handled in a safe manner and with compassion. Pathogenic (anything able to cause a disease) substances should not be used in lab experiments.

Lab Notebooks

A **lab notebook** is a record of all pre-lab work and lab work. It differs from a lab report, which is prepared after lab work is completed. A lab notebook is a formal record of lab preparations and what was done. **Observational recordings** should not be altered, erased, or whited-out to make corrections. Drawing a single line through an entry is sufficient to make changes. Pages should be numbered and should not be torn out. Entries should be made neatly, but don't necessarily have to be complete sentences. **Entries** should provide detailed information and be recorded in such a way that another person could use them to replicate the experiment. **Quantitative data** may be recorded in tabular form, and may include calculations made during an experiment. Lab book entries can also include references and research performed before the experiment.

Entries may also consist of information about a lab experiment, including the objective or purpose, the procedures, data collected, and the results.

Lab Reports

A **lab report** is an item developed after an experiment that is intended to present the results of a lab experiment. Generally, it should be prepared using a word processor, not hand-written or recorded in a notebook. A lab report should be formally presented. It is intended to persuade others to accept or reject a hypothesis. It should include a brief but descriptive **title** and an **abstract**. The abstract is a summary of the report. It should include a purpose that states the problem that was explored or the question that was answered. It should also include a **hypothesis** that describes the anticipated results of the experiment. The experiment should include a **control** and one **variable** to ensure that the results can be interpreted correctly. Observations and results can be presented using written narratives, tables, graphs, and illustrations. The report should also include a **summation** or **conclusion** explaining whether the results supported the hypothesis.

Types of Laboratory Glassware

Two types of flasks are Erlenmeyer flasks and volumetric flasks. **Volumetric flasks** are used to accurately prepare a specific volume and concentration of a solution. **Erlenmeyer flasks** can be used for mixing, transporting, and reacting, but are not appropriate for accurate measurements.

A **pipette** can be used to accurately measure small amounts of liquid. Liquid is drawn into the pipette through a bulb. The liquid measurement is read at the **meniscus**. There are also plastic disposable pipettes. A **repipette** is a hand-operated pump that dispenses solutions.

Beakers can be used to measure mass or dissolve a solvent into a solute. They do not measure volume as accurately as a volumetric flask, pipette, graduated cylinder, or burette.

Graduated cylinders are used for precise measurements and are considered more accurate than Erlenmeyer flasks or beakers. To read a graduated cylinder, it should be placed on a flat surface and read at eye level. The surface of a liquid in a graduated cylinder forms a lens-shaped curve. The measurement should be taken from the bottom of the curve. A ring may be placed at the top of tall, narrow cylinders to help avoid breakage if they are tipped over.

A **burette**, or buret, is a piece of lab glassware used to accurately dispense liquid. It looks similar to a narrow graduated cylinder, but it includes a stopcock and tip. It may be filled with a funnel or pipette.

Microscopes

There are different kinds of microscopes, but **optical** or **light microscopes** are the most commonly used in lab settings. Light and lenses are used to magnify and view samples. A specimen or sample is placed on a slide, and the slide is placed on a stage with a hole in it. Light passes through the hole and illuminates the sample. The sample is magnified by lenses and viewed through the eyepiece. A simple microscope has one lens, while a typical compound microscope has three lenses. The light source can be room light redirected by a mirror, or the microscope can have its own independent light source that passes through a condenser. In this case, there are diaphragms and filters to allow light intensity to be controlled. Optical microscopes also have coarse and fine adjustment knobs.

Other types of microscopes include **digital microscopes**, which use a camera and a monitor to allow viewing of the sample. **Scanning electron microscopes (SEMs)** provide greater detail in terms of a sample's surface topography and can produce magnifications much greater than those possible with optical microscopes. The technology of an SEM is quite different from an optical microscope in that it does not rely on lenses to magnify objects, but uses samples placed in a chamber. In one type of SEM, a beam of electrons from an electron gun scans and actually interacts with the sample to produce an image.

Wet mount slides designed for use with a light microscope typically require a thin portion of the specimen to be placed on a standard glass slide. A drop of water is added, and a cover slip or cover glass is placed on top. Air bubbles and fingerprints can make viewing difficult. Placing the cover slip at a 45-degree angle and allowing it to drop into place can help avoid the problem of air bubbles. A **cover slip** should always be used when viewing wet mount slides. The viewer should start with the objective in its lowest position and then fine-focus. The microscope should be carried with two hands and stored with the low-power objective in the down position. **Lenses** should be cleaned with lens paper only. A **graticule slide** is marked with a grid line, and is useful for counting or estimating a quantity.

Balances

Balances such as triple-beam balances, spring balances, and electronic balances measure mass and force. An **electronic balance** is the most accurate, followed by a **triple-beam balance** and then a **spring balance**. One part of a **triple-beam balance** is the plate, which is where the item to be weighed is placed. There are also three beams, which have hash marks indicating amounts and which hold the weights that rest in the notches. The front beam measures weights between 0 and 10 grams, the middle beam measures weights in 100-gram increments, and the far beam measures weights in 10-gram increments. The sum of the weight of each beam is the total weight of the object. A triple beam balance also includes a set screw to calibrate the equipment, as well as a mark indicating that the object and counterweights are in balance.

Chromatography

Chromatography refers to a set of laboratory techniques used to separate or analyze **mixtures**. Mixtures are dissolved in their mobile phases. In the stationary or bonded phase, the desired component is separated from other molecules in the mixture. In chromatography, the analyte is the substance to be separated. **Preparative chromatography** refers to the type of chromatography that involves purifying a substance for further use rather than further analysis. **Analytical chromatography** involves analyzing the isolated substance. Other types of chromatography include column, planar, paper, thin layer, displacement, supercritical fluid, affinity, ion exchange, and size exclusion chromatography. Reversed phase, two-dimensional, simulated moving bed, pyrolysis, fast protein, counter current, and chiral are also types of chromatography. **Gas chromatography** refers to the separation technique in which the mobile phase of a substance is in gas form.

Review Video: Paper Chromatography
Visit mometrix.com/academy and enter code: 543963

Reagents and Reactants

A **reagent** or **reactant** is a chemical agent for use in chemical reactions. When preparing for a lab, it should be confirmed that glassware and other equipment have been cleaned and/or sterilized. There should be enough materials, reagents, or other solutions needed for the lab for every group of students completing the experiment. Distilled water should be used instead of tap water when performing lab experiments because distilled water has most of its impurities removed. Other needed apparatus such as funnels, filter paper, balances, Bunsen burners, ring stands, and/or microscopes should also be set up. After the lab, it should be confirmed that sinks, workstations, and any equipment used have been cleaned. If chemicals or specimens need to be kept at a certain temperature by refrigerating them or using another storage method, the temperature should be checked periodically to ensure the sample does not spoil.

Diluting Acids

When preparing a solution of **dilute acid**, always add the concentrated acid solution to water, not water to concentrated acid. Start by adding approximately $\frac{2}{3}$ of the total volume of water to the graduated cylinder or volumetric flask. Next, add the concentrated acid to the water. Add additional water to the diluted acid to bring the solution to the final desired volume.

Cleaning After Acid Spills

In the event of an **acid spill**, any clothes that have come into contact with the acid should be removed and any skin contacted with acid must be rinsed with clean water. To the extent a window can be opened or a fume hood can be turned on, do so. Do not try to force air circulation, such as by adding a fan, as acid fumes can be harmful if spread.

Next, pour one of the following over the spill area: sodium bicarbonate, baking soda, soda ash, or cat litter. Start from the outside of the spill and then move towards the center, in order to prevent splashing. When the clumps have thoroughly dried, sweep up the clumps and dispose of them as chemical waste.

Centrifuges

A centrifuge is used to separate the components of a heterogeneous mixture (consisting of two or more compounds) by spinning it. The solid precipitate settles in the bottom of the container, and the liquid component of the solution, called the **centrifugate**, is at the top. A well-known application of this process is using a centrifuge to separate blood cells and plasma. The heavier cells settle on the bottom of the test tube, and the lighter plasma stays on top. Another example is using a salad spinner to help dry lettuce.

Electrophoresis, Calorimetry, and Titration

- **Electrophoresis** is the separation of molecules based on electrical charge. This is possible because particles dispersed in a fluid usually carry electric charges on their surfaces. Molecules are pulled through the fluid toward the positive end if the molecules have a negative charge and are pulled through the fluid toward the negative end if the molecules have a positive charge.
- **Calorimetry** is used to determine the heat released or absorbed in a chemical reaction.
- **Titration** helps determine the precise endpoint of a reaction. With this information, the precise quantity of reactant in the titration flask can be determined. A burette is used to deliver the second reactant to the flask and an indicator or pH meter is used to detect the endpoint of the reaction.

Field Studies and Research Projects

Field studies may facilitate scientific inquiry in a manner similar to indoor lab experiments. Field studies can be interdisciplinary in nature and can help students learn and apply scientific concepts and processes. **Research projects** can be conducted in any number of locations, including school campuses, local parks, national parks, beaches, or mountains. Students can practice the general techniques of observation, data collection, collaborative planning, and analysis of experiments. Field studies give students the chance to learn through hands-on applications of scientific processes, such as map making in geography, observation of stratification in geology, observation of life cycles of plants and animals, and analysis of water quality.

Students should watch out for obvious outdoor **hazards**. These include poisonous flora and fauna such as poison ivy, poison oak, and sumac. Depending on the region of the United States in which the field study is being conducted, hazards may also include rattlesnakes and black widow or brown recluse spiders. Students should also be made aware of potentially hazardous situations specific to **geographic locales** and the possibility of coming into contact with **pathogens**.

Field studies allow for great flexibility in the use of traditional and technological methods for **making observations** and **collecting data**. For example, a nature study could consist of a simple survey of bird species within a given area. Information could be recorded using still photography or a video camera. This type of activity gives students the chance to use technologies other than computers. Computers could still be used to create a slide show of transferred images or a digital lab report. If a quantitative study of birds was being performed, the simple technique of using a pencil and paper to tabulate the number of birds counted in the field could also be used. Other techniques used during field studies could include collecting specimens for lab study, observing coastal ecosystems and tides, and collecting weather data such as temperature, precipitation amounts, and air pressure in a particular locale.

Scientific Concepts Related to Biology

Chemical Nature of Biology

All organisms are made up of matter and display the typical physical and chemical properties of matter. Every cell of an organism is composed of molecules, atoms, and ions. **Chemistry** is needed to explain the structure and function of all cellular processes at the molecular level. **Organic chemistry** involves many large and complex molecules including biochemical compounds like carbohydrates, lipids, proteins, and nucleic acids. Chemical reactions occur in the daily function of organisms even at the cellular level. Chemical reactions that are important for life include oxidation-reduction, dehydration synthesis, hydrolysis, phosphorylation, and acid-base reactions.

Use of Mathematics in Biology

Mathematics is becoming increasingly prevalent in modern biology, especially with the use of computers for statistical programs. Mathematics is used in the **studies of populations**. For example, biologists study human population growth, bacteria growth, and virus growth. Populations of organisms in feeding relationships such as predator and prey are studied. Mathematics is used in classical genetics. For example, biologists use probability theory to predict offspring in **genetic crosses**. Mathematics, with the help of computer science, is used extensively in bioinformatics to analyze large amounts of biological information. For example, biological data are extracted and analyzed using sophisticated computer programing. Mathematics is also used in studies of epidemics. For example, studies concerning the spread of the flu and acquired immune deficiency syndrome (AIDS) have been performed.

Physical Laws and Principles Governing Biological Systems

Biological systems are governed by the same physical laws and principles that govern the rest of the universe. For example, biological systems must obey the laws of thermodynamics. These laws govern energy and the transformations of energy. The first law of thermodynamics is the law of **conservation of energy**, which states that energy is neither created nor destroyed but can change forms. The energy needed for life on Earth comes from the Sun. Sunlight reaches the Earth and is transformed by green plants and cyanobacteria (producers) during photosynthesis into the chemical bonds of ATP molecules, which can be used by these organisms for energy. Consumers eat the producers or other consumers in order to obtain energy. The second law of thermodynamics states that systems tend toward more disorder or randomness, also known as **entropy**. This is evident in the fact that organisms must continually acquire or transfer energy to sustain life and, as such, the energy is dispersed through the whole biosphere. This diffusion of energy isn't perfectly efficient and much of the energy becomes heat and is essentially unusable.

Cell Theory

Cell theory states that all living things are composed of cells, which are the basic unit of structure and function in living things, and that cells come from preexisting cells. Cells were first observed in 1655 by Robert Hooke when he was studying thin slices of a piece of cork under his primitive microscope. Because the cork cells were dead, Hooke actually only observed the cell walls of the cork cells. Hooke was the first to use the word "cell," which comes from the Latin word *cellula*, which means small compartment. Hooke documented his observations with sketches and published his work in his book commonly called *Micrographia.*

Germ Theory of Disease

The **germ theory of disease** states that most infectious diseases are caused by germs or disease-causing microbes or pathogens. The germ theory is the foundation of microbiology and modern medicine. Pasteur studied the fermentation of wine and the spoiling of milk. He discovered that yeast caused the fermentation of wine and bacteria caused the spoiling of milk. He developed the process of pasteurization of milk that killed the harmful microbes without ruining the taste of the milk. Then he studied diseases in silkworms and was able to determine that the causes of those diseases were protozoa and bacteria. Pasteur also thought that microbes in hospitals came from preexisting microbes instead of **spontaneous generation**. He disproved spontaneous generation with his work with bacteria and broth. He discovered that weakened microbes could be used in **vaccines** or **immunizations** to prevent or protect against the diseases caused by those microbes. Pasteur discovered viruses in his work, developing the rabies vaccine and treatments for those already infected with the rabies virus.

MENDEL'S CONTRIBUTIONS TO GENETICS

Johann Gregor Mendel is known as the **father of genetics**. Mendel was an Austrian monk who performed thousands of experiments involving the breeding of the common pea plant in the monastery garden. Mendel kept detailed records including seed color, pod color, seed type, flower color, and plant height for eight years and published his work in 1865. Unfortunately, his work was largely ignored until the early 1900s. Mendel's work showed that genes come in pairs and that dominant and recessive traits are inherited independently of each other. His work established the law of segregation, the law of independent assortment, and the law of dominance.

DARWIN'S CONTRIBUTIONS TO THEORY OF EVOLUTION

Charles Darwin's **theory of evolution** by natural selection is the unifying concept in biology today. From 1831 to 1836, Darwin traveled as a naturalist on a five-year voyage on the *H.M.S. Beagle* around the tip of South America and to the Galápagos Islands. He studied finches, took copious amounts of meticulous notes, and collected thousands of plant and animal specimens. He collected 13 species of finches, each with a unique bill for a distinct food source These similarities between the finches led him to believe that the finches shared a common ancestor. The similarities and differences of fossils of extinct rodents and modern mammal fossils led him to believe that the mammals had changed over time. Darwin believed that these changes were the result of random genetic changes called **mutations**. He believed that mutations could be beneficial and eventually result in a different organism over time. In 1859, in his first book, *On the Origin of Species*, Darwin coined the term "**natural selection**" and proposed that it was the means by which adaptations would arise over time. He said that it is the mechanism of evolution. Because variety exists among individuals of a species, he stated that those individuals must compete for the same limited resources. Some would die, and others would survive. According to Darwin, evolution is a slow, gradual process. In 1871, Darwin published his second book, *Descent of Man, and Selection in Relation to Sex*, in which he discussed the evolution of man.

CONTRIBUTION TO GENETICS BY ALFRED HERSHEY AND MARTHA CHASE

Alfred Hershey and Martha Chase did a series of experiments in 1952 known as the **Hershey-Chase experiments**. These experiments showed that deoxyribonucleic acid (DNA), not protein, is the genetic material that transfers information for inheritance. The Hershey-Chase experiments used a bacteriophage, a virus that infects bacteria, to infect the bacteria *Escherichia coli.* The bacteriophage T2 is basically a small piece of DNA enclosed in a protein coating. The DNA contains phosphorus, and the protein coating contains sulfur. In the first set of experiments, the T2 was marked with radioactive phosphorus-32. In the second set of experiments, the T2 was marked with radioactive sulfur-35. For both sets of experiments, after the *E. coli* was infected by the T2, the *E. coli* was isolated using a centrifuge. In the first set of experiments, the radioactive isotope (P-32) was found in the *E. coli*, showing that the genetic information was transferred by the DNA. In the second set of experiments, the radioactive isotope (S-35) was not found in the *E. coli*, showing that the genetic information was not transferred by the protein as was previously thought. Hershey and Chase conducted further experiments allowing the bacteria from the first set of experiments to reproduce, and the offspring was also found to contain the radioactive isotope (P-32) further confirming that the DNA transferred the genetic material.

CONTRIBUTIONS TO THE KNOWLEDGE OF DNA

The three-dimensional double-helix structure of the DNA molecule was formulated by James Watson and Francis Crick in 1953. But the actual discovery of DNA took place in 1869 when Friedrich Miescher discovered DNA, which he called "nuclein" in the nuclei of human white blood cells while attempting to isolate proteins. Years later in 1919, Phoebus Levene identified the components of a nucleotide. Then in 1950, Erwin Chargaff published his discovery that DNA varies among species and states what is now known as **Chargaff's rule**:

Adenine always combines with thymine, and cytosine always combines with guanine. In 1951, Rosalind Franklin studied the molecular structure of DNA using x-rays. Her work laid the foundation for the work that Watson and Crick did in 1953, in which they discovered the three-dimensional double-helix structure of DNA. Watson and Crick showed that the complementary bases are joined by hydrogen bonds. Franklin also studied the structure of RNA and discovered that RNA is a single-strand helix structure, not a double strand like DNA.

Population Models

Ecologists use population models to study the populations in an ecosystem and their interactions of populations with the environment. **Population models** are mathematical models that are designed to study population dynamics. Ecologists can model the growth of a population. For example, models can be designed to describe increases, decreases, or fluctuations in the size of populations due to births, deaths, and migrations. Ecologists can model the interactions of populations with other populations. For example, models of the interactions between predator and prey describe the fluctuating cycles associated with these relationships. Models can also include other factors such as diseases and limiting resources.

Ethical Concerns of Embryonic Stem Cells for Research

Research involving the use of embryonic stem cells offers hope for genetics-related health issues. However, ethical issues are seriously debated. New therapies could be developed using embryonic stem cells that would greatly alleviate suffering for many people. However, that benefit comes at the cost of human embryos. Proponents of embryonic stem cell research argue that an early embryo is not yet a person because the embryo cannot survive without being implanted in the uterus. Some believe that the embryo should have no moral status and that fertilized eggs should be treated as the property of the parents who should have the right to donate that property to research. Opponents of embryonic stem cell research argue that the embryo is a human life at fertilization and should have full moral status at fertilization, and that a human embryo is a human being. Opponents argue that judgments determining when an embryo is viable or when an embryo is fully human cannot be made. Some opponents of stem cell research do not believe that the fertilized egg is a human being, but they still argue that by removing the stem cells from the early embryo, the embryo is prevented from becoming a human being. They argue that embryonic stem cell research destroys potential life.

Ethical and Societal Concerns Regarding Genetically Modified Food

Genetically modified (GM) foods are transgenic crops that have had their genes altered by technology. For example, herbicide-tolerant soybeans and insect-resistant corn have been grown for years in the United States. Several issues have been raised concerning GM foods. Some people do not want to go against nature. Even scientists may feel that because the genes in organisms have evolved over millions of years that man should not interfere. Others would argue that man has been selectively breeding plants and animals for hundreds of years, and genetic modification is just an extension of that concept. Scientists are concerned about introducing new allergens into the food supply. For example, if a gene from a peanut plant is introduced into a soybean plant, there may be a potential for allergic reactions. Proteins from microorganisms may have never been tested as allergens. Many are concerned that the genetic modifications will not be contained. Pollen from fields of genetically modified crops may be carried by insects or wind to other fields. In some cases, traits such as herbicide resistance might pass from the cultivated plants to the wild populations of those plants. Insect-resistant plants may harm insects other than those that were being targeted. For example, studies show that pollinators such as the monarch butterfly may be harmed from GM corn.

Ethical Concerns Regarding Human Cloning and Animal Cloning

Many issues are raised with the topic of human cloning and animal cloning. Disagreements arise over who, if any, should be allowed to produce human clones. Many are concerned about how clones would integrate into families and societies. Some believe that human cloning for procreation purposes should be regulated based on motivation. For example, individuals interested in raising a genetically-related child should be granted approval, but those seeking immortality or viewing cloning as a novelty should be denied. Many believe that mandatory counseling and a waiting period should be enforced. Others argue that individuals do not have a right to a genetically-related child, that cloning is not safe, and that cloning is not medically necessary.

Proponents argue that cloning is needed to generate tissues and whole organs that eliminate the need for immunosuppressive drugs. Cloned tissues and organs could be used to counter the effects of aging. Others fear that this will lead to the generation of humans solely for the purpose of harvesting tissues and organs. Animals are being cloned in laboratories and in livestock production. Animal rights activists are opposed to the cloning of animals and argue that many cloned animals suffer from defects before they die. Some believe that animals have moral rights and should be treated with the same ethical consideration given to humans.

Societal Concerns About Genetic Testing

Society has not fully embraced genetic testing. Many people do not consider genetic testing to be a medical test and many feel pressure from family members who do not want the family genes revealed. Some do not want to know of potential health problems they may face later in life. Many are concerned about the psychological impact and stigma associated with carrying gene mutations. Others fear genetic discrimination from employers such as not being hired, losing a job, or being denied promotions. Some people fear being denied services from health insurers, while others fear being denied educational opportunities. However, the Genetic Information Nondiscrimination Act of 2008 protects Americans from discrimination due to differences in their DNA.

Concerns about privacy and confidentiality in regard to genetic testing raise questions that have yet to be answered. For example, who owns an individual's genetic information and who has access to that information? Should courts and schools have access to that information? Genetic testing also raises philosophical issues. Do genes determine behavior? If so, then are people responsible for their behavior?

Genetic Engineering

Genetic engineering is putting DNA from one species into another species. DNA from a species with desirable traits is spliced into the chromosomes in cells of other species. Through mitosis, those transgenic cells produce other similar cells, which are cultured to produce new organisms. Food produced by using these transgenic organisms is called GM (genetically modified) food. There is controversy over the safety of GM foods.

Genetic engineering is much faster than the older process—artificial selection—used to make better agricultural plants and animals. In agriculture, desirable traits include better resistance to pests and disease, quicker growth, and development of more of the edible parts. Genetic engineering may also produce plants that need less investment of water or fertilizer, are more resistant to drought and poor soil conditions, and spoil less when stored or transported.

Scientific Inquiry and Reasoning

Scientific Inquiry

The concept of **scientific inquiry** refers to the idea of how one thinks and asks questions in a logical way to gain trustworthy information. The underlying motivation of science is to try to understand the natural world. Much of human thought is based on assumptions about how things work that may or may not be true. The goal of scientific inquiry is to test those assumptions to gain a greater understanding of the world with good questions and objective tests, and then re-use what was learned to ask better questions. The more we understand about the natural world, the better the questions we can ask, and that is the general idea behind scientific inquiry. The applied practice of scientific inquiry is to ask questions in a systematic method, called the scientific method.

Scientific Knowledge

Scientific knowledge refers to any topic that is studied **empirically**, meaning that it is based on observation of a **phenomenon** in an objective way. The body of **scientific knowledge** is often broken down into several domains including biology, ecology, Earth science, space science, physics, and chemistry. These each have further subdomains and are overlapping in many ways. For instance, ecology is the study of ecosystems, which are made up of biological factors and geological factors, so it contains elements of both biology and Earth science. Each of these domains is subject to the concepts of scientific inquiry, such as the scientific method, scientific facts, hypotheses, and scientific laws.

IMPORTANT TERMINOLOGY

- A **phenomenon** is an event or effect that is observed.
- A **scientific fact** is considered an objective and verifiable observation. Usually, a fact can be repeated or demonstrated to others.
- A **scientific theory** is a proposition explaining why or how something happens and is built on scientific facts and laws. Scientific theories can be tested, but are not fully proven. If new evidence is found that disproves the theory, it is no longer considered true.
- A **hypothesis** is an educated guess that is not yet proven. It is used to predict the outcome of an experiment in an attempt to solve a problem or answer a question.
- A **law** is an explanation of events that always leads to the same outcome. It is a fact that an object falls. The law of gravity explains why an object falls. The theory of relativity, although generally accepted, has been neither proven nor disproved.
- A **model** is used to explain something on a smaller scale or in simpler terms to provide an example. It is a representation of an idea that can be used to explain events or applied to new situations to predict outcomes or determine results.

HISTORY OF SCIENTIFIC KNOWLEDGE

When one examines the history of **scientific knowledge**, it is clear that it is constantly **evolving**. The body of facts, models, theories, and laws grows and changes over time. In other words, one scientific discovery leads to the next. Some advances in science and technology have important and long-lasting effects on science and society. Some discoveries were so alien to the accepted beliefs of the time that not only were they rejected as wrong, but were also considered outright blasphemy. Today, however, many beliefs once considered incorrect have become an ingrained part of scientific knowledge, and have also been the basis of new advances. Examples of advances include: Copernicus's heliocentric view of the universe, Newton's laws of motion and planetary orbits, relativity, geologic time scale, plate tectonics, atomic theory, nuclear physics, biological evolution, germ theory, industrial revolution, molecular biology, information and communication, quantum theory, galactic universe, and medical and health technology.

SCIENTIFIC INQUIRY AND SCIENTIFIC METHOD

Scientists use a number of generally accepted techniques collectively known as the **scientific method**. The scientific method generally involves carrying out the following steps:

- Identifying a problem or posing a question
- Formulating a hypothesis or an educated guess
- Conducting experiments or tests that will provide a basis to solve the problem or answer the question
- Observing the results of the test
- Drawing conclusions

An important part of the scientific method is using acceptable experimental techniques. Objectivity is also important if valid results are to be obtained. Another important part of the scientific method is peer review. It is essential that experiments be performed and data be recorded in such a way that experiments can be reproduced to verify results. Historically, the scientific method has been taught with a more linear approach, but it is important to recognize that the scientific method should be a cyclical or **recursive process**. This means that as hypotheses are tested and more is learned, the questions should continue to change to reflect the changing body of knowledge. One cycle of experimentation is not enough.

Review Video: The Scientific Method
Visit mometrix.com/academy and enter code: 191386

Metric and International System of Units

The **metric system** is the accepted standard of measurement in the scientific community. The **International System of Units (SI)** is a set of measurements (including the metric system) that is almost globally accepted. The United States, Liberia, and Myanmar have not accepted this system. **Standardization** is important because it allows the results of experiments to be compared and reproduced without the need to laboriously convert measurements. The SI is based partially on the **meter-kilogram-second (MKS) system** rather than the **centimeter-gram-second (CGS) system**. The MKS system considers meters, kilograms, and seconds to be the basic units of measurement, while the CGS system considers centimeters, grams, and seconds to be the basic units of measurement. Under the MKS system, the length of an object would be expressed as 1 meter instead of 100 centimeters, which is how it would be described under the CGS system.

Review Video: Metric System Conversions
Visit mometrix.com/academy and enter code: 163709

Basic Units of Measurement

Using the **metric system** is generally accepted as the preferred method for taking measurements. Having a **universal standard** allows individuals to interpret measurements more easily, regardless of where they are located. The basic units of measurement are: the **meter**, which measures length; the **liter**, which measures volume; and the **gram**, which measures mass. The metric system starts with a base unit and increases or decreases in units of 10. The prefix and the base unit combined are used to indicate an amount. For example, deka- is 10 times the base unit. A dekameter is 10 meters; a dekaliter is 10 liters; and a dekagram is 10 grams. The prefix hecto- refers to 100 times the base amount; kilo- is 1,000 times the base amount. The prefixes that indicate a fraction of the base unit are deci-, which is $\frac{1}{10}$ of the base unit; centi-, which is $\frac{1}{100}$ of the base unit; and milli-, which is $\frac{1}{1,000}$ of the base unit.

Common Prefixes

The prefixes for multiples are as follows:

Deka	(da)	10^1 (deka is the American spelling, but deca is also used)
Hecto	(h)	10^2
Kilo	(k)	10^3
Mega	(M)	10^6
Giga	(G)	10^9
Tera	(T)	10^{12}

The prefixes for subdivisions are as follows:

Deci	(d)	10^{-1}
Centi	(c)	10^{-2}
Milli	(m)	10^{-3}
Micro	(μ)	10^{-6}
Nano	(n)	10^{-9}
Pico	(p)	10^{-12}

The rule of thumb is that prefixes greater than 10^3 are capitalized when abbreviating. Abbreviations do not need a period after them. A decimeter (dm) is a tenth of a meter, a deciliter (dL) is a tenth of a liter, and a decigram (dg) is a tenth of a gram. Pluralization is understood. For example, when referring to 5 mL of water, no "s" needs to be added to the abbreviation.

Basic SI Units of Measurement

SI uses **second(s)** to measure time. Fractions of seconds are usually measured in metric terms using prefixes such as millisecond ($\frac{1}{1,000}$ of a second) or nanosecond ($\frac{1}{1,000,000,000}$ of a second). Increments of time larger than a second are measured in **minutes** and **hours**, which are multiples of 60 and 24. An example of this is a swimmer's time in the 800-meter freestyle being described as 7:32.67, meaning 7 minutes, 32 seconds, and 67 one-hundredths of a second. One second is equal to $\frac{1}{60}$ of a minute, $\frac{1}{3,600}$ of an hour, and $\frac{1}{86,400}$ of a day. Other SI base units are the **ampere** (A) (used to measure electric current), the **kelvin** (K) (used to measure thermodynamic temperature), the **candela** (cd) (used to measure luminous intensity), and the **mole** (mol) (used to measure the amount of a substance at a molecular level). **Meter** (m) is used to measure length and **kilogram** (kg) is used to measure mass.

Significant Figures

The mathematical concept of **significant figures** or **significant digits** is often used to determine the accuracy of measurements or the level of confidence one has in a specific measurement. The significant figures of a measurement include all the digits known with certainty plus one estimated or uncertain digit. There are a number of rules for determining which digits are considered "important" or "interesting." They are:

- All non-zero digits are *significant.*
- Zeros between digits are *significant.*
- Leading and trailing zeros are *not significant* unless they appear to the right of the non-zero digits in a decimal.

For example, in 0.01230, the significant digits are 1230, and this number would be said to be accurate to the hundred-thousandths place. The zero indicates that the amount has actually been measured as 0. Other zeros are considered placeholders and are not important. A decimal point may be placed after zeros to indicate their importance (in "100." for example).

Graphs and Charts

Graphs and charts are effective ways to present scientific data such as observations, statistical analyses, and comparisons between dependent variables and independent variables. On a line chart, the **independent variable** (the one that is being manipulated for the experiment) is represented on the horizontal axis (the x-axis). Any **dependent variables** (the ones that may change as the independent variable changes) are represented on the y-axis. An **XY** or **scatter plot** is often used to plot many points. A "best fit" line is drawn, which allows outliers to be identified more easily. Charts and their axes should have titles. The x and y interval units should be evenly spaced and labeled. Other types of charts are **bar charts** and **histograms**, which can be used to compare differences between the data collected for two variables. A **pie chart** can graphically show the relation of parts to a whole.

Review Video: Identifying Variables
Visit mometrix.com/academy and enter code: 627181

Review Video: Data Interpretation of Graphs
Visit mometrix.com/academy and enter code: 200439

Data Presentation

Data collected during a science lab can be organized and **presented** in any number of ways. While **straight narrative** is a suitable method for presenting some lab results, it is not a suitable way to present numbers and quantitative measurements. These types of observations can often be better presented with **tables** and **graphs**. Data that is presented in tables and organized in rows and columns may also be used to make graphs quite easily. Other methods of presenting data include illustrations, photographs, video, and even audio formats. In a **formal report**, tables and figures are labeled and referred to by their labels. For example, a picture of a bubbly solution might be labeled Figure 1, Bubbly Solution. It would be referred to in the text in the following way: "The reaction created bubbles 10 mm in size, as shown in Figure 1, Bubbly Solution." Graphs are also labeled as figures. Tables are labeled in a different way. Examples include: Table 1, Results of Statistical Analysis, or Table 2, Data from Lab 2.

Statistical Precision and Errors

Errors that occur during an experiment can be classified into two categories: random errors and systematic errors. **Random errors** can result in collected data that is wildly different from the rest of the data, or they may result in data that is indistinguishable from the rest. Random errors are not consistent across the data set. In large data sets, random errors may contribute to the variability of data, but they will not affect the average. Random errors are sometimes referred to as noise. They may be caused by a student's inability to take the same measurement in exactly the same way or by outside factors that are not considered variables, but influence the data. A **systematic error** will show up consistently across a sample or data set, and may be the result of a flaw in the experimental design. This type of error affects the average, and is also known as bias.

Scientific Notation

Scientific notation is used because values in science can be very large or very small, which makes them unwieldy. A number in **decimal notation** is 93,000,000. In **scientific notation**, it is 9.3×10^7. The first number, 9.3, is the **coefficient**. It is always greater than or equal to 1 and less than 10. This number is followed by a multiplication sign. The base is always 10 in scientific notation. If the number is greater than ten, the exponent is positive. If the number is between zero and one, the exponent is negative. The first digit of the number is followed by a decimal point and then the rest of the number. In this case, the number is 9.3, and the decimal point was moved seven places to the right from the end of the number to get 93,000,000. The number of places moved, seven, is the exponent.

Statistical Terminology

- **Mean**—The average, found by taking the sum of a set of numbers and dividing by the number of numbers in the set.
- **Median**—The middle number in a set of numbers sorted from least to greatest. If the set has an even number of entries, the median is the average of the two in the middle.
- **Mode**—The value that appears most frequently in a data set. There may be more than one mode. If no value appears more than once, there is no mode.
- **Range**—The difference between the highest and lowest numbers in a data set.
- **Standard deviation**—Measures the dispersion of a data set, or how far from the mean a single data point is likely to be.
- **Regression analysis**—A method of analyzing sets of data and sets of variables. It involves studying how the typical value of the dependent variable changes when any one of the independent variables is varied and the other independent variables remain fixed.

Review Video: Mean, Median, and Mode
Visit mometrix.com/academy and enter code: 286207

Review Video: Standard Deviation
Visit mometrix.com/academy and enter code: 419469

Chapter Quiz

Ready to see how well you retained what you just read? Scan the QR code to go directly to the chapter quiz interface for this study guide. If you're using a computer, simply visit the online resources page at **mometrix.com/resources719/abctebio** and click the Chapter Quizzes link.

Biochemical Basis of Life

Chemical Structures and Properties of Biologically Important Molecules

Chemical Bonding Properties of Carbon

Carbon is considered to be the central atom of organic compounds. Carbon atoms each have four valence electrons and require four more electrons to have a stable outer shell. Due to the repulsion between the valence electrons, the bond sites are all equidistant from each other. This enables carbon to form longs chains and rings. Carbon atoms can form four single covalent bonds with other atoms. For example, methane (CH_4) consists of one carbon atom singly bonded to four separate hydrogen atoms. Carbon atoms can also form double or triple covalent bonds. For example, an oxygen atom can form a double bond with a carbon atom, and a nitrogen atom can form a triple bond with a carbon atom.

Organic and Inorganic Molecules

Organic molecules contain carbon and hydrogen. Because carbon can form four covalent bonds, organic molecules can be very complex structures. Organic molecules can have carbon backbones that form long chains, branched chains, or even rings. Organic compounds tend to be less soluble in water than inorganic compounds. Organic compounds are often classified as either natural (found in plants and animals) or as synthetic (made via laboratory or industrial processes). **Inorganic molecules** generally do not contain carbon-carbon or carbon-hydrogen bonds, but there are some exceptions. Inorganic compounds include salts and metals. Specific examples of inorganic molecules include sodium chloride, oxygen, and carbon dioxide.

Covalent Bonds

Chemical bonds are the attractive forces that bind atoms together to form molecules. Chemical bonds include covalent bonds, ionic bonds, and metallic bonds. **Covalent bonds** are formed from the sharing of electron pairs between two atoms in a molecule. In organic molecules, carbon atoms form single, double, or triple covalent bonds. Organic compounds including proteins, carbohydrates, lipids, and nucleic acids are molecular compounds formed by covalent bonds.

Review Video: Covalent Bonds
Visit mometrix.com/academy and enter code: 482899

Hydrogen Bonds

Intermolecular forces are the attractive forces between molecules. Intermolecular forces include hydrogen bonds, London or dispersion forces, and dipole-dipole forces. **Hydrogen bonds** are the attractive forces between molecules containing hydrogen atoms covalently bonded to oxygen, fluorine, or nitrogen. Hydrogen bonds bind the two strands of a DNA molecule to each other. Two hydrogen bonds join each adenosine and thymine, and three hydrogen bonds join each cytosine and guanine.

ATP

Adenosine triphosphate (ATP) is the energy source for most cellular functions. Each ATP molecule is a nucleotide consisting of a central ribose sugar flanked by a purine base and a chain of three phosphate groups. The purine base is adenine, and when adenine is joined to ribose, an adenosine is formed, explaining the name adenosine triphosphate. If one phosphate is removed from the end of the molecule, adenosine diphosphate (ADP) is formed.

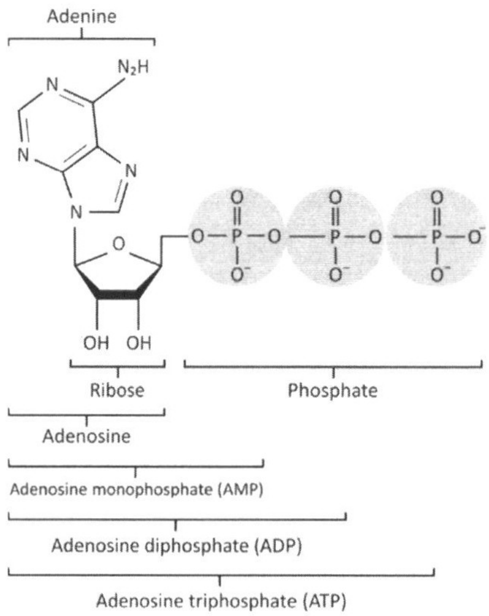

Properties of Water

Water exhibits numerous properties. Water has a high surface tension due to the cohesion between water molecules from the hydrogen bonds between the molecules. The capillary action of water is also due to this cohesion, and the adhesion of water is due to its polarity. Water is an excellent solvent due to its polarity and is considered the universal solvent. Water exists naturally as a solid, liquid, and gas. The density of water decreases as ice freezes and forms crystals in the solid phase. Water is most dense at 4 °C. Water can act as an acid or base in chemical reactions. Pure water is an insulator because it has virtually no ions. Water has a high specific heat capacity due to its low molecular mass and bent molecular shape.

Review Video: Properties of Water
Visit mometrix.com/academy and enter code: 279526

Biological Macromolecules

Macromolecules are large molecules made up of smaller organic molecules. Four classes of macromolecules include carbohydrates, nucleic acids, proteins, and lipids. Carbohydrates, proteins, and nucleic acids are polymers that are formed when the monomers are joined together in a dehydration process. In this dehydration process, the monomers are joined by a covalent bond and a water molecule is released. The monomers in carbohydrates are simple sugars such as glucose, while polysaccharides are polymers of carbohydrates. The monomers in proteins are amino acids. The amino acids form polypeptide chains, which are folded into proteins. The monomers in nucleic acids are nucleotides. Lipids are not actually considered to be polymers. Lipids typically are classified as fats, phospholipids, or steroids.

Review Video: Macromolecules
Visit mometrix.com/academy and enter code: 220156

Biological Processes Dependent on Chemical Principles

Biochemical Pathways

Autotrophs that use light to produce energy use **photosynthesis** as a biochemical pathway. In eukaryotic autotrophs photosynthesis takes place in chloroplasts. Prokaryotic autotrophs that use inorganic chemical reactions to produce energy use **chemosynthesis** as a biochemical pathway. Heterotrophs require food and use **cellular respiration** to release energy from chemical bonds in the food. All organisms use cellular respiration to release energy from stored food. Cellular respiration can be aerobic or anaerobic. Most eukaryotes use cellular respiration that takes place in the mitochondria.

Photosynthesis

Photosynthesis is a food-making process that occurs in three processes: light-capturing events, light-dependent reactions, and light-independent reactions. In light-capturing events, the thylakoids of the chloroplasts, which contain chlorophyll and accessory pigments, absorb light energy and produce excited electrons. Thylakoids also contain enzymes and electron-transport molecules. Molecules involved in this process are arranged in groups called photosystems. In light-dependent reactions, the excited electrons from the light-capturing events are moved by electron transport in a series of steps in which they are used to split water into hydrogen and oxygen ions. The oxygen is released, and the $NADP^+$ bonds with the hydrogen atoms and forms NADPH. ATP is produced from the excited elections. The light-independent reactions use this ATP, NADPH, and carbon dioxide to produce sugars.

Review Video: Photosynthesis
Visit mometrix.com/academy and enter code: 227035

C_3 and C_4 Photosynthesis

Plants undergo an additional process during photosynthesis that is known as photorespiration. Photorespiration is a wasteful process that uses energy and decreases sugar synthesis. This process occurs when the enzyme rubisco binds to oxygen rather than atmospheric carbon dioxide. There are three different processes that plants use to fix carbon during photosynthesis and these include C_3, C_4, and crassulacean acid metabolism (CAM). Some plants, such as C_4 and CAM plants, can decrease photorespiration and therefore minimize energy lost while C_3 plants, which make up more than 85% of plants, have no special adaptations to stop photorespiration from occuring. C_3 and C_4 plants are named for the type of carbon molecule (three-carbon or four-carbon) that is made during the first step of the reaction. The first step of the C_3 process involves the formation of two three-carbon molecules (3-phosphoglycerate; 3-PGA) from carbon dioxide being fixed by the enzyme. The first step of C_4 photosynthesis is carbon dioxide beign fixed by the enzyme PEP carboxylase, which unlike rubisco does not have the ability to bind to oxygen. This fixation forms a four-carbon molecule (oxaloaceate) and these initial steps occur in the mesophyll cell. Next, oxaloacetate is converted into a malate, a molecule that can enter the bundle sheath cells, and then is broken down to release carbon dioxide. From there, the carbon dioxide is fixed by rubisco as it undergoes the Calvin cycle seen in C_3 photosynthesis. Because C_4 plants undergo an initial step that allows carbon dioxide to be more readily available, with the use of malate, photorespiration is minimized.

Crassulacean Acid Metabolism

Crassulacean acid metabolism (CAM) is a form of photosynthesis adapted to dry environments. While C_4 plants separate the Calvin cycle via space, or by having different cells for different functions and processes, CAM plants separate the processes by time of day. During the night, pores of the plant leaves, called stomata, open to receive carbon dioxide, which combines with PEP carboxylase to form oxaloacetate. Oxaloacetate is eventually converted into malate, which is stored in vacuoles until the next day. During the following day, the stomata are closed and the malate is transported to chloroplasts, where malate is broken down into pyruvate (three-carbon molecule) and carbon dioxide. The carbon dioxide released from malate is used in photosynthesis during the daytime. One advantage of the CAM cycle is that it minimizes loss of water through the stomata during the daytime. A second advantage is that concentrating carbon dioxide in the chloroplasts in this manner increases the efficiency of the enzyme rubisco to fix carbon dioxide and complete the Calvin cycle.

Aerobic Respiration

Aerobic cellular respiration is a series of enzyme-controlled chemical reactions in which oxygen reacts with glucose to produce carbon dioxide and water, releasing energy in the form of adenosine triphosphate (ATP). Cellular respiration occurs in a series of three processes: glycolysis, the Krebs cycle, and the electron-transport system.

Review Video: Aerobic Respiration
Visit mometrix.com/academy and enter code: 770290

Glycolysis

Glycolysis is a series of enzyme-controlled chemical reactions that occur in the cell's cytoplasm. Each glucose molecule is split in half to produce two pyruvic acid molecules, four ATP molecules, and two NADH molecules. Because two ATP molecules are used to split the glucose molecule, the net ATP yield for glycolysis is two ATP molecules.

Review Video: Glycolysis
Visit mometrix.com/academy and enter code: 466815

Krebs Cycle

The **Krebs cycle** is also called the citric acid cycle or the tricarboxylic acid cycle (TCA). It is a **catabolic pathway** in which the bonds of glucose and occasionally fats or lipids are broken down and reformed into ATP. It is a respiration process that uses oxygen and produces carbon dioxide, water, and ATP. Cells require energy from ATP to synthesize proteins from amino acids and replicate DNA. The cycle is acetyl CoA, citric acid, isocitric acid, ketoglutaric acid (products are amino acids and CO_2), succinyl CoA, succinic acid, fumaric acid, malic acid, and oxaloacetic acid. One of the products of the Krebs cycle is NADH, which is then used in the electron chain transport system to manufacture ATP. From glycolysis, pyruvate is oxidized in a step linking to the Krebs cycle. After the Krebs cycle, NADH and succinate are oxidized in the electron transport chain.

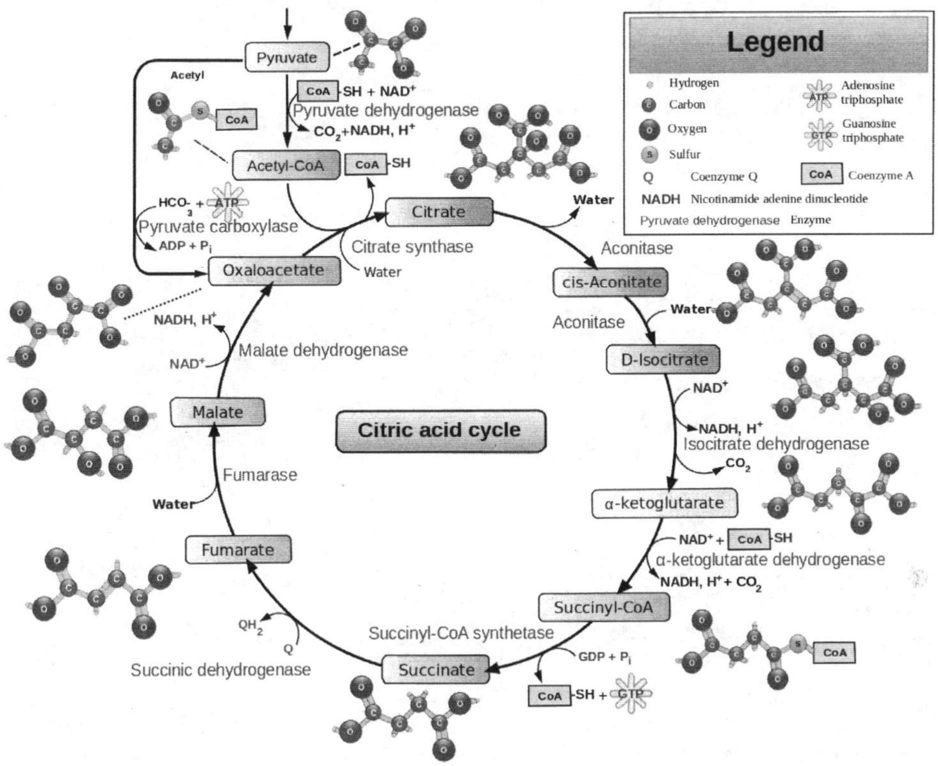

Electron Transport Chain

The **electron transport chain** is part of phosphorylation, whereby electrons are transported from enzyme to enzyme until they reach a final acceptor. The electron transport chain includes a series of oxidizing and reducing molecules involved in the release of energy. In **redox reactions**, electrons are removed from a substrate (oxidative) and H^+ (protons) can also be simultaneously removed. A substrate gains electrons during reduction. For example, when glucose is oxidized, electrons are lost and energy is released. There are enzymes in the membranes of mitochondria. The electrons are carried from one enzyme to another by a co-enzyme. Protons are also released to the other side of the membrane. For example, FAD and $FADH_2$ are used in oxidative phosphorylation. FAD is reduced to $FADH_2$. Electrons are stored there and then sent onward, and the

$FADH_2$ becomes FAD again. In aerobic respiration, the final electron acceptor is O_2. In anaerobic respiration, it is something other than O_2.

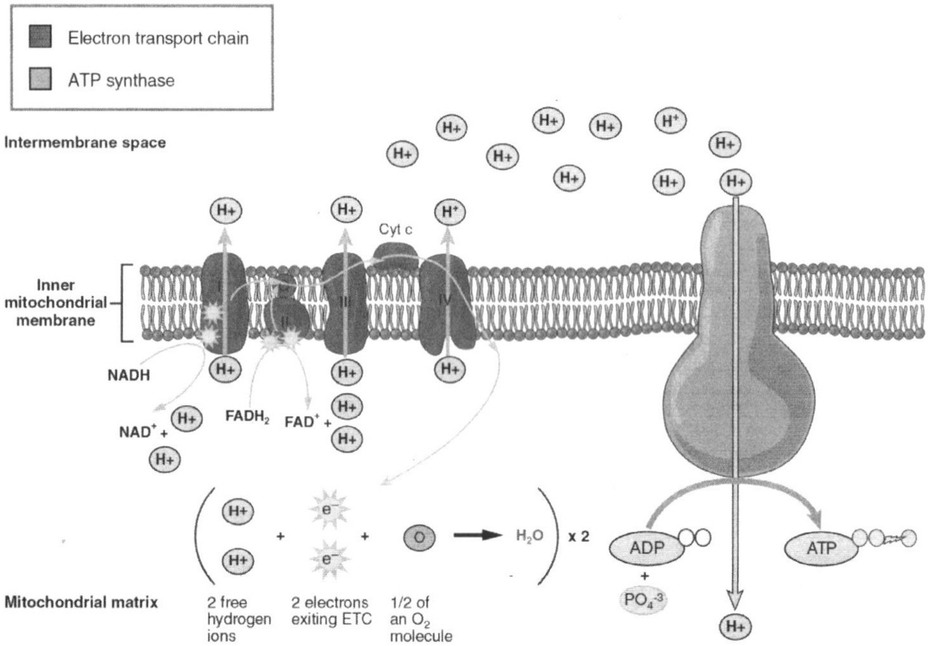

FERMENTATION

Fermentation is an anaerobic reaction in which glucose is only partially broken down. It releases energy through the oxidation of sugars or other types of organic molecules. Oxygen is sometimes involved, but not always. It is different from respiration in that it uses neither the Krebs cycle nor the electron transport chain and the final electron acceptor is an organic molecule. It uses **substrate-level phosphorylation** to form ATP. NAD^+ is reduced to NADH and NADH further reduces pyruvic acid to various end products. Fermentation can lead to excess waste products and is less efficient than aerobic respiration. **Homolactic fermentation** refers to lactic acid fermentation in which the sugars are converted to lactic acid only (there is one end product). In **heterolactic fermentation**, the sugars are converted to a range of products.

EXAMPLES OF FERMENTATION

Lactic acid fermentation is the breakdown of glucose and six-carbon sugars into lactic acid to release energy. It is an anaerobic process, meaning that it does not require oxygen. It can occur in muscle cells and is also performed by streptococcus and lactobacillus bacteria. It can also be used to making yogurt and other food products.

Alcohol fermentation is the breakdown of glucose and six-carbon sugars into ethanol and carbon dioxide to release energy. It is an anaerobic process. It is performed by yeast and used in the production of alcoholic beverages.

CHEMOSYNTHESIS

Chemosynthesis is the food-making process of chemoautotrophs in extreme environments such as deep-sea-vents, or hydrothermal vents. Unlike photosynthesis, chemosynthesis does not require light. In general, chemosynthesis involves the oxidation of inorganic substances to make a sugar, but there are several species that use different pathways or processses. For example, sulfur bacteria live near or in deep-sea vents and oxidize hydrogen sulfide released from those vents to make a sugar. Instead of sunlight, chemosynthesis uses the energy stored in the chemical bonds of chemicals such as hydrogen sulfide to produce food. During chemosynthesis, the electrons that are removed from the inorganic molecules are combined with carbon dioxide and oxygen to produce sugar, sulfur, and water. Some bacteria use metal ions such as iron and magnesium to obtain the needed electrons. For example, methanobacteria such as those found in human intestines combine carbon dioxide and hydrogen gas and release methane as a waste product. Nitrogen bacteria such as nitrogen-fixing bacteria in the nodules of legumes convert atmospheric nitrogen into nitrates.

Structure and Function of Enzymes

Active Site Structure and Substrate Binding

Each enzyme has a complex three-dimensional shape that is specifically designed to fit to a particular reactant, which is called the **substrate**. The enzyme and the substrate join temporarily forming the enzyme-substrate complex. This complex is unstable, and the chemical bonds are likely to be altered to produce a new molecule or molecules. Each enzyme can only combine with specific substrates because of this "lock-and-key" fit. Each enzyme has a designated binding site on the surface that binds to the substrate. Often, the binding site and the active site are at the same location. The enzyme and the substrate are specifically designed for each other, and as the substrate binds to the active site of the enzyme, that active site can bend and fold to form around the substrate. This concept of the active site slightly altering its shape is the **induced fit hypothesis**. The active site of the enzyme with return to its original shape after the products are released.

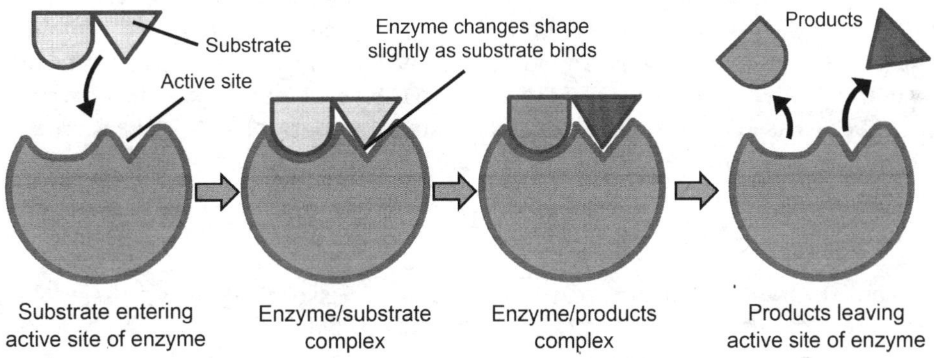

Effects of Temperature, pH, and Inhibitors on Enzyme Activity

The rate of an enzyme-controlled reaction is affected by factors such as temperature, pH, and inhibitors. According to kinetic-molecular theory, increasing the temperature increases the rate of molecular motion. Typically, increasing the temperature increases the rate of these reactions. The optimum temperature is the temperature at which the rate is the fastest and the most product is formed. Increasing the temperature above the optimum temperature actually decreases the reaction rate due to changes on the enzyme's structure that affect substrate binding. The pH also affects enzyme activity due to hydrogen ions binding to the enzyme's surface and changing the enzyme's surface shape. Because enzymes must have a specific shape for their specific substrate, enzymes have a certain pH range in which they can function. Inhibitors are molecules that attach to the enzymes and interfere with substrate binding, thus decreasing or even halting enzyme-controlled reactions.

Regulation of Enzymes by Feedback Inhibition

Enzyme-controlled reactions can be regulated by feedback inhibition, or negative feedback. **Feedback inhibition** can be illustrated by a furnace and thermostat. The inhibitor in this system is the heat. When the furnace runs, the temperature increases. When the temperature reaches a specific level, the thermostat switches the furnace off. When the temperature decreases below a specific level, the thermostat switches the furnace back on, and the cycle begins again. In enzyme-controlled reactions, the end products of a metabolic pathway bind to the enzymes that initiate the metabolic pathway. This causes the reaction rate to decrease. The more product there is, the less product is produced. The less product there is, the more product is produced. This process of feedback inhibition enables a stable range of concentrations that are necessary for homeostasis.

Biochemical Processes Within an Organism

Concentration Gradients

Concentration gradients, also called diffusion gradients, are differences in the concentration (i.e., the number of molecules of solutes in a solution) between two regions. A gradient can also result from an unequal distribution of ions across a cell membrane. Solutes move along a concentration gradient by random motion from the region of high concentration toward the region of low concentration in a process called diffusion. In other words, **diffusion** is the movement of molecules or ions down a concentration gradient. Diffusion is the method by which oxygen, carbon dioxide, and other nonpolar molecules cross a cell membrane. The steepness of the concentration gradient affects the rate of diffusion. **Passive transport** makes use of concentration gradients as well as electric gradients to move substances across the cell membrane, while **active transport** can move a substance against its concentration gradient.

Laws of Thermodynamics and Gibbs Free Energy

The **first law of thermodynamics** states that energy can neither be created nor destroyed. Energy may change forms, but the energy in a closed system is constant. The **second law of thermodynamics** states that systems tend toward a state of lower energy and greater disorder. This disorder is called **entropy**. According to the second law of thermodynamics, entropy is increasing. **Gibbs free energy** is the energy a system that is available or "free" to be released to perform work at a constant temperature. Organisms must be able to use energy to survive, and biological processes such as the chemical reactions involved in metabolism are governed by these laws.

Anabolic and Catabolic Reactions

Anabolism and catabolism are metabolic processes. **Anabolism** is essentially the synthesis of large molecules from monomers, whereas **catabolism** is the decomposition of large molecules into their component monomers. Anabolism uses energy, whereas catabolism produces energy. Anabolism typically builds and repair tissues, and catabolism typically burns stored food to produce energy. Protein synthesis, which is the polymerization of amino acids to form proteins, is an anabolic reaction. Another anabolic process is the mineralization of bones. An example of a catabolic reaction is hydrolysis, which is the decomposition of polymers into monomers that releases a water molecule and energy. Cellular respiration is a catabolic process in which typically glucose combines with oxygen to release energy in the form of adenosine triphosphate (ATP).

Oxidation-Reduction Reactions

Oxidation-reduction reactions, or redox reactions, involve the transfer of electrons from one substance to another. Reduction occurs in the substance that gains the electrons. Oxidation occurs in the substance that loses the electrons. Cellular respiration and photosynthesis are examples of redox reactions. During cellular respiration, glucose molecules are oxidized and oxygen molecules are reduced. Because electrons lose energy when being transferred to oxygen, the electrons are usually first transferred to the coenzyme NAD^+, which is reduced to NADH. The NADH then releases the energy to oxygen. During photosynthesis, water molecules are split and oxidized and carbon dioxide molecules are reduced. When the water molecules are split, electrons are transferred with the hydrogen ions to the carbon dioxide molecules.

Chapter Quiz

Ready to see how well you retained what you just read? Scan the QR code to go directly to the chapter quiz interface for this study guide. If you're using a computer, simply visit the online resources page at **mometrix.com/resources719/abctebio** and click the Chapter Quizzes link.

Cell Biology and Microbiology

Differences Between Prokaryotic and Eukaryotic Cells

Prokaryotes and Eukaryotes

Sizes and Metabolism

Cells of the domains of Bacteria and Archaea are **prokaryotes**. Bacteria cells and Archaea cells are much smaller than cells of eukaryotes. Prokaryote cells are usually only 1 to 2 micrometers in diameter, but eukaryotic cells are usually at least 10 times and possibly 100 times larger than prokaryotic cells. Eukaryotic cells are usually 10 to 100 micrometers in diameter. Most prokaryotes are unicellular organisms, although some prokaryotes live in colonies. Because of their large surface-area-to-volume ratios, prokaryotes have a very high metabolic rate. **Eukaryotic cells** are much larger than prokaryotic cells. Due to their larger sizes, they have a much smaller surface-area-to-volume ratio and consequently have much lower metabolic rates.

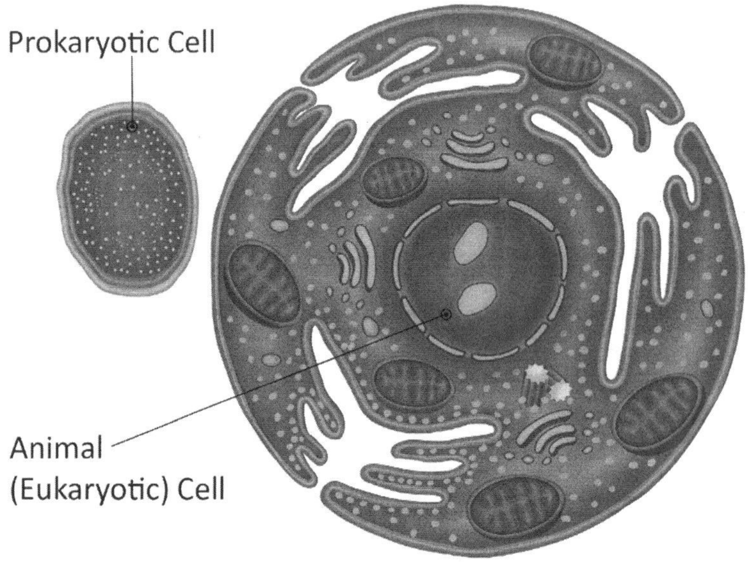

Review Video: Eukaryotic and Prokaryotic Cells
Visit mometrix.com/academy and enter code: 231438

Review Video: Cell Structure
Visit mometrix.com/academy and enter code: 591293

Membrane-Bound Organelles

Prokaryotic cells are much simpler than eukaryotic cells. Prokaryote cells do not have a nucleus due to their small size and their DNA is located in the center of the cell in a region referred to as a **nucleoid**. Eukaryote cells have a **nucleus** bound by a double membrane. Eukaryotic cells typically have hundreds or thousands of additional **membrane-bound organelles** that are independent of the cell membrane. Prokaryotic cells do not have any membrane-bound organelles that are independent of the cell membrane. Once again, this is probably due to the much larger size of the eukaryotic cells. The organelles of eukaryotes give them much higher levels of intracellular division than is possible in prokaryotic cells.

CELL WALLS

Not all cells have cell walls, but most prokaryotes have cell walls. The cell walls of organisms from the domain Bacteria differ from the cell walls of the organisms from the domain Archaea. Some eukaryotes, such as some fungi, some algae, and plants, have cell walls that differ from the cell walls of the Bacteria and Archaea domains. The main difference between the cell walls of different domains or kingdoms is the composition of the cell walls. For example, most bacteria have cell walls outside of the plasma membrane that contains the molecule peptidoglycan. **Peptidoglycan** is a large polymer of amino acids and sugars. The peptidoglycan helps maintain the strength of the cell wall. Some of the Archaea cells have cell walls containing the molecule pseudopeptidoglycan, which differs in chemical structure from the peptidoglycan but basically provides the same strength to the cell wall. Some fungi cell walls contain **chitin**. The cell walls of diatoms, a type of yellow algae, contain silica. Plant cell walls contain cellulose, and woody plants are further strengthened by lignin. Some algae also contain lignin. Animal cells do not have cell walls.

CHROMOSOME STRUCTURE

Prokaryote cells have DNA arranged in a **circular structure** that should not be referred to as a chromosome. Due to the small size of a prokaryote cell, the DNA material is simply located near the center of the cell in a region called the nucleoid. A prokaryotic cell may also contain tiny rings of DNA called plasmids. Prokaryote cells lack histone proteins, and therefore the DNA is not actually packaged into chromosomes. Prokaryotes reproduce by binary fission, while eukaryotes reproduce by mitosis with the help of **linear chromosomes** and histone proteins. During mitosis, the chromatin is tightly wound on the histone proteins and packaged as a chromosome. The DNA in a eukaryotic cell is located in the membrane-bound nucleus.

Review Video: Chromosomes
Visit mometrix.com/academy and enter code: 132083

Structure and Function of Cells and Organelles

CELLS AND ORGANELLES OF PLANT CELLS AND ANIMAL CELLS

Plant cells and animal cells both have a nucleus, cytoplasm, cell membrane, ribosomes, mitochondria, endoplasmic reticulum, Golgi apparatus, and vacuoles. Plant cells have only one or two extremely large vacuoles. Animal cells typically have several small vacuoles. Plant cells have chloroplasts for photosynthesis and use this process to produce their own food, distinguishing plants as **autotrophs**. Animal cells do not have chloroplasts and therefore cannot use photosynthesis to produce their own food. Instead animal cells rely on other sources for food, which classifies them as **heterotrophs**. Animal cells have centrioles, which are used to help organize microtubules and in in cell division, but only some plant cells have centrioles. Additionally, plant cells have a rectangular and more rigid shape due to the cell wall, while animal cells have more of a circular shape because they lack a cell wall.

Review Video: Difference Between Plant and Animal Cells
Visit mometrix.com/academy and enter code: 115568

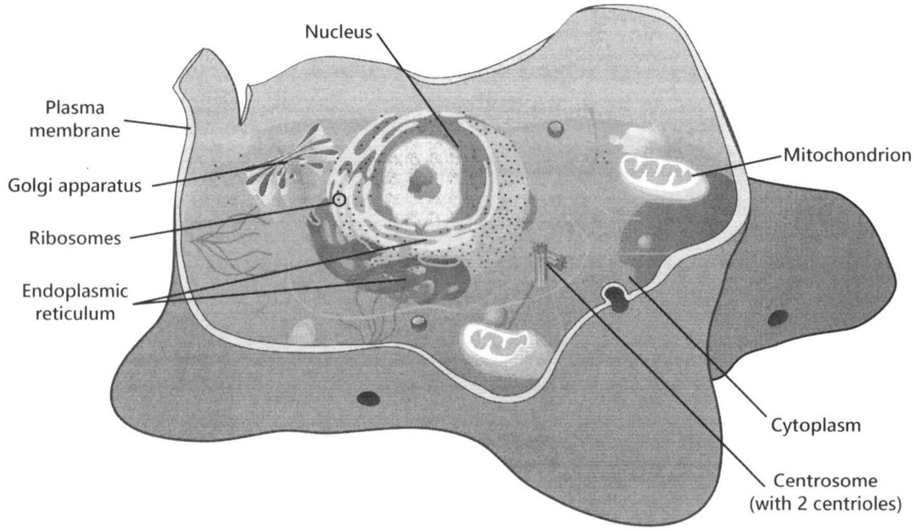

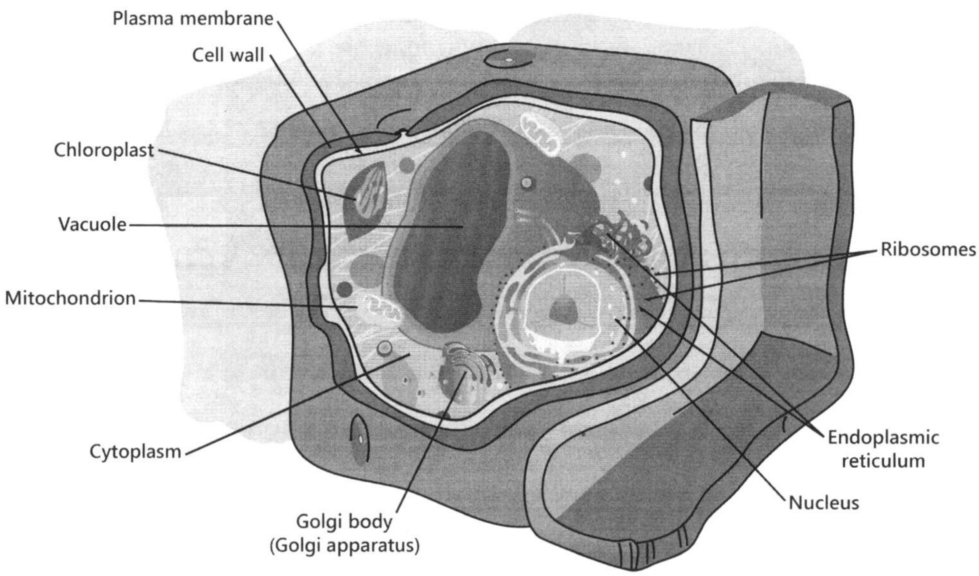

Cell Membranes

The **cell membrane**, also referred to as the plasma membrane, is a thin semipermeable membrane of lipids and proteins. The cell membrane isolates the cell from its external environment while still enabling the cell to communicate with that outside environment. It consists of a phospholipid bilayer, or double layer, with the hydrophilic ("water-loving") ends of the outer layer facing the external environment, the inner layer facing the inside of the cell, and the hydrophobic ("water-fearing") ends facing each other. Cholesterol in the cell membrane adds stiffness and flexibility. Glycolipids help the cell to recognize other cells of the organisms. The proteins in the cell membrane help give the cells shape. Special proteins help the cell communicate with its external environment, while other proteins transport molecules across the cell membrane.

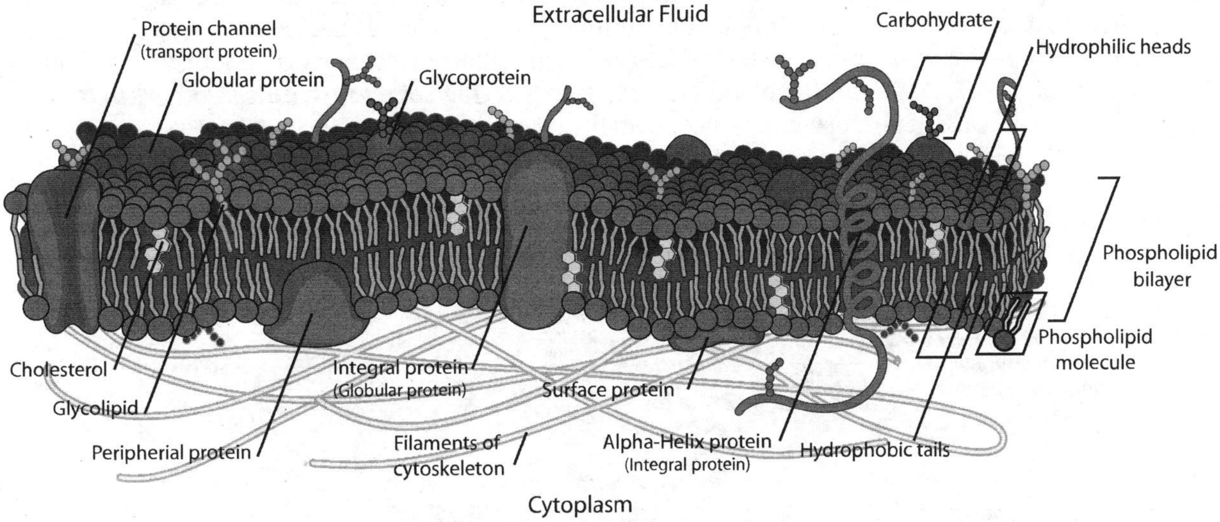

Review Video: Function of the Plasma Membrane
Visit mometrix.com/academy and enter code: 943095

Nucleus

Typically, a eukaryote has a single nucleus that takes up approximately 10% of the volume of the cell. Components of the nucleus include the nuclear envelope, nucleoplasm, chromatin, and nucleolus. The **nuclear envelope** is a double-layered membrane with the outer layer connected to the endoplasmic reticulum. The nucleus can communicate with the rest of the cell through several nuclear pores. The chromatin consists of deoxyribonucleic acid (DNA) and histones that are packaged into chromosomes during mitosis. The **nucleolus**, which is the dense central portion of the nucleus, produced and assembles ribosomes with the help of ribosomal RNA and proteins. Functions of the nucleus include the storage of genetic material, production of ribosomes, and transcription of ribonucleic acid (RNA).

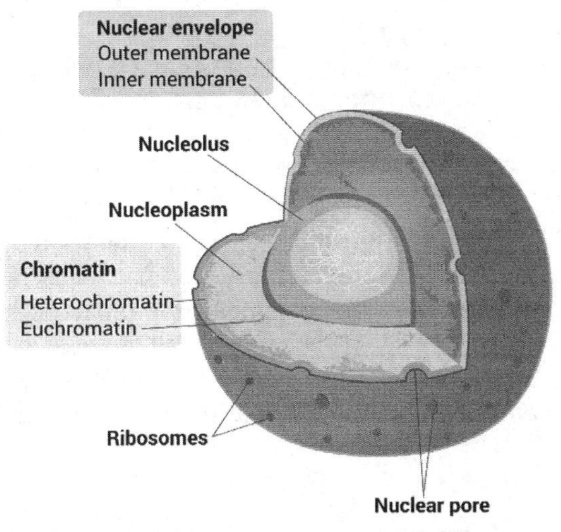

Review Video: Nucleic Acids
Visit mometrix.com/academy and enter code: 503931

CHLOROPLASTS

Chloroplasts are large organelles that are enclosed in a double membrane. Just as cells contain a fluid called cytoplasm, chloroplasts contain a fluid called the **stroma**. Within the stroma, there are discs called **thylakoids**, which are arranged in stacks called **grana** (singular: granum). The thylakoids have chlorophyll molecules on their surfaces. **Stromal lamellae** separate the thylakoid stacks. Chloroplasts perform photosynthesis and make food (in the form of sugars) for the plant. The light reaction stage of photosynthesis occurs in the grana, and the dark reaction stage of photosynthesis occurs in the stroma. Sugars are formed in the stroma. Chloroplasts have their own DNA and can reproduce by fission independently.

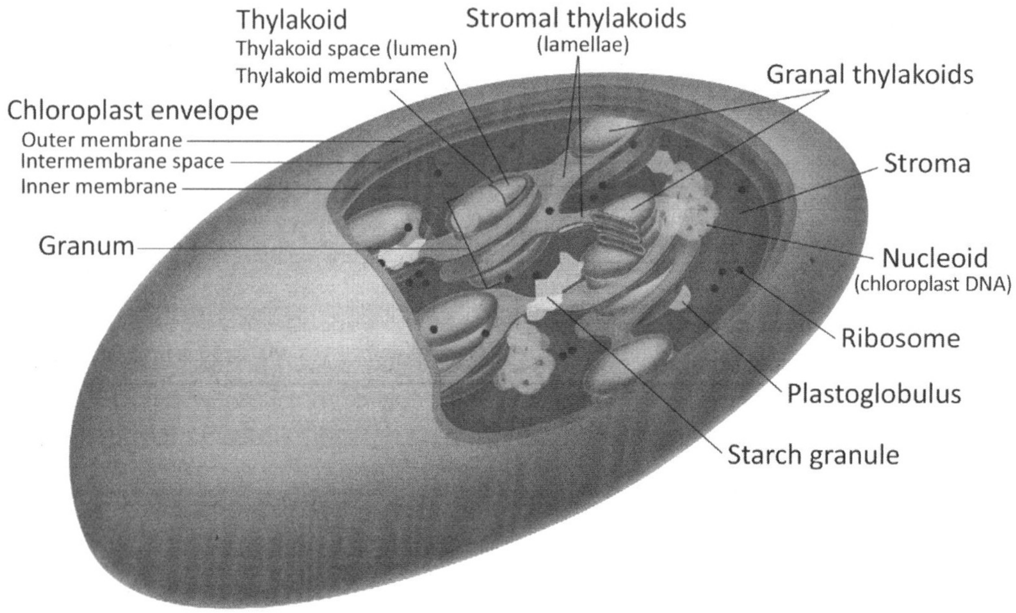

PLASTIDS

Plastids are major organelles found in plants and algae that are used to synthesize and store food. Because plastids can differentiate, there are many forms of plastids. Specialized plastids can store pigments, starches, fats, or proteins. Two examples of plastids are amyloplasts and chloroplasts. **Amyloplasts** are the plastids that store the starch formed from long chains of glucose produced during photosynthesis. Amyloplasts synthesize and store the starch granules through the polymerization of glucose. When needed, amyloplasts also convert these starch granules back into sugar. Fruits and potato tubers have large numbers of amyloplasts. **Chloroplasts** can synthesize and store starch. Interestingly, amyloplasts can redifferentiate and transform into chloroplasts.

MITOCHONDRIA

Mitochondria break down sugar molecules and produce energy in the form of molecules of adenosine triphosphate (ATP). Both plant and animal cells contain mitochondria. Mitochondria are enclosed in a bilayer semi-membrane of phospholipids and proteins. The intermembrane space is the space between the two layers. The outer membrane has proteins called porins, which allow small molecules through. The inner membrane contains proteins that aid in the synthesis of ATP. The matrix consists of enzymes that help synthesize ATP. Mitochondria have their own DNA and can reproduce by fission independently. Mitochondria also help to maintain calcium concentrations, form blood components and hormones, and are involved in activating cell death pathways.

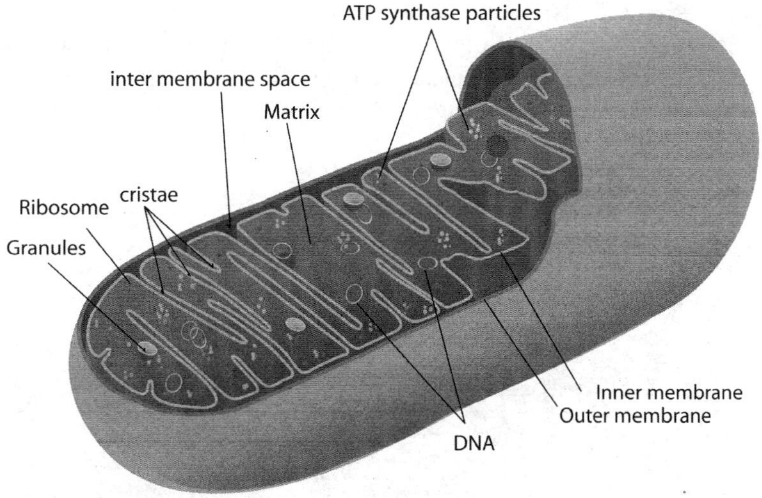

Review Video: Mitochondria
Visit mometrix.com/academy and enter code: 444287

Ribosomes

A **ribosome** consists of RNA and proteins. The RNA component of the ribosome is known as ribosomal RNA (rRNA). Ribosomes consist of two subunits, a large subunit and a small subunit. Few ribosomes are free in the cell. Most of the ribosomes in the cell are embedded in the rough endoplasmic reticulum located near the nucleus. Ribosomes are protein factories and translate the code of DNA into proteins by assembling long chains of amino acids. **Messenger RNA** (mRNA) is used by the ribosome to generate a specific protein sequence, while **transfer RNA** (tRNA) collects the needed amino acids and delivers them to the ribosome.

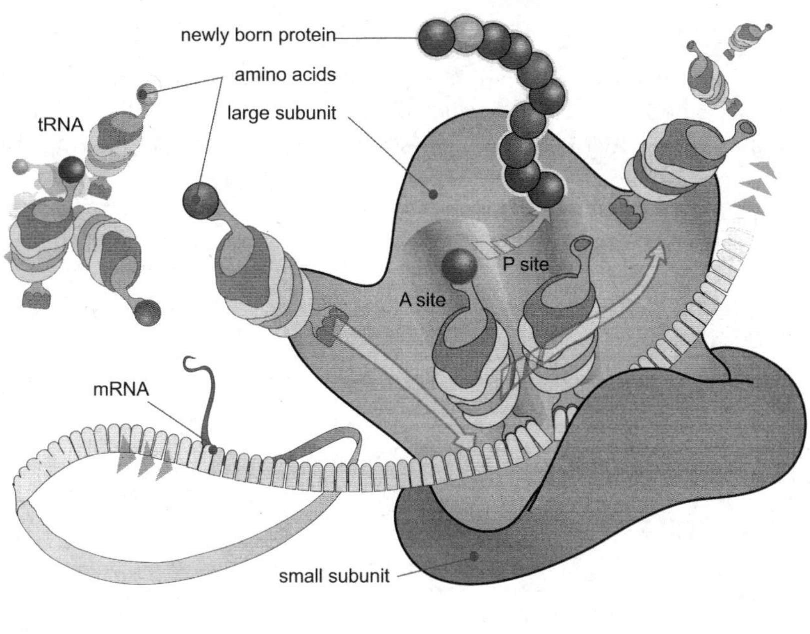

Golgi Apparatus

The **Golgi apparatus**, also called the Golgi body or Golgi complex, is a stack of flattened membranes called **cisternae** that package, ship, and distribute macromolecules such as carbohydrates, proteins, and lipids in shipping containers called **vesicles**. It also helps modify proteins and lipids before they are shipped. Most Golgi apparatuses have six to eight cisternae. Each Golgi apparatus has four regions: the cis region, the endo region, the medial region, and the trans region. Transfer vesicles from the rough endoplasmic reticulum (ER) enter at the cis region, and secretory vesicles leave the Golgi apparatus from the trans region.

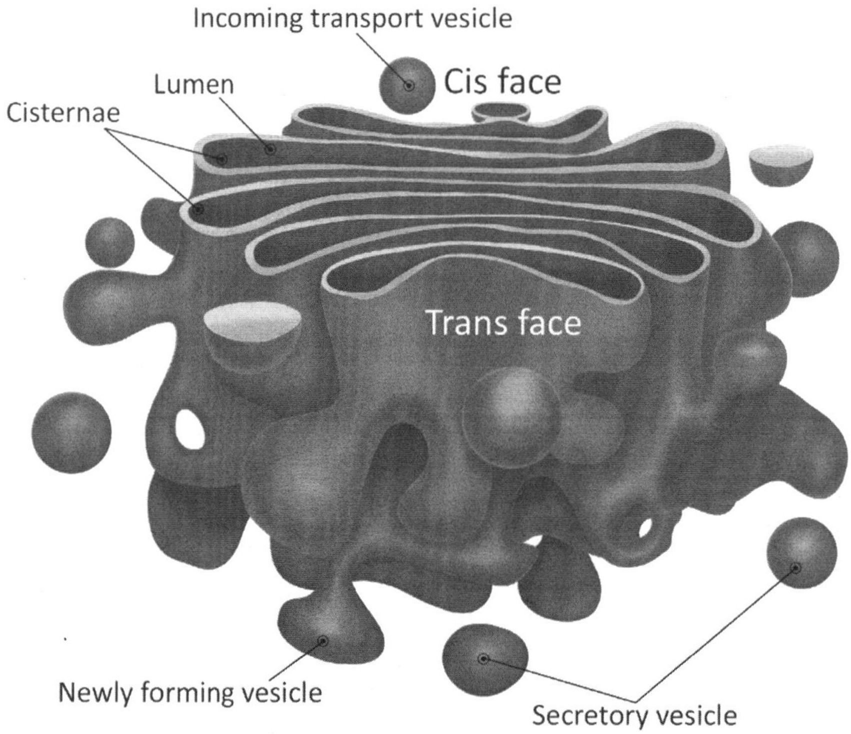

Cytoskeleton

The **cytoskeleton** is a scaffolding system located in the cytoplasm. The cytoskeleton consists of elongated organelles made of proteins called microtubules, microfilaments, and intermediate filaments. These organelles provide shape, support, and the ability to move. These structures also assist in moving the chromosomes during mitosis. Microtubules and microfilaments help transport materials throughout the cell and are the major components in cilia and flagella.

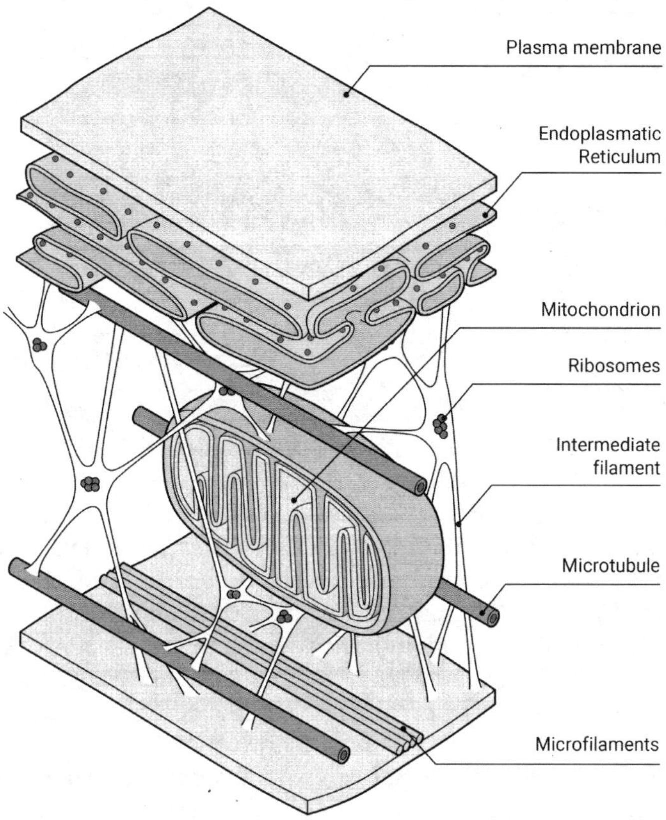

Cellular Homeostasis

Selective Permeability

The cell membrane, or plasma membrane, has selective permeability with regard to size, charge, and solubility. With regard to molecule size, the cell membrane allows only small molecules to diffuse through it. Oxygen and water molecules are small and typically can pass through the cell membrane. The charge of the ions on the cell's surface also either attracts or repels ions. Ions with like charges are repelled, and ions with opposite charges are attracted to the cell's surface. Molecules that are soluble in phospholipids can usually pass through the cell membrane. Many molecules are not able to diffuse the cell membrane, but, if needed, those molecules must be moved through by active transport and vesicles.

ACTIVE AND PASSIVE TRANSPORT

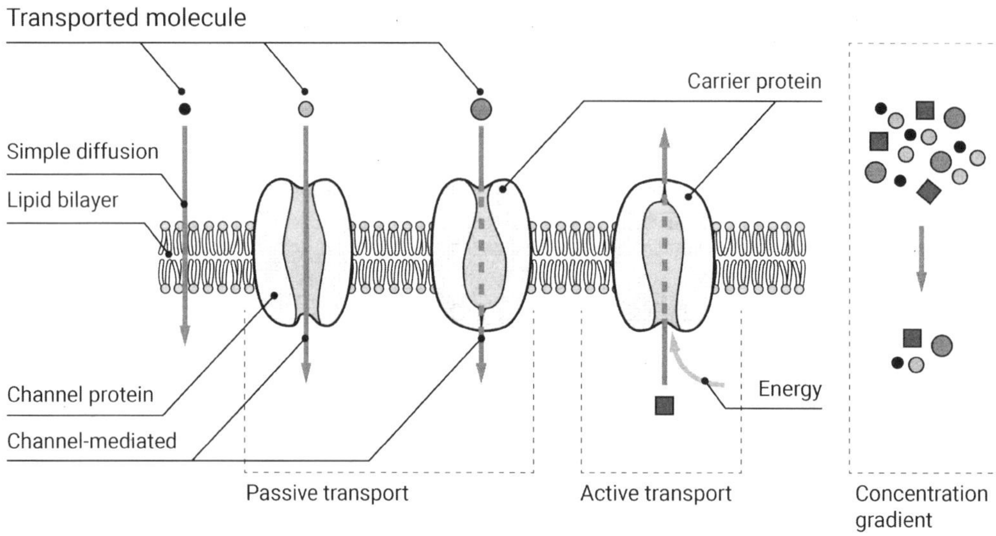

Cells can move materials in and out through the cell membrane by active and passive transport. In **passive transport**, the molecules diffuse across the cell membrane by osmosis. These molecules are moving from a region where they have a high concentration to a region where the concentration is lower. In passive transport, the molecules move across the cell membrane without the cell expending any extra energy. Diffusion and facilitated diffusion are considered passive transport. **Facilitated diffusion** occurs when molecules are helped across the membrane by certain proteins called channel proteins or carrier proteins. Because facilitated diffusion is still from a region of high to low concentration, it does not require additional energy and is therefore a type of passive transport. In active transport, molecules are forcibly moved from regions where the concentration is low into a region where the concentration is higher. Carrier proteins must carry these ions and molecules, and this requires an expenditure of energy. Some ions are actively pumped across the cell membrane by proteins. Sodium ions are pumped out of the cell and potassium ions are pumped into the cell in this manner.

Review Video: Passive Transport: Diffusion and Osmosis
Visit mometrix.com/academy and enter code: 642038

WATER MOVEMENT TO MAINTAIN INTERNAL ENVIRONMENTS OF CELLS

Cells must maintain their water balance for **homeostasis**. If cells have too little water, wastes and poisons can build up in the cells. If cells have too much water, the chemicals in the cells may be diluted. Water is moved in and out of cells by **osmosis**. Because osmosis is a type of passive transport, the cell cannot actually control this diffusion of water in and out of the cells. The amount of water that diffuses into or out of cells depends on the cell's environment. When the cell's concentration of water and dissolved solids equals that of its environment, the cells are **isotonic** with their environment. Cells with a lower concentration of water than their environment tend to rapidly gain water by osmosis. These cells are **hypotonic** with their environment. Cells with a higher concentration of water than their environment tend to rapidly lose water by osmosis. The cells are **hypertonic** with their environment. If cells are hypotonic or hypertonic, they must expend energy to maintain the proper water balance.

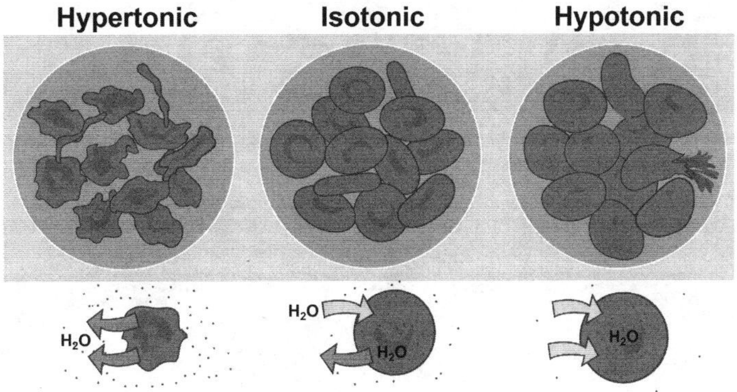

Use of Cell Surface Proteins and Cell Communication

In order to maintain a stable internal environment, cells need to send and receive signals from the external environment. Cells have specialized surface proteins called **receptors** embedded in the cell membrane that allow them to communicate with this external environment. Surface proteins are exposed to the external side of the membrane. Some surface proteins allow entry to specific materials, and others trigger chemical signals inside the cell. Because these proteins have attached carbohydrates, they are called **glycoproteins**. Due to the cholesterol in the cell membrane, fat-soluble materials can pass straight through the membrane, but water-soluble materials cannot diffuse. Sodium, calcium, and potassium must use these specialized surface proteins to gain entry to the cell. These surface proteins bind to specific chemicals in the materials seeking access to the cell. This triggers a chemical signal to the interior of the cell.

Exocytosis and Endocytosis

Larger particles or groups of particles can be transported whole across the cell membrane by being packaged in a piece of cell membrane. **Endocytosis** is the process by which large particles are moved into the cell, and **exocytosis** is the process by which large molecules are moved out of the cell. The three main types of endocytosis are phagocytosis, pinocytosis, and receptor-mediated endocytosis. **Phagocytosis**, or "cell eating," is the process by which large solid particles are engulfed. **Pinocytosis**, or "cell drinking," is the process by which liquids and dissolved substances are surrounded by small sacs of cell membrane. **Receptor-mediated endocytosis** is the process by which molecules enter cells through receptor molecules on the cell membrane.

Endocytosis

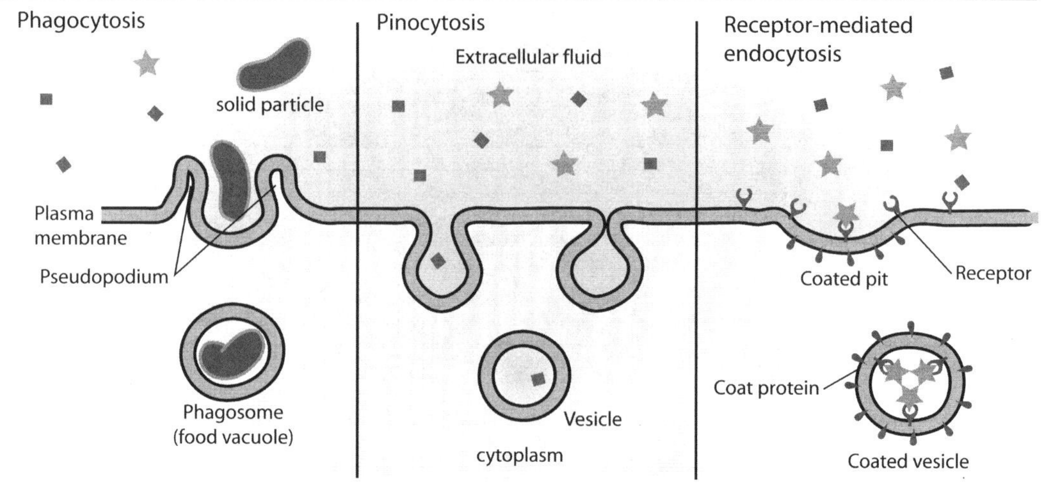

HORMONE ACTION AND FEEDBACK

In order to maintain homeostasis, the endocrine system often employs negative-feedback inhibition or positive-feedback regulation. In **negative-feedback inhibition**, an increase in an output of a reaction to a stimulus triggers a decrease in the stimulus, which in turn causes a decrease in the original output. In **positive-feedback regulation**, an increase in an output leads to further increase of the stimulus. An example of negative-feedback inhibition is the release of the hormones insulin and glucagon to maintain the level of glucose in the blood.

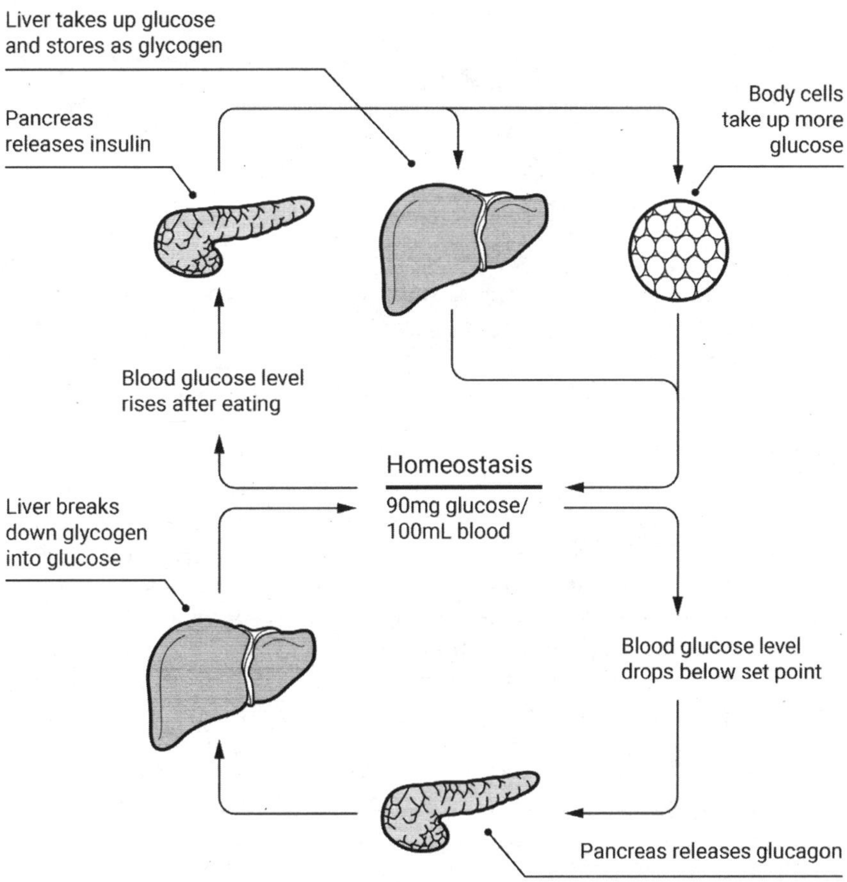

Cell Cycle and Cellular Division

Cell Cycle Stages

The cell cycle consists of three stages: interphase, mitosis, and cytokinesis. **Interphase** is the longest stage of the cell cycle and involves the cell growing and making a copy of its DNA. Cells typically spend more than 90% of the cell cycle in interphase. Interphase includes two growth phases called G_1 and G_2. The order of interphase is the first growth cycle, **GAP 1** (G_1 phase), followed by the **synthesis phase** (S), and ending with the second growth phase, **GAP 2** (G_2 phase). During the G_1 phase of interphase, the cell increases the number of organelles by forming diploid cells. During the S phase of interphase, the DNA is replicated, and the chromosomes are doubled. During the G_2 phase of interphase, the cell synthesizes needed proteins and organelles, continues to increase in size, and prepares for mitosis. Once the G_2 phase ends, mitosis can begin.

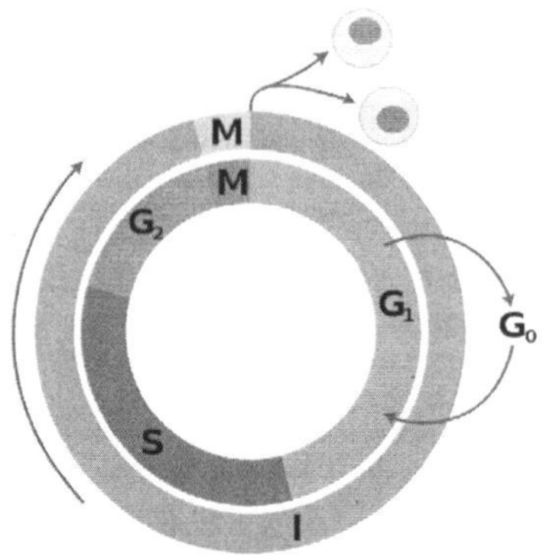

MITOSIS

Mitosis is the asexual process of cell division. During mitosis, one parent cell divides into two identical daughter cells. Mitosis is used for growth, repair, and replacement of cells. Some unicellular organisms reproduce asexually by mitosis. Some multicellular organisms can reproduce by fragmentation or budding, which involves mitosis. Mitosis consists of four phases: prophase, metaphase, anaphase, and telophase. During **prophase**, the spindle fibers appear and the DNA is condensed and packaged as chromosomes that become visible. The nuclear membrane also breaks down, and the nucleolus disappears. During **metaphase**, the spindle apparatus is formed and the centromeres of the chromosomes line up on the equatorial plane. During **anaphase**, the centromeres divide and the two chromatids separate and are pulled toward the opposite poles of the cell. During **telophase**, the spindle fibers disappear, the nuclear membrane reforms, and the DNA in the chromatids is decondensed.

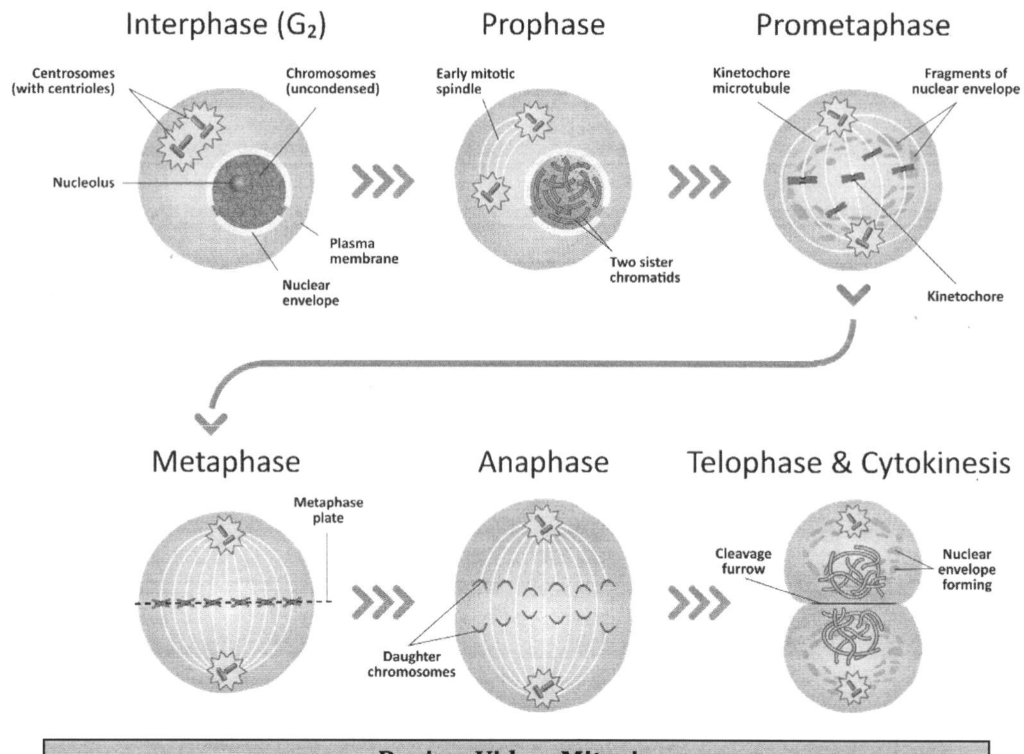

Review Video: Mitosis
Visit mometrix.com/academy and enter code: 849894

Cytokinesis

Cytokinesis is the dividing of the cytoplasm and cell membrane by the pinching of a cell into two new daughter cells at the end of mitosis. This occurs at the end of telophase when the actin filaments in the cytoskeleton form a contractile ring that narrows and divides the cell. In plant cells, a cell plate forms across the phragmoplast, which is the center of the spindle apparatus. In animal cells, as the contractile ring narrows, the cleavage furrow forms. Eventually, the contractile ring narrows down to the spindle apparatus joining the two cells and the cells eventually divide. Diagrams of the cleavage furrow of an animal cell and cell plate of a plant are shown below.

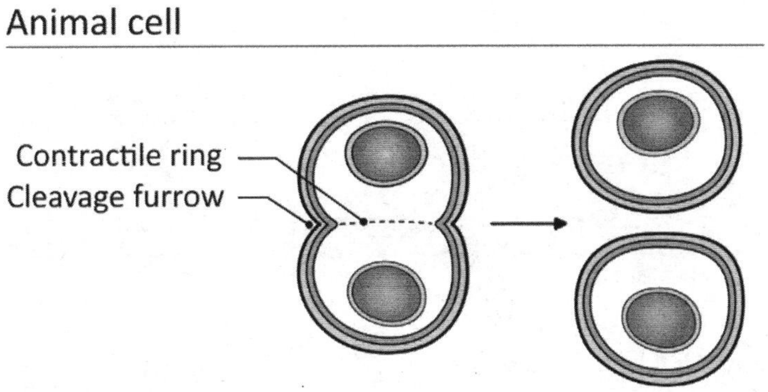

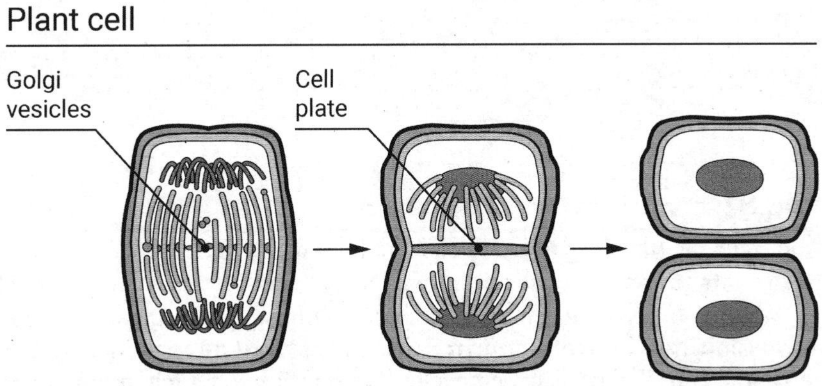

Meiosis

Meiosis is a type of cell division in which the number of chromosomes is reduced by half. Meiosis produces gametes, or egg and sperm cells. Meiosis occurs in two successive stages, which consist of a first mitotic division followed by a second mitotic division. During **meiosis I**, or the first meiotic division, the cell replicates its DNA in interphase and then continues through prophase I, metaphase I, anaphase I, and telophase I. At the end of meiosis I, there are two haploid daughter cells, each with half the number of chromosomes as the original diploid parent cell. Each chromosome consists of two sister chromatids, but these are considered a single chromosome. During **meiosis II**, the cell enters a brief interphase but does not replicate its DNA. Then, the cell continues through prophase II, metaphase II, anaphase II, and telophase II. During prophase II, the unduplicated chromosomes split. At the end of telophase II, there are four daughter cells that have half the number of chromosomes as the parent cell.

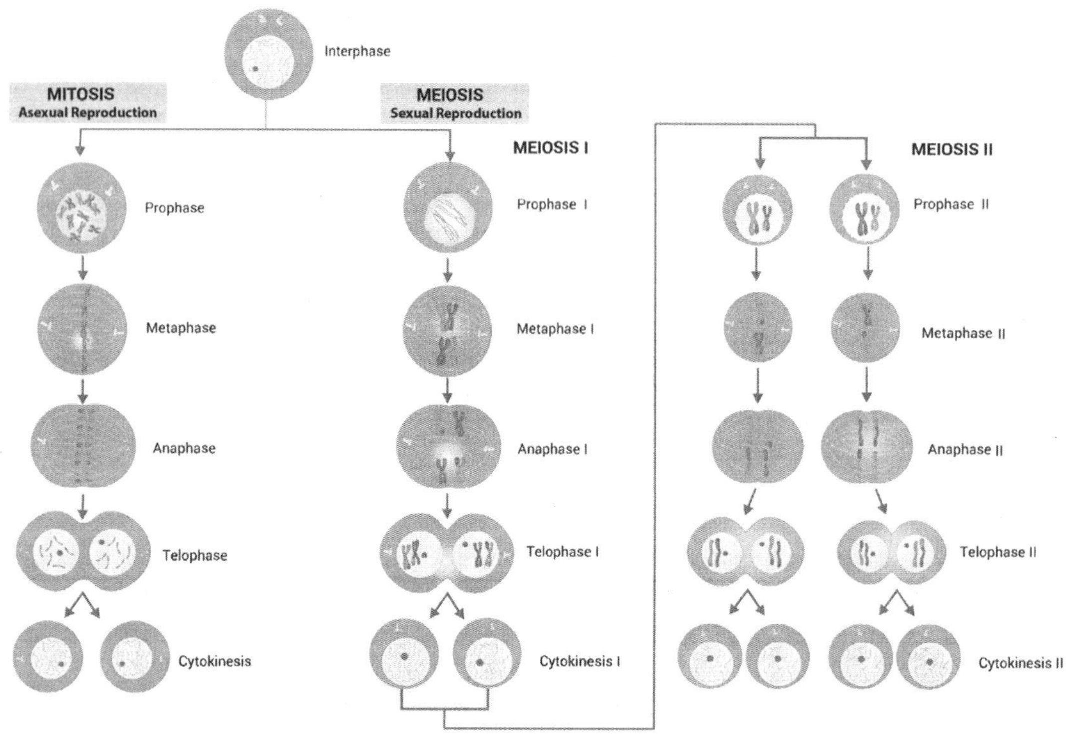

Cell Cycle Checkpoints

During the cell cycle, the cell goes through three checkpoints to ensure that the cell is dividing properly at each phase, that it is the appropriate time for division, and that the cell has not been damaged. The **first checkpoint** is at the end of the G_1 phase just before the cell undergoes the S phase, or synthesis. At this checkpoint, a cell may continue with cell division, delay the division, or rest. This **resting phase** is called G_0. In animal cells, the G_1 checkpoint is called **restriction**. Proteins called cyclin D and cyclin E, which are dependent on enzymes cyclin-dependent kinase 4 and cyclin-dependent kinase 2 (CDK4 and CDK2), respectively, largely control this first checkpoint. The **second checkpoint** is at the end of the G_2 phase just before the cell begins prophase during mitosis. The protein cyclin A, which is dependent on the enzyme CDK2, largely controls this checkpoint. During mitosis, the **third checkpoint** occurs at metaphase to check that the chromosomes are lined up along the equatorial plane. This checkpoint is largely controlled by cyclin B, which is dependent upon the enzyme CDK1.

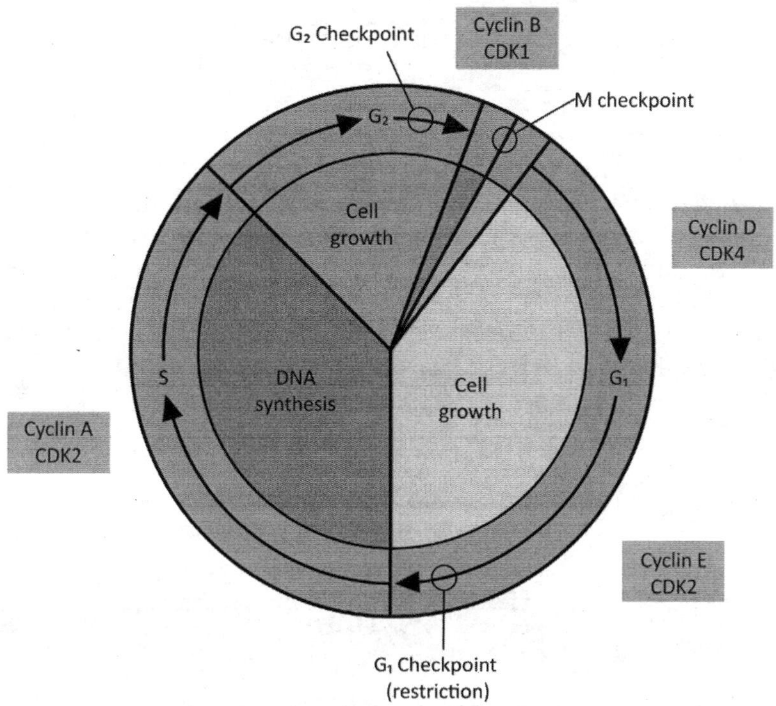

Chapter Quiz

Ready to see how well you retained what you just read? Scan the QR code to go directly to the chapter quiz interface for this study guide. If you're using a computer, simply visit the online resources page at **mometrix.com/resources719/abctebio** and click the Chapter Quizzes link.

Classical Genetics

Mendel's Laws

Law of Segregation

The **law of segregation** states that the alleles for a trait separate when gametes are formed, which means that only one of the pair of alleles for a given trait is passed to the gamete. This can be shown in monohybrid crosses, which can be used to show which allele is **dominant** for a single trait. A **monohybrid cross** is a genetic cross between two organisms with a different variation for a single trait. The first monohybrid cross typically occurs between two **homozygous** parents. Each parent is homozygous for a separate allele (gg or GG) for a particular trait. For example, in pea plants, green seeds (G) are dominant over yellow seeds (g). Therefore, in a genetic cross of two pea plants that are homozygous for seed color, the F_1 generation will be 100% **heterozygous** green seeds.

	g	**g**
G	Gg	Gg
G	Gg	Gg

Review Video: Punnett Square
Visit mometrix.com/academy and enter code: 853855

Monohybrid Cross for a Cross Between Two Gg Parents

If the plants with the heterozygous green seeds are crossed, the F_1 generation should be 50% heterozygous green (Gg), 25% homozygous green (GG), and 25% homozygous yellow (gg).

	G	**g**
G	GG	Gg
g	Gg	gg

Law of Independent Assortment

Mendel's law of independent assortment states that alleles of one characteristic or trait separate independently of the alleles of another characteristic. Therefore, the allele a gamete receives for one gene does not influence the allele received for another gene due to the allele pairs separating independently during gamete formation. This means that traits are transmitted independently of each other. This can be shown in dihybrid crosses.

Gene, Genotype, Phenotype, and Allele

A **gene** is a portion of DNA that identifies how traits are expressed and passed on in an organism. A gene is part of the genetic code. Collectively, all genes form the **genotype** of an individual. The genotype includes genes that may not be expressed, such as recessive genes. The **phenotype** is the physical, visual manifestation of genes. It is determined by the basic genetic information and how genes have been affected by their environment.

An **allele** is a variation of a gene. Also known as a trait, it determines the manifestation of a gene. This manifestation results in a specific physical appearance of some facet of an organism, such as eye color or height. The genetic information for eye color is a gene. The gene variations responsible for blue, green, brown, or black eyes are called alleles. **Locus** (plural, *loci*) refers to the location of a gene or alleles.

Review Video: Genotype vs Phenotype
Visit mometrix.com/academy and enter code: 922853

DOMINANT AND RECESSIVE GENES

Gene traits are represented in pairs with an uppercase letter for the **dominant trait** (A) and a lowercase letter for the **recessive trait** (a). Genes occur in pairs (AA, Aa, or aa). There is one gene on each chromosome half supplied by each parent organism. Since half the genetic material is from each parent, the offspring's traits are represented as a combination of these. A dominant trait only requires one gene of a gene pair for it to be expressed in a phenotype, whereas a recessive requires both genes in order to be manifested. For example, if the mother's genotype is Dd and the father's is dd, the possible combinations are Dd and dd. The dominant trait will be manifested if the genotype is DD or Dd. The recessive trait will be manifested if the genotype is dd. Both DD and dd are **homozygous** pairs. Dd is **heterozygous**.

DIHYBRID CROSS FOR THE F_2 GENERATION OF A CROSS BETWEEN GGRR AND ggrr PARENTS

A **dihybrid cross** is a genetic cross for two traits that each have two alleles. For example, in pea plants, green seeds (G) are dominant over yellow seeds (g), and round seeds (R) are dominant over wrinkled seeds (r). In a genetic cross of two pea plants that are homozygous for seed color and seed shape (GGRR or ggRR), the F_1 generation will be 100% heterozygous green and round seeds (GgRr). If these F_1 plants (GgRr) are crossed, the resulting F_2 generation is shown below. Out of the 16 total genotypes for the cross of green, round seeds, there are only four possible phenotypes, or physical traits of the seed: green and round seed (GGRR, GGRr, GgRR, or GgRr), green and wrinkled seed (GGrr or Ggrr), yellow and round seed (ggRR or ggRr) , or yellow and wrinkled seed (ggrr). There are nine green and round seed plants, three green and wrinkled seed plants, three yellow and round seed plants, and only one yellow and wrinkled seed plant. This cross has a **9:3:3:1 ratio**.

	GR	gR	Gr	gr
GR	GGRR	GgRR	GGRr	GgRr
gR	GgRR	ggRR	GgRr	ggRr
Gr	GGRr	GgRr	GGrr	Ggrr
gr	GgRr	ggRr	Ggrr	ggrr

PEDIGREE

Pedigree analysis is a type of genetic analysis in which an inherited trait is studied and traced through several generations of a family to determine how that trait is inherited. A **pedigree** is a chart arranged as a type of family tree using symbols for people and lines to represent the relationships between those people. Squares usually represent males, and circles represent females. Horizontal lines represent a male and female mating, and the vertical lines beneath them represent their children. Usually, family members who possess the trait are fully shaded and those who only carry the trait are half-shaded. Genotypes and phenotypes are determined for each individual if possible. The pedigree below shows the family tree of a family in which the first male who was red-green color blind mated with the first female who was unaffected. They had five children. The three sons were unaffected, and the two daughters were carriers.

Inheritance of Red-Green Color Blindness: an X-linked Recessive Trait

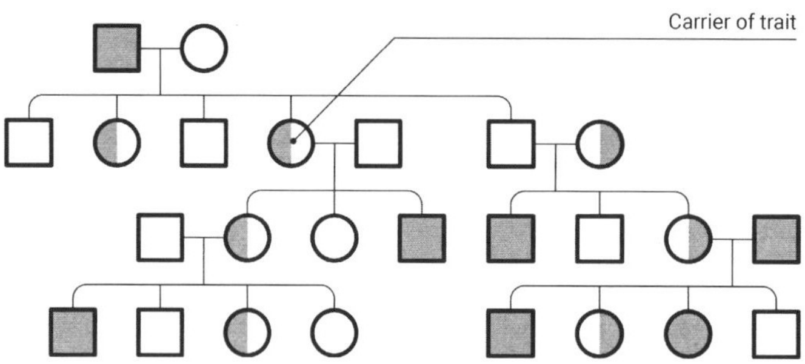

Non-Mendelian Inheritance

Non-Mendelian Inheritance Concepts

Linkage

Linkage is an exception to Mendel's law of independent assortment. Linkage can occur when two genes are located on the same chromosome. Each chromosome has several genes, and those genes tend to be inherited together. Genes that are located on the same chromosome and tend to be inherited together are called **linkage groups**. Because the genes are on the same chromosome, they do not separate during meiosis. During meiosis, the genes in a linkage group always go into the same gamete together. Due to linkage, genes with different characteristics are inherited together more frequently than is predicted using the laws of probability. An example of a linkage group is found on chromosome number 4. This linkage group includes genes for Parkinson's disease, narcolepsy, and Huntington's disease.

Review Video: Mendelian and Non-Mendelian Genetics
Visit mometrix.com/academy and enter code: 113159

Sex-Linked Inheritance

Sex-linked inheritance is an exception to Mendel's law of independent assortment. In human genetics, females have two X chromosomes, and males have one X and one Y chromosome. **Sex-linked traits** are carried on the X chromosome. Because females have two X chromosomes, they have two copies of genes found on the X chromosome. Females may possess a recessive allele for various disorders on one X chromosome, but as long as they possess the dominant allele for normal functioning on the other X chromosome, they will not have the disorder. Females who are heterozygous for a trait such as color blindness or hemophilia are only carriers. Because males have only one X chromosome, if they possess the recessive allele for a disorder, it will be expressed. Examples of traits that are a result of sex linkage are color blindness, hemophilia, a form of muscular dystrophy, and some forms of anemia.

Multiple Alleles

Multiple alleles result in a type of non-Mendelian inheritance. In Mendelian inheritance, only two alleles for each gene exist. For example, Mendel's pea plants were either tall or short, and the plants had either yellow or green pods. Often, there are more than two possibilities for a particular trait. For example, in human genetics, blood type has many variations. Multiple allele inheritance occurs where there are more than two different alleles of a gene for a particular trait. Even though there may be several alleles for a particular trait, each individual can still only possess two of those possible alleles. For example, the three human blood alleles are I^A

(blood contains type A antigens), I^B (blood contains type B antigens), and *i* (blood contains neither type A nor type B antigens).

Blood types and their possible genotypes are shown below.

Blood Type (Phenotype)	Genotype
A	I^AI^A, I^AI^O
B	I^BI^B, I^BI^O
AB	I^AI^B
O	*ii*

Incomplete Dominance

Incomplete dominance is an exception to Mendel's law of dominance. In these situations, there is no dominant or recessive allele. Instead, both alleles of a heterozygote are expressed, and when they are, they blend or mix. For example, there are two alleles for petal color for snapdragons: red (C^R) and white (C^W). Crossing a red snapdragon with a white snapdragon yields an F_1 generation that is 100% heterozygous pink. Crossing two pink snapdragons yields an F_2 generation that is 50% heterozygous pink (C^RC^W), 25% homozygous white (C^WC^W), and 25% homozygous red (C^RC^R).

Laws of Dominance and Codominance

The **law of dominance** states that a dominant trait is always expressed. **Codominance** is an exception to the law of dominance. In codominance, a heterozygote simultaneously expresses both genes for a trait without blending. For example, in certain horses, the hair colors red (D^R) and white (D^W) are codominant. Horses with the genotype D^RD^W have coats composed of both red hairs and white hairs, which—when mixed together—causes their coats to have a golden color.

Polygenic Inheritance

Polygenic inheritance occurs when a trait is determined by the interaction of many different genes. In Mendelian genetics, traits are determined by just one pair of genes with two alleles. For example, Mendel's pea plants had either red or white flowers, and his plants were either tall or short. An example of polygenic genetic inheritance in human genetics is skin color and height. Each is controlled by at least four pairs of genes. Skin color has many variations between very light and very dark. Height has many variations between very short and very tall. Eye color and intelligence are also polygenic.

Epistasis

Epistasis occurs when a gene at one locus inhibits the expression of a gene at another locus. For example, in mice, black hair (B) is dominant over brown hair (b). But a different gene at a different locus determines whether or not pigment is deposited (C for deposited and c for not deposited) on the mouse hair. A black mouse with genotypes BB or Bb will only have that color deposited if the pigment genotype is CC or Cc. A black mouse with genotype BBcc will be white. A brown mouse can have genotypes bbCC or bbCc, but a mouse with genotype bbcc will also be white.

Pleiotropy

In Mendelian inheritance, each gene can influence only one trait. Most genes can affect many traits or have multiple phenotypes. **Pleiotropy** is the situation in which one gene influences several seemingly unrelated traits. A gene that affects multiple traits is **pleiotropic**. Pleiotropy can be due to normal or mutated genes. Genes code for proteins. Because proteins are often used in more than one tissue or more than one area of the body, a missing protein can cause many complications. For example, the hormone insulin is a protein. If the insulin receptors are faulty, then the cells cannot recognize and use the insulin. Other examples of pleiotropy include inherited diseases such as cystic fibrosis, sickle-cell anemia, phenylketonuria (PKU), and albinism.

MITOCHONDRIAL INHERITANCE

Mitochondria are cellular organelles that produce energy for the cell. Mitochondria contain their own DNA consisting of 37 genes arranged in a circular structure. Mitochondrial DNA is transmitted maternally, which means that these mitochondrial genes are only inherited from the mother. The offspring's mitochondria only come from the oocyte (egg cell), not from the sperm. Sperm cells only contain mitochondria in their tails, which does not enter the egg during fertilization. Mitochondrial inheritance is not consistent with Mendelian inheritance in which the zygote derives half of the genetic material from the mother and half from the father. Most of these genes code for proteins related to muscular disorders.

Common Human Genetic Disorders

CHROMOSOMAL CHANGES THAT LEAD TO DOWN SYNDROME

Down syndrome is a type of **aneuploidy** (abnormal number of chromosomes) in which an individual has three copies of chromosome 21, as shown in the karyotype below. When a gamete with an extra 21st chromosome unites with a normal gamete, the result is a group of three chromosomes instead of a diploid set. A **trisomy** can occur as a result of nondisjunction, which occurs when a pair of chromosomes fails to separate during meiosis in the formation of an egg or sperm cell.

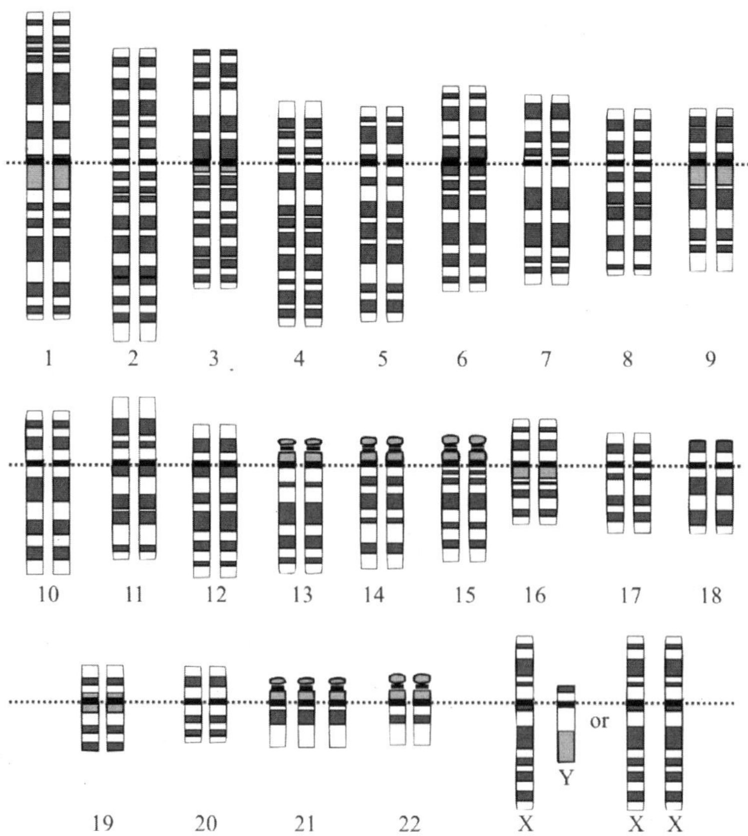

GENETICS OF SICKLE-CELL ANEMIA

Sickle cell anemia is a genetic disorder that is the result of a gene mutation. Specifically, sickle cell anemia is the result of the point mutation in which adenine is substituted for thymine. This results in a defective form of hemoglobin. Sickle-cell anemia occurs when a person is homozygous for the defective gene. Sickle-cell trait occurs when a person is heterozygous for the defective gene, and this person is a carrier but usually suffers no ill effects. Sickle cell anemia is an example of **pleiotropy**, in which a change in one gene affects multiple aspects of a person's health. These health problems are due to the abnormally sickle-shaped red blood cells that block the flow of blood, damaging tissues and organs. The sickle-shaped cells tend to rupture, leading to anemia.

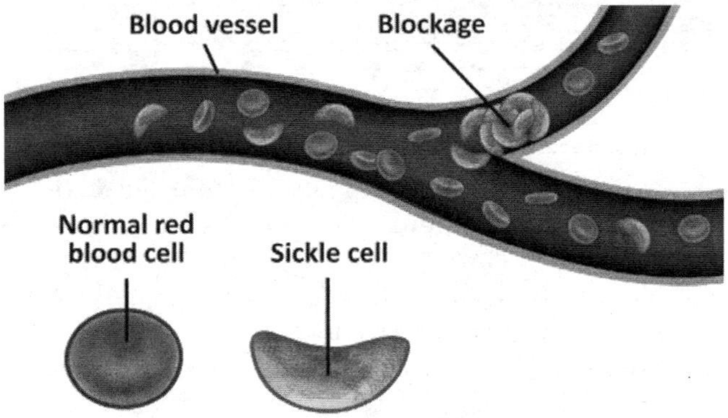

Sources of Genetic Variation

Genetic Variation

Mutations

Mutations are changes in DNA. Mutations are one of the main sources of genetic variation and can introduce new genetic information into the genome. The changes can be gene mutations such as the **point mutations** of substitution, addition, or deletion, or the changes can be on the chromosomal level such as the chromosomal aberrations of translocations, deletions, inversions, and duplications. Mutations are random and can benefit, harm, or have no effect on the individual. **Somatic mutations** do not affect inheritance and therefore do not affect genetic variation with regard to evolution. **Germline mutations** that occur in gametes (eggs and sperm) can be passed to offspring and therefore are very important to genetic variation and evolution.

Crossing Over

Crossing over is a major source of genetic variation. **Crossing over** is the exchange of equivalent segments of DNA between homologous chromosomes. Crossing over occurs during meiosis in prophase I. During synapsis, a **tetrad** is formed when homologous chromosomes pair up. Also during synapsis, the chromatids are extremely close together and sometimes the chromatids swap genes. Because genes have more than one allele, this allows for an exchange of genetic information. Crossing over is that exchange of genes. Crossing over can occur several times along the length of the chromosomes. Although crossing over does not introduce new information, it does introduce new combinations of the information that is available. Without crossing over during meiosis, only two genetically different gametes can be formed. With just one instance of crossing over, four genetically different gametes can be formed. With crossing over, each gamete contains genes from both the father and the mother. Crossing over leads to variation in traits among gametes, which leads to variation in traits among offspring.

Independent Assortment During Sexual Reproduction

Independent assortment during sexual reproduction is a source of genetic variation. Mutations originally brought about changes in DNA leading to alleles or different forms of the same gene. During sexual reproduction, these alleles are "shuffled" or "independently sorted," producing individuals with unique combinations of traits. Gametes are produced during meiosis, which consists of two cell divisions: meiosis I and meiosis II. Meiosis I is a reduction division in which the diploid parent cell divides into two haploid daughter cells. During the metaphase of meiosis I, the homologous pairs (one from the mother and one from the father) align on the equatorial plane. The orientation of the homologous pairs is random, and each placement is independent of another's placement. The number of possible arrangements increases exponentially as the number of chromosomes increases. The independent assortment of chromosomes during metaphase in meiosis I provides a variety of gametes with tremendous differences in their combinations of chromosomes.

Review Video: Gene Mutation
Visit mometrix.com/academy and enter code: 955485

Chromosomal Aberrations

Chromosomal aberrations are changes in DNA sequences on the chromosomal level. These mutations typically involve many genes and often result in miscarriages. Chromosomal aberrations include translocations, deletions, inversions, and duplications. **Translocations** occur when a piece of DNA breaks off of one chromosome and is joined to another chromosome. **Deletions** occur when a piece of DNA breaks off on a chromosome and is lost without reattaching. **Inversions** occur when a piece of DNA breaks off of one chromosome and becomes reattached to that same chromosome but with an inverted or flipped orientation. **Duplications** occur when a piece of DNA is replicated and attached to the original piece of DNA in sequence.

Sources of Genetic Exchange

Genetic exchange, or the transfer of DNA from one organism to another, is a source of genetic variation. Three general types of genetic exchange are transduction, transformation, and conjugation. **Transduction** occurs when genetic material is transferred from one bacterium to another by a bacteriophage. A bacteriophage is a virus that infects a bacterium. As the new bacteriophages are replicated, some of the host bacteria DNA can be added to the virus particles. **Transformation** occurs when a cell obtains new genetic information from its environment or surroundings. Many bacteria take up DNA fragments such as plasmids from their surroundings to obtain new genes. **Conjugation** occurs when bacteria or single-celled organisms are in direct contact with each other. Genes can be transferred from one into the other while the two cells are joined.

Processes Affecting the Gene Pool

Genetic Drift

Genetic drift is a microevolutionary process that causes random changes in allele frequencies that are not the result of natural selection. Genetic drift can result in a loss of genetic diversity. Genetic drift greatly impacts small populations. Two special forms of genetic drift are the genetic bottleneck and the founder effect. A **genetic bottleneck** occurs when there is a drastic reduction in population due to some change such as overhunting, disease, or habitat loss. When a population is greatly reduced in size, many alleles can be lost. Even if the population size greatly increases again, the lost alleles represent lost genetic diversity. The **founder effect** occurs when one individual or a few individuals populate a new area such as an island. This new population is limited to the alleles of the founder(s) unless mutations occur or new individuals immigrate to the region.

Gene Flow

Gene flow is a microevolutionary process in which alleles enter a population by immigration and leave a population by emigration. Gene flow helps counter genetic drift. When individuals from one genetically distinct population immigrate to a different genetically distinct population, alleles and their genetic information are added to the new population. The added alleles will change the gene frequencies within the population. This increases genetic diversity. If individuals with rare alleles emigrate from a population, the genetic diversity is decreased. Gene flow reduces the genetic differences between populations.

Hardy-Weinberg Equilibrium

HW EQUILIBRIUM

Hardy–Weinberg (HW) equilibrium is a theoretical concept that uses a mathematical relationship to study gene frequencies. According to HW, if specific conditions are met, the proportions of genotypes in a population can be described by the equation: $p^2 + 2pq + q^2 = 1$, in which p is the frequency of the dominant allele and q is the frequency of the recessive allele. Also, p^2 is the frequency of the homozygous dominant genotype, $2pq$ is the frequency of the heterozygous genotype, and q^2 is the frequency of the homozygous recessive genotype. In addition, the sum of p and q must be equal to one. If the frequencies on the left side of the equation have a sum of one, then the population is in equilibrium, and evolution is not taking place. If the frequencies on the left side of the equation do not have a sum of one, then evolution is taking place. Therefore, the HW equation is only true for populations that are in equilibrium.

The HW equilibrium requires the following five conditions to be met:

1. The population must be very large.
2. Mating is random.
3. There are no mutations.
4. No immigration or emigration can occur.
5. All individuals of the population have an equal chance to survive and reproduce.

According to this concept, if all five conditions are met, the gene frequencies will remain constant. In reality, these five conditions are rarely met except in a laboratory situation.

CALCULATION OF ALLELE FREQUENCY

> Explain how to calculate allele frequencies of a simple genetic locus at which there are two alleles (A and a) in a population of 1,000 individuals given that the population consists of 120 individuals homozygous for the dominant allele (AA), 480 heterozygous individuals (Aa), and 400 individuals homozygous for the recessive allele (aa).

To calculate the frequency of an allele, divide the total number of those alleles in the population by the total number of alleles in the population for that locus as shown in the following equation:

$$\text{allele frequency} = \frac{\text{total \# of allelles in population}}{\text{total \# of alleles in the population for that locus}}$$

First, find the total number of each type of allele. The 120 AA individuals produce 240 A alleles. The 480 heterozygous individuals produce 480 A alleles and 480 a alleles. The 400 aa individuals produce 800 a alleles. Therefore, there is a total of 720 A alleles and 1,280 a alleles. Adding the 720 and 1,280 yields a total of 2,000 alleles in the population for that locus. The allele frequency for $A = \frac{720}{2{,}000}$ or 0.36. The allele frequency for $a = \frac{1{,}280}{2{,}000}$ or 0.64.

Chapter Quiz

Ready to see how well you retained what you just read? Scan the QR code to go directly to the chapter quiz interface for this study guide. If you're using a computer, simply visit the online resources page at **mometrix.com/resources719/abctebio** and click the Chapter Quizzes link.

Molecular Biology

Nucleic Acids

Nucleotide Structure

A **nucleotide**, whether DNA or RNA, contains three components: a phosphate group, a ringed, five-carbon sugar (deoxyribose in DNA, ribose in RNA), and a nitrogen-containing base. The **phosphate group** binds to one side of the **ringed, five-carbon sugar**. The **nitrogen-containing base** binds to the opposite side of the ringed, five-carbon sugar. A nucleotide strand is formed by covalently linking the phosphate groups of the nucleotides into a linear sequence.

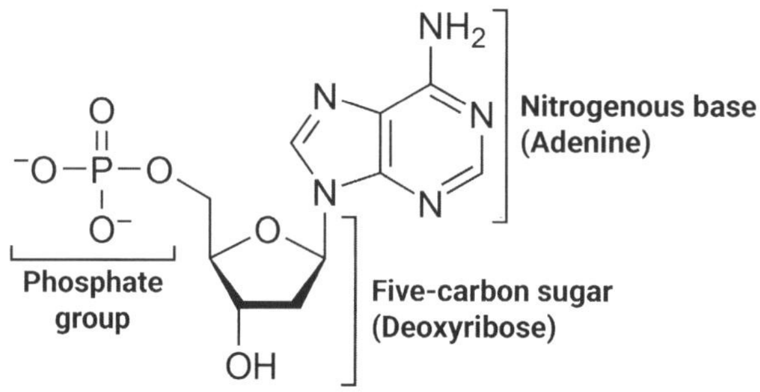

DNA and RNA

Structural Similarities

Structural similarities between DNA and RNA:

- DNA and RNA are both **nucleic acids** composed of nucleotides made up of a sugar, a base, and a phosphate molecule.
- DNA and RNA have three of their four bases in common: guanine, cytosine, and adenine.

Review Video: DNA Vs. RNA
Visit mometrix.com/academy and enter code: 184871

Structural, Locational, and Functional Differences

Structural differences between DNA and RNA:

- DNA contains the base thymine, but RNA replaces thymine with uracil.
- DNA contains the sugar deoxyribose, but RNA contains the sugar ribose.
- DNA is double stranded, but RNA is single stranded.

Locational: DNA is located in the nucleus and mitochondria. RNA is found in the nucleus, ribosomes, and cytoplasm.

Functional: DNA contains the genetic blueprint and instructions for the cell. RNA carries out those instructions and synthesizes proteins.

TYPES AND FUNCTIONS OF RNA

Types of RNA include ribosomal RNA (rRNA), transfer RNA (tRNA), and messenger RNA (mRNA).

- **rRNA** forms the RNA component of the ribosome. It is evolutionarily conserved, which means it can be used to study relationships in organisms.
- **mRNA** is used by the ribosome to generate proteins (translation). The mRNA contains three-nucleotide "codons" that code for specific amino acids in a protein sequence.
- **tRNA** functions in translation by transferring an amino acid to the corresponding codon on the mRNA strand.

Review Video: DNA
Visit mometrix.com/academy and enter code: 639552

COMPLEMENTARY BASE PAIRING

According to **Chargaff's rule**, a DNA molecule always has a 1:1 ratio of purine to pyrimidine within it. The amount of adenine always equals the amount of thymine, and the amount of guanine always equals the amount of cytosine. (Note that the same rule holds for RNA, but the thymine is replaced with uracil.) In DNA, adenine always pairs with thymine, and guanine always pairs with cytosine. In RNA, adenine always pairs with uracil, and guanine always pairs with cytosine. The pairs are bonded together with hydrogen bonds.

DOUBLE HELIX STRUCTURE OF DNA

Double-stranded DNA consists of two complementary strands that adopt the shape of a double helix, which resembles a twisted ladder. The "sides" of the ladder are the sugar-phosphate backbones of the complementary strands. The "rungs" of the ladder are the nitrogenous bases, which are held together (base paired) by hydrogen bonds between the complementary nitrogenous bases in the opposite strand. In DNA, **adenine** (A) base pairs with **thymine** (T) and **guanine** (G) base pairs with **cytosine** (C). DNA also has an antiparallel structure, consisting of a 5' end and a 3' end, where the two strands of the DNA run in opposite directions for one another. The two ends of the DNA strand are coined 5' or 3' based on the specific carbon atom within the purine or pyrimidine ring that makes up the deoxyribose sugar. The 5' end of a DNA strand has a free phosphate group attached to the 5'-carbon atom of the deoxyribose sugar, while the 3' end of DNA has a free hydroxyl group at the 3'-carbon.

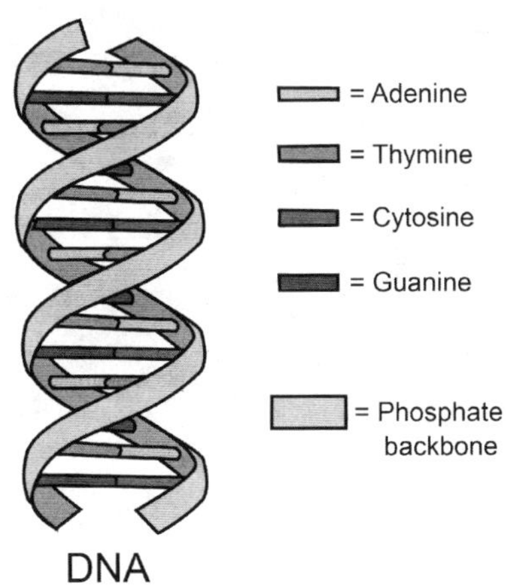

ORGANIZATION OF PROKARYOTIC DNA

Prokaryotes lack a nucleus and therefore prokaryotic DNA is organized primarily into a central loop contained in the cytoplasm. Prokaryotes may also contain smaller loops of DNA known as **plasmids** that contain other genes. Most prokaryotes lack histones, but Archaea are an example of prokaryotes that do contain histones.

Organization of Eukaryotic DNA

Eukaryotes have a nucleus with multiple chromosomes, each containing a tightly-compacted, double-helix DNA molecule. The structural sub-components of chromosomes include histones, nucleosomes, and chromatin.

- **Histones** are positively-charged, DNA-binding proteins.
- A **nucleosome** is composed of eight histone proteins around which approximately 146 base pairs of DNA are wrapped. The nucleosome is often called a "beads on a string" structure.
- **Chromatin** is made up of compacted nucleosomes.
- **Chromosomes** are made up of compacted chromatin.

RNA is also thought to play a role in chromatin structure.

Telomeres

Eukaryotic chromosomes have **telomeres** located at their tips. Telomeres are repetitive sequences of DNA that maintain the ends of the linear chromosomes and keep those ends from deteriorating.

DNA Replication

DNA replication begins when the double strands of the parent DNA molecule are unwound and unzipped. The enzyme **helicase** separates the two strands by breaking the hydrogen bonds between the base pairs that make up the rungs of the twisted ladder. These two single strands of DNA are called the **replication fork**. Each separate DNA strand provides a template for the complementary DNA bases, G with C and A with T. The opposite ends of DNA are called the 5' and 3' ends. After the DNA is separated, the enzyme **RNA primase** lays down an RNA primer that the enzyme **DNA polymerase** binds to initiate replication. DNA polymerase only synthesizes DNA from the 5' end towards the 3' end. Of the two strands open during replication, the strand with the 3' end will be replicated as a single, continuous strand, also known as the **leading strand**. The strand with the 5' end, which runs away from the fork, is known as the **lagging strand**, and will be replicated into shorter, unlinked segments known as Okazaki fragments. After bases are joined to the complementary base, the enzyme **exonuclease** removes the RNA primers used to initiate replication of the two strands. A separate

DNA polymerase fills in gaps after the RNA primer is removed. The Okazaki fragments are joined by the enzyme DNA ligase.

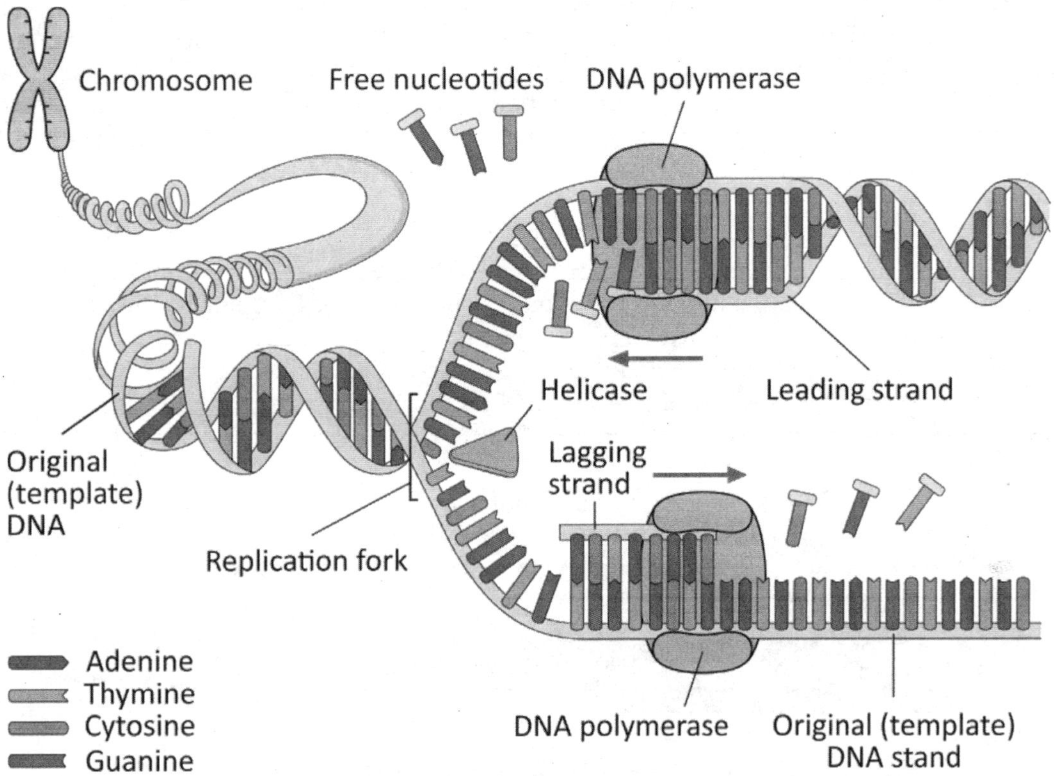

Protein Synthesis

Transcription

Transcription is the process by which a segment of DNA is copied onto a working blueprint called RNA. Each gene has a special region called a **promoter** that guides the beginning of the transcription process. **RNA polymerase** unwinds the DNA at the promoter region and makes an RNA copy of the DNA gene by adding the **complementary nucleotides**, G with C, C with G, T with A, and A with U. This forms a single strand of messenger RNA or mRNA.

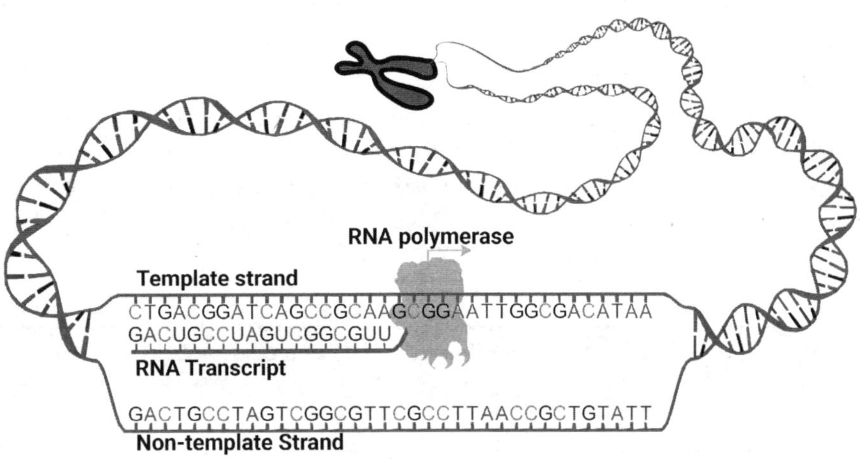

PROCESSING MRNA

In addition to being transcribed, the mRNA must also be processed. First, a 5' cap (modified guanine nucleotide) is added, which helps promote ribosome recognition and preventing mRNA degradation. Second, a string of adenosine ribonucleotides are added to the 3' end of the mRNA, forming a structure known as a **poly(A) tail**. The poly(A) tail helps prevent mRNA degradation. The mRNA transcript may contain regions that do not code for protein, called **introns**. The regions that do code for protein are called **exons**. If introns are present, they will be removed in a process called splicing by a structure known as the **spliceosome**. After addition of the 5' cap, addition of the poly(A) tail, and splicing, the mRNA is ready for translation.

TRANSLATION

Ribosomes synthesize proteins from mRNA in a process called **translation**. The ribosome has three tRNA binding sites—A, P, and E. Translation initiates when the "**A site**" becomes occupied by the tRNA molecule corresponding to the mRNA start codon. The ribosome then moves the first tRNA from the "A site" to the "**P site**." The "A site" is then occupied by the tRNA molecule corresponding to the second mRNA codon. The ribosome then transfers the amino acid on the "P site" tRNA to the amino acid on the "A site" tRNA. The first tRNA, which now has no amino acid, is moved from the "P site" the "**E site**." The second tRNA, complexed to a chain of two amino acids, is moved from the "A site" to the "P site." The "A site" is then occupied by the tRNA corresponding to the third mRNA codon. The "P site" amino acid chain is transferred to the amino acid bound to the "A site" tRNA. The first tRNA then exits from the "E site" and the second and third tRNA molecules shift, opening the "A site" for the next tRNA. The growing amino acid chain continues to be transferred from the "P site" to the "A site" until translation is complete.

Review Video: Amino Acids
Visit mometrix.com/academy and enter code: 190385

Regulation of Gene Expression

REGULATION OF GENE EXPRESSION

ROLE OF PROMOTERS

Promoters are DNA sequences located upstream of the gene needed for transcription. Promoters signal the beginning of transcription. Special proteins called **transcription factors**, which bind to promoters, subsequently provide binding sites for the **RNA polymerase**, which is the enzyme that transcribes the RNA. Promoters in the Archaea and Eukaryota domains often contain a nucleotide sequence TATA, which is called a **TATA box**. The TATA box is usually 25 nucleotides upstream of the transcription start site, and it is the location at which the DNA is unwound.

ROLE OF ENHANCERS

Enhancers are DNA sequences that regulate gene expression by providing a binding site for proteins that regulate RNA polymerase in transcribing proteins. Enhancers can greatly increase the expression of genes in their range. Enhancers are functional over large distances. Some enhancers are located within the gene they control while others can be hundreds or thousands of base pairs upstream or downstream from the genes they control. Most genes are controlled by two or three enhancers, but some may be controlled by more. Enhancers provide binding sites for regulatory proteins that either promote or inhibit RNA polymerase activity. Enhancers are more common in eukaryotes than prokaryotes.

Review Video: Regulation of Gene Expression
Visit mometrix.com/academy and enter code: 651793

ROLE OF TRANSCRIPTION FACTORS

Transcription factors are DNA-binding proteins that help regulate gene expression in eukaryotes and prokaryotes. In eukaryotes that have promoter or enhancer regions, transcription factors bind near these regions and increase the ability of the RNA polymerase to start transcription. In eukaryotes, because genes are typically turned "off," transcription factors typically work to turn genes "on." The opposite is often true in bacteria, and transcription factors often work to turn genes off.

Role of Operons

Operons are segments of DNA or groups of genes that are controlled by one promoter. Operons consist of an operator, a promoter, and one or more structural genes. The **operator** provides a binding side for a repressor that inhibits the binding of RNA polymerase. The **promoter** provides the binding site for the RNA polymerase. The **structural genes** provide the sequence that codes for a protein. Operons are transcribed as single units and code for a single mRNA molecule, which produces proteins with related functions. Operons have been found in prokaryotes, eukaryotes, and viruses. For example, the lac (lactose) operon in certain bacteria controls the production of the enzymes needed to digest lactose. If lactose is already available in the cell, the lactose binds to the repressor protein to prevent the repressor protein from binding to the operator. The gene is transcribed, and the enzymes necessary for the digestion of the lactose are produced. If there is no lactose that needs to be digested, the repressor protein binds to the operator. The gene is not transcribed, and the enzyme is not produced. This allows the cell to only code for proteins as needed by the cell.

Role of Epigenetics

Epigenetics studies factors or mechanisms that determine if genes are active (switched on) or dormant (switched off). These mechanisms can alter gene function or gene expression without altering the sequences of the DNA itself. An example is the addition of a methyl group (**methylation**) to the histones. **Acetylation**, the addition of an acetyl group, and **phosphorylation**, the addition of a phosphoryl group, are also modifications to the proteins associated with DNA that can switch genes on or off or affect their activity level.

Differentiation and Specialization of Cells

Differential Gene Expression

Differential gene expression is the expression of different sets of gene by cells with identical DNA molecules. The unused genes in a differentiated cell remain in the cell but are not expressed. Actually, only a few genes are expressed in each cell. For example, during mammalian embryonic development, the undifferentiated zygote undergoes cell division through mitosis. As the number of cells increases, selected cells undergo differentiation to become specialized components in the developing tissues of the embryo.

Stem Cells

Stem cells are undifferentiated cells that can divide without limit and that can differentiate to produce the specialized cells that each organism needs. **Embryonic stem cells** are harvested from the embryo at the blastocyst stage or from the developing gonads of the embryo. Stem cells can be pluripotent or multipotent depending on their source. Early embryonic stem cells are **pluripotent**, which means they have not undergone any differentiation and have the ability to become any special type of cell. After embryonic stem cells begin to differentiate, they may be limited to specializing into a specific tissue type. These stem cells are considered to be **multipotent** because they can only develop into a few different types of cells. Adult stem cells, also called **somatic stem cells**, are harvested from organs and tissues and can differentiate into those types of cells in that particular organ or tissue. Umbilical cord blood stem cells can be harvested from the umbilical cord of a newborn baby. Adult stem cells and umbilical cord blood stem cells are multipotent. **Induced pluripotent cells** (iPS) are somatic cells that have been manipulated to act like pluripotent cells. Experiments have shown that iPS may be useful in treating diseases.

Mutations

Missense Mutations, Silent Mutations, and Nonsense Mutations

Mutations are changes in DNA sequences. **Point mutations** are changes in a single nucleotide in a DNA sequence. Three types of point mutations are missense, silent, and nonsense.

- **Missense mutations** result in a codon for a different amino acid. An example is mutating TGT (Cysteine codon) to TGG (Tryptophan codon).
- **Silent mutations** result in a codon for the same amino acid as the original sequence. An example is mutating TGT (Cysteine codon) to TGC (a different Cysteine codon).
- **Nonsense mutations** insert a premature stop codon, typically resulting in a non-functional protein. An example is mutating TGT (Cysteine codon) to TGA (STOP codon).

Review Video: Codons
Visit mometrix.com/academy and enter code: 978172

Frameshift Mutations and Inversion Mutations

Deletions and insertions can result in the addition of amino acids, the removal of amino acids, or cause a frameshift mutation. A **frameshift mutation** changes the reading frame of the mRNA (a new group of codons will be read), resulting in the formation of a new protein product. Mutations can also occur on the chromosomal level. For example, an **inversion** is when a piece of the chromosome inverts or flips its orientation.

Germline Mutations and Somatic Mutations

Mutations can occur in somatic (body) cells and germ cells (egg and sperm). **Somatic mutations** develop after conception and occur in an organism's body cells such as bone cells, liver cells, or brain cells. Somatic mutations cannot be passed on from parent to offspring. The mutation is limited to the specific descendent of the cell in which the mutation occurred. The mutation is not in the other body cells unless they are descendants of the originally mutated cell. Somatic mutations may cause cancer or diseases. Some somatic mutations are silent. **Germline mutations** are present at conception and occur in an organism's germ cells, which are only egg and sperms cells. Germline mutations may be passed on from parent to offspring. Germline mutations will be present in every cell of an offspring that inherits a germline mutation. Germline mutations may cause diseases. Some germline mutations are silent.

Mutagens

Mutagens are physical and chemical agents that cause changes or errors in DNA replication. Mutagens are external factors to an organism. Examples include ionizing radiation such as ultraviolet radiation, x-rays, and gamma radiation. Viruses and microorganisms that integrate their DNA into host chromosomes are also mutagens. Mutagens include environmental poisons such as asbestos, coal tars, tobacco, and benzene. Alcohol and diets high in fat have been shown to be mutagenic. Not all mutations are caused by mutagens. **Spontaneous mutations** can occur in DNA due to molecular decay.

Lab Techniques for Studying Biological Processes

Gel Electrophoresis

Gel electrophoresis is a technique used to separate macromolecules such as nucleic acids and proteins with regard to size. Fragments of DNA and RNA, as well as proteins, are separated according to length. Using different types of gel electrophoresis, proteins can also be separated according to electrical charge. The technique for gel electrophoresis is relatively simple. For example, to separate DNA strands, a solution containing the DNA strand is placed in a gel. When an electric current is passed through the gel, the DNA strands migrate from the negative end of the container to the positive end due to their negative charge because of their phosphate ions. Shorter DNA strands migrate faster than the longer DNA strands. This results in a series of bands. Each band contains DNA strands of a specific length. A DNA standard, commonly called a DNA ladder, is placed in the gel to provide a reference to determine the strand length. Lengths are measured in base pairs (bps).

Microscopy

Microscopy is used in many fields of biology, including microbiology. Bacteria, viruses, cell components, and molecules are too small to be seen by the naked eye. Several types of microscopes are available to examine these samples. There are **light microscopes**, which use visible light to study samples, and electron microscopes, which use beams of electrons. The light microscope (also called the compound microscope) uses two types of lenses (ocular and objective) to magnify objects. These are typically used when studying samples at the cellular level. Basic compound light microscopes are typically used in high school biology classes. Other compound light microscopes such as the dark-field microscope, phase-contrast microscope, and the fluorescent microscope are available for more specific uses. For tiny samples, such as viruses, cell components, or individual molecules, electron microscopes can be used. **Electron microscopes** use beams of electrons instead of light. Because beams of electrons have shorter wavelengths, electron microscopes have greater resolution than light microscopes. Resolution is the ability of a lens to reveal two points as being distinct. The two types of electron microscopy are transmission electron microscopy (TEM) and scanning electron microscopy (SEM). SEM is a newer technology than TEM and produces three-dimensional images.

Spectrophotometry

Spectrophotometry involves measuring the amount of visible light absorbed by a colored solution. There are **analog** and **digital spectrometers** that measure absorbance and transmittance. A **single beam spectrometer** measures relative light intensity. A **double beam spectrometer** compares light intensity between a reference sample and a test sample. Spectrometers measure the wavelength of light. Spectrometry not only involves working with visible light, but also near-ultraviolet and near-infrared light. A **spectrophotometer** includes an illumination source. An output wavelength is selected and beamed at the sample, the sample absorbs light, and the detector responds to the light and outputs an analog electronic current in a usable form. A spectrophotometer may require calibration. Some types can be used to identify unknown chemicals.

Review Video: Spectrophotometer
Visit mometrix.com/academy and enter code: 104413

DNA Technologies and Genetic Engineering

PCR

The **polymerase chain reaction (PCR)** is a laboratory technique used to rapidly copy selected segments of DNA. PCR can be performed on the DNA from a single cell. PCR is a hot-and-cold cycled reaction that uses a special heat-tolerant polymerase. The DNA sample is combined with this special DNA polymerase, primers, and free nucleotides. Primers are synthetic strands of DNA containing just a few bases. The first step is a high-temperature **denaturation step** (90–95°C) that causes the DNA strands to unwind. The second step is a low-temperature **annealing step** (~60°C) in which the primers anneal to the single-stranded DNA. The final step is an **activation step** that matches the activation temperature for the heat-resistant DNA polymerase (~70°C, depending on the enzyme). This final step results in the formation of newly-synthesized, double-stranded DNA. These steps will be repeated on the same sample for multiple cycles, typically about 30. The number of DNA copies generated is 2^N, where N is the number of cycles.

DNA Sequencing

DNA sequencing is a laboratory technique used to determine the order or linear sequence of nucleotides of DNA fragments. A PCR is used to isolate the needed DNA segment or DNA template. During PCR, some of each of the nucleotides containing the four bases (G, C, A, and T) are chemically altered and fluorescently tagged with different colors of dye. Also, the chemically altered nucleotides have the dideoxyribose sugar, which contains one less oxygen atom than the usual deoxyribose. When synthesis begins, the polymerase randomly adds either a regular nucleotide or an altered nucleotide. If the polymerase adds an altered nucleotide, synthesis stops. This way, each DNA fragment of the same length is tagged with the same color. Then, electrophoresis is used to separate DNA fragments according to length. The DNA sequence can be read by reading the tags of the shortest fragments to the tags of the longest fragments.

Human Genome Project

In 1990, the **Human Genome Project (HGP)** was launched to map the human genome. The project involved scientists from 16 laboratories located in at least 6 different countries, and it was completed in 2003. The human genome consists of approximately 3.12 billion paired nucleotides. The genomes of several plants, animal, fungi, protists, bacteria, viruses, and even cell organelles have also been studied and mapped. Interesting comparisons can be made between these genomes. For example, the number of genes in an organism's genome does not indicate the complexity of that organism. Humans have approximately 21,000 genes, but the simpler roundworms have approximately 26,000 genes.

Gene Therapy

Gene therapy is an experimental but promising technique that introduces new genes into an organism to correct a specific disease caused by a defective gene. In gene therapy, the defective gene is replaced by a properly functioning gene. Gene therapy is most promising for diseases that are caused by a single defective gene. For example, gene therapy was first successfully used to treat severe combined immunodeficiency (SCID). One type of SCID is caused by a single defective gene on the X chromosome. Doctors removed some bone marrow from the test subjects, injected a retrovirus that was carrying the gene, and then re-implanted the bone marrow. The bone marrow cells then have the correct DNA sequence for the production of proteins for much-needed enzymes. Unfortunately, some of the first recipients developed leukemia, and the trials were halted. Later, researchers discovered that the leukemia was related to the location of the insertion of the retroviral vectors.

Cloning

Clones are exact biological copies of genes, cells, or multicellular organisms. There are natural clones and artificial clones. Many clones are produced in nature. For example, animals that can reproduce asexually by fragmentation or budding produce natural clones. Some plants such as strawberries can reproduce by stolons. Typically, in biology, cloning refers to gene cloning or the cloning of organisms. Gene cloning is the process of splicing genes that are needed to code for a specific protein and introducing them into a new cell with a DNA vector. Gene cloning has been used with bacteria in the production of human insulin and a human growth hormone replacement.

Cloning can also occur with an entire organism. This type of cloning is called a **somatic cell nuclear transfer**. The first mammal clone was Dolly the sheep. In this procedure, a nucleus of a somatic cell from the sheep to be cloned was transferred or injected into a denucleated egg cell of the surrogate mother sheep. The egg was stimulated to divide by electric shock, and then the embryo was implanted into the uterus of the surrogate mother. Dolly was born identical to the egg nucleus donor, not the surrogate mother. Dolly and other cloned mammals typically have serious health problems. Dolly aged prematurely possibly due to the shortened telomeres from the adult somatic cell nucleus.

Review Video: Genetic Cloning
Visit mometrix.com/academy and enter code: 289634

Genetic Engineering and Genetically Engineered Cells

Genetic engineering is the manipulation of DNA outside of normal reproduction. This modified DNA is called **recombinant DNA**. Genetic engineering is prevalent in gene cloning, which is used in the production of genetically modified (GM) organisms and the production of GM food. **Gene cloning** involves cloning a specific gene that is needed for a specific purpose. Genes can be inserted into cells of an entirely different species. Genetically engineered cells are also called transgenic cells. GM organisms such as plants or crops contain recombinant DNA. Many types of organisms such as plants, animals, fungi, and bacteria have been genetically modified. GM crops such as corn and soybeans can be engineered to be herbicide resistant to ensure that herbicides kill the weeds but not the crop plants. Crops can also be modified to be pest resistant in order to kill the insects that might damage the crops. In addition, several foods can be genetically modified to increase nutritional value.

Review Video: Genetic Engineering and Genetically Engineered Cells
Visit mometrix.com/academy and enter code: 548687

Chapter Quiz

Ready to see how well you retained what you just read? Scan the QR code to go directly to the chapter quiz interface for this study guide. If you're using a computer, simply visit the online resources page at **mometrix.com/resources719/abctebio** and click the Chapter Quizzes link.

Evolution

Mechanics of Evolution

Mechanisms of Evolution

Natural and Artificial Selection

Natural selection and artificial selection are both mechanisms of evolution. **Natural selection** is a process of nature in which a population can change over generations. Every population has variations in individual heritable traits and organisms best suited for survival typically reproduce and pass on those genetic traits to offspring to increase the likelihood of them surviving. Typically, the more advantageous a trait is, the more common that trait becomes in a population. Natural selection brings about evolutionary **adaptations** and is responsible for biological diversity. Artificial selection is another mechanism of evolution. **Artificial selection** is a process brought about by humans. Artificial selection is the selective breeding of domesticated animals and plants such as when farmers choose animals or plants with desirable traits to reproduce. Artificial selection has led to the evolution of farm stock and crops. For example, cauliflower, broccoli, and cabbage all evolved due to artificial selection of the wild mustard plant.

Sexual Selection

Sexual selection is a special case of natural selection in animal populations. **Sexual selection** occurs because some animals are more likely to find mates than other animals. The two main contributors to sexual selection are **competition** of males and **mate selection** by females. An example of male competition is in the mating practices of the redwing blackbird. Some males have huge territories and numerous mates that they defend. Other males have small territories, and some even have no mates. An example of mate selection by females is the mating practices of peacocks. Male peacocks display large, colorful tail feathers to attract females. Females are more likely to choose males with the larger, more colorful displays.

Coevolution

Coevolution describes a rare phenomenon in which two populations with a close ecological relationship undergo reciprocal adaptations simultaneously and evolve together, affecting each other's evolution. General examples of coevolution include predator and prey, or plant and pollinator, and parasites and their hosts. A specific example of coevolution is the yucca moths and the yucca plants. Yucca plants can only be pollinated by the yucca moths. The yucca moths lay their eggs in the yucca flowers, and their larvae grow inside the ovary.

Adaptive Radiation

Adaptive radiation is an evolutionary process in which a species branches out and adapts and fills numerous unoccupied ecological niches. The adaptations occur relatively quickly, driven by natural selection and resulting in new phenotypes and possibly new species eventually. An example of adaptive radiation is the finches that Darwin studied on the Galápagos Islands. Darwin recorded 13 different varieties of finches, which differed in the size and shape of their beaks. Through the process of natural selection, each type of finch adapted to the specific environment and specifically the food sources of the island to which it belonged. On newly formed islands with many unoccupied ecological niches, the adaptive radiation process occurred quickly due to the lack of competing species and predators.

Evidence Supporting Evolution

Molecular Evidence

Because all organisms are made up of cells, all organisms are alike on a fundamental level. Cells share similar components, which are made up of molecules. Specifically, all cells contain DNA and RNA. This should indicate that all species descended from a **common ancestor**. Humans and chimpanzees share approximately 98% of their genes in common, while humans and bacteria share approximately 7% of their genes in common suggesting that bacteria and humans are not closely related. Biologists have been able to use DNA sequence comparisons of modern organisms to reconstruct the "root" of the tree of life. The fact that RNA can store information, replicate itself, and code for proteins suggests that RNA could have could have evolved first, followed by DNA.

Homology

Homology is the similarity of structures of different species based on a similar anatomy in a common evolutionary ancestor. For instance, the forelimbs of humans, dogs, birds, and whales all have the same basic pattern of the bones. Specifically, all of these organisms have a humerus, radius, and ulna. They are all modifications of the same basic evolutionary structure from a common ancestor. Tetrapods resemble the fossils of extinct transitional animal called the *Eusthenopteron*. This would seem to indicate that evolution primarily modifies preexisting structures.

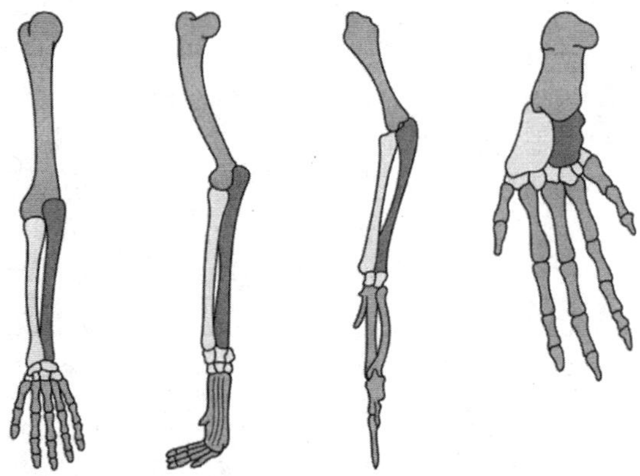

Review Video: Homologous vs Analogous Structures
Visit mometrix.com/academy and enter code: 355157

Embryology

The stages of **embryonic development** reveal homologies between species. These homologies are evidence of a **common ancestor**. For example, in chicken embryos and mammalian embryos, both include a stage in which slits and arches appear in the embryo's neck region that are strikingly similar to gill slits and gill arches in fish embryos. Adult chickens and adult mammals do not have gills, but this embryonic homology indicates that birds and mammals share a common ancestor with fish. As another example, some species of toothless whales have embryos that initially develop teeth that are later absorbed, which indicates that these whales have an ancestor with teeth in the adult form. Finally, most tetrapods have five-digit limbs, but birds have three-digit limbs in their wings. However, embryonic birds initially have five-digit limbs in their wings, which develop into a three-digit wing. Tetrapods such as reptiles, mammals, and birds all share a common ancestor with five-digit limbs.

Endosymbiosis Theory

The endosymbiosis theory is foundational to evolution. Endosymbiosis provides the path for prokaryotes to give rise to eukaryotes. Specifically, **endosymbiosis** explains the development of the organelles of mitochondria in animals and chloroplasts in plants. This theory states that some eukaryotic organelles such as mitochondria and chloroplasts originated as free living cells. According to this theory, primitive, heterotrophic eukaryotes engulfed smaller, autotrophic bacteria prokaryotes, but the bacteria were not digested. Instead, the eukaryotes and the bacteria formed a symbiotic relationship. Eventually, the bacteria transformed into mitochondrion or chloroplasts.

Supporting Evidence

Several facts support the endosymbiosis theory. Mitochondria and chloroplasts contain their own DNA and can both only arise from other preexisting mitochondria and chloroplasts. The genomes of mitochondria and chloroplasts consist of single, circular DNA molecules with no histones. This is similar to bacteria genomes, not eukaryote genomes. Also, the RNA, ribosomes, and protein synthesis of mitochondria and chloroplasts are remarkably similar to those of bacteria, and both use oxygen to produce ATP. These organelles have a double phospholipid layer that is typical of engulfed bacteria. This theory also involves a secondary endosymbiosis in which the original eukaryotic cells that have engulfed the bacteria are then engulfed themselves by another free-living eukaryote.

Convergent Evolution

Convergent evolution is the evolutionary process in which two or more unrelated species become increasingly similar in appearance. In convergent evolution, similar adaptations in these unrelated species occur due to these species inhabiting the same kind of environment. For example, the mammals shown below, although found in different parts of the world, developed similar appearances due to their similar environments.

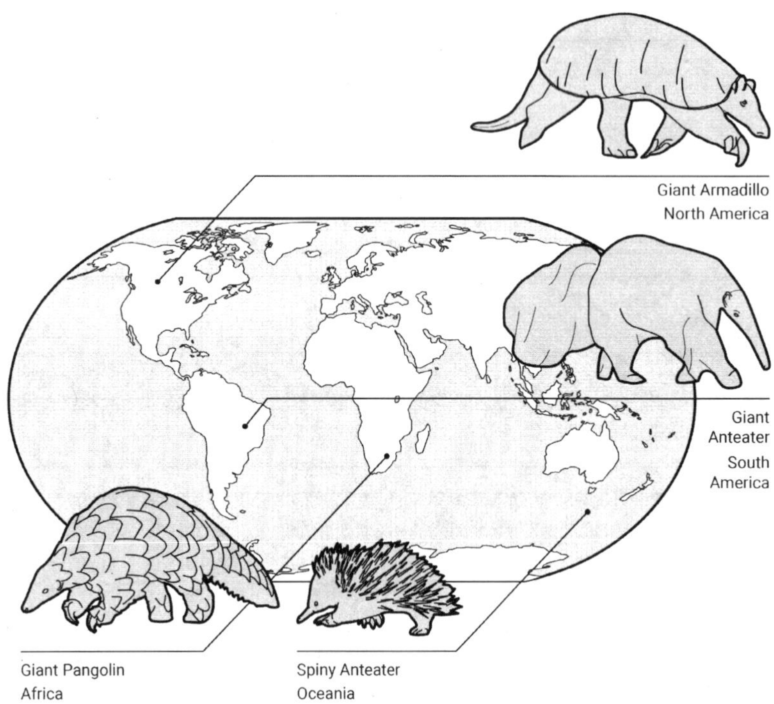

Divergent Evolution

Divergent evolution is the evolutionary process in which organisms of one species become increasingly dissimilar in appearance. As several small adaptations occur due to natural selection, the organisms will finally reach a point at which two new species are formed, also known as **speciation**. Then, these two species will further diverge from each other as they continue to evolve. Adaptive radiation is an example of divergent evolution. Another example is the divergent evolution of the wooly mammoth and the modern elephant from a common ancestor.

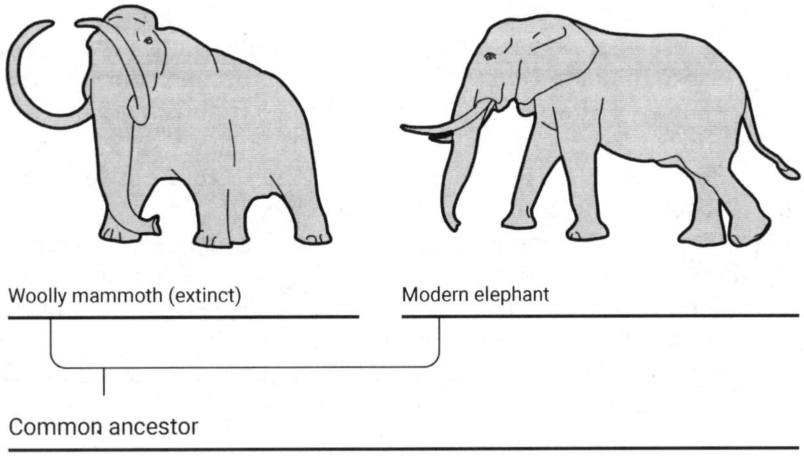

Fossil Record

The **fossil record** provides many types of support for evolution including comparisons from rock layers, transition fossils, and homologies with modern organisms. First, fossils from rock layers from all over the world have been compared, enabling scientists to develop a sequence of life from simple to complex. Based on the fossil record, the **geologic timeline** chronicles the history of all living things. For example, the fossil record clearly indicates that invertebrates developed before vertebrates and that fish developed before amphibians. Second, numerous transitional fossils have been found. **Transitional fossils** show an intermediate state between an ancestral form of an organism and the form of its descendants. These fossils show the path of evolutionary change. For example, many transition fossils documenting the evolutionary change from fish to amphibians have been discovered. In 2004, scientists discovered *Tiktaalik roseae*, or the "fishapod," which is a 375-million-year-old fossil that exhibits both fish and amphibian characteristics. Another example would be *Pakicetus,* an extinct land mammal, that scientists determined is an early ancestor of modern whales and dolphins based on the specialized structures of the inner ear. Most fossils exhibit homologies with modern organisms. For example, extinct horses are similar to modern horses, indicating a common ancestor.

Cephalization and Multicellularity

Cephalization is the evolutionary trend that can be summarized as "the evolution of the head." In most animals, nerve tissue has been concentrated into a brain at one end of an organism over many generations. Eventually, a head enclosing a brain and housing sensory organs was produced at one end of the organism. Many invertebrates, such as arthropods and annelids and all vertebrates, have undergone cephalization. However, some invertebrates, such as echinoderms and sponges, have not undergone cephalization, and these organisms literally do not have a head.

Another evolutionary trend is **multicellularity**. Life has evolved from simple, single-celled organisms to complex, multicellular organisms. Over millions of years, single-celled organisms gave rise to biofilms, which gave rise to multicellular organisms, which gave rise to all of the major phyla of multicellular organisms present today.

Genetic Basis of Speciation

SPECIATION

SIGNIFICANCE OF REPRODUCTIVE ISOLATION

A biological species is a group of similar organisms that can breed and produce viable offspring. If gene flow between two groups of a species is hindered or stopped completely through **reproductive isolation**, more significant genetic differences between the two groups can accumulate and a new species may originate. This process is known as **speciation**. For the two incipient species to completely split, one of two things must occur: either successful mating between the incipient species cannot occur or the offspring must be nonviable or sterile. **Prezygotic barriers** occur before fertilization and stop or hinder species from mating. These barriers include, but are not limited to, habitat isolation, behavioral isolation, or temporal isolation. For instance, a change in the mating location or a change in the mating rituals can keep mating from occurring. **Postzygotic barriers** occur after fertilization but prevent the offspring or hybrid from living or being fertile. Some examples of postzygotic barriers include differences in chromosome numbers or the arrangement of genes on certain chromosomes. Various modes of geographic and population isolation may occur, but the key to speciation in each type is still the reduced gene flow.

MODES

Speciation has various modes that bring about the reduced gene flow needed for incipient species to fully separate. **Allopatric speciation** occurs between two incipient species that become geographically isolated populations. This would include if, for some geographic reason, two or more groups within a species cannot mate with each other due to a barrier like a desert or river. Some may still mate, but the gene flow is greatly reduced. Peripatric speciation is a more specific type of allopatric speciation. **Peripatric speciation** occurs when an extremely small group is geographically isolated at the edge of the rest of the population. This small population size brings about genetic drift relatively quickly, with unique characteristics of the smaller group getting passed on to future generations of that group and further diffientiating them from their original population. **Parapatric speciation** occurs within a population that is distributed over a large geographic area, thus creating "barrier" of space to distance. Individuals in the population simply choose to mate with close neighbors in their specific region, leading to a reduced gene flow. Natural selection in the range of those individuals brings about further differentiation among members of the species spread out across the population. **Sympatric speciation** occurs when a new species develops in a population, even though there is no geographic isolation or physical barrier separating or preventing this species from mating. Sympatric speciation is uncommon but may occur when a species inhabits a new niche.

Models of Evolutionary Rates

GRADUALISM

Gradualism is a model of evolutionary rates that states that evolutionary changes occurred slowly or gradually by a divergence of lineages due largely to natural selection. These accumulated changes occurred over millions of years at a slow and consistent rate. Many transitional forms occurred between ancestors and modern descendants. Although not all of these transitional forms were preserved in the fossil record, the fossil record clearly supports gradualism. Many transition fossils show adaptations as organisms evolve. The geologic time scale describes this gradual change from simple to complex organisms over millions of years.

PUNCTUATED EQUILIBRIUM

Punctuated equilibrium is a model of evolutionary rates that states that in some instances, evolutionary changes occurred in relatively short bursts that "punctuate" long periods of equilibrium of little or no change. These "short" periods would still consist of hundreds of thousands of years, but include one or more substantial changes. Most scientists believe that punctuated equilibrium occurred along with gradualism. The fossil record supports punctuated equilibrium for many organisms. Punctuated equilibrium provides an explanation for the supposed numerous "missing links" in the fossil record. If punctuated equilibrium is validated, then there actually are no missing links.

Scientific Explanations for the Origin of Life on Earth

Explanations for the Origin of Life on Earth

Panspermia

The word *panspermia* is a Greek work that means "seeds everywhere." **Panspermia** is one possible explanation for the origin of life on Earth that states that "seeds" of life exist throughout the universe and can be transferred from one location to another. Three types of panspermia based on the seed-dispersal method have been proposed. **Lithopanspermia** is described as rocks or dust transferring microorganisms between solar systems. **Ballistic panspermia** is described as rocks or dust transferring microorganisms between planets within the same solar system. **Directed panspermia** is described as intelligent extraterrestrials purposely spreading the seeds to other planets and solar systems. The panspermia hypothesis only proposes the origin of life on Earth. It does not offer an explanation for the origin of life in the universe or explain the origin of the seeds themselves.

Abiotic Synthesis of Organic Compounds

Scientists have performed sophisticated experiments to determine how the first organic compounds appeared on Earth. First, scientists performed controlled experiments that closely resembled the conditions similar to an early Earth. In the classic **Miller–Urey experiment** (1953), the Earth's early atmosphere was simulated with water, methane, ammonia, and hydrogen that were stimulated by an electric discharge. The Miller–Urey experiment produced complex organic compounds including several amino acids, sugars, and hydrocarbons. Later experiments by other scientists produced nucleic acids. Recently, Jeffrey Bada, a former student of Miller, was able to produce amino acids in a simulation using the Earth's current atmospheric conditions with the addition of iron and carbonate to the simulation. This is significant because in previous studies using Earth's current atmosphere, the amino acids were destroyed by the nitrites produced by the nitrogen.

Atmospheric Composition

The early atmosphere of Earth had little or possibly no oxygen. Early rocks had high levels of iron at their surfaces. Without oxygen, the iron just entered into the early oceans as ions. In the same time frame, early photosynthetic algae were beginning to grow abundantly in the early ocean. During photosynthesis, the algae would produce oxygen gas, which oxidized the iron at the rocks' surfaces, forming an iron oxide. This process basically kept the algae in an oxygen-free environment. As the algae population grew much larger, it eventually produced such a large amount of oxygen that it could not be removed by the iron in the rocks. Because the algae at this time were intolerant to oxygen, the algae became extinct. Over time, a new iron-rich layer of sediments formed, and algae populations reformed, and the cycle began again. This cycle repeated itself for millions of years. Iron-rich layers of sediment alternated with iron-poor layers. Gradually, algae and other life forms evolved that were tolerant to oxygen, stabilizing the oxygen concentration in the atmosphere at levels similar to those of today.

Development of Self-Replication

Several hypotheses for the origin of life involve the self-replication of molecules. In order for life to have originated on Earth, proteins and RNA must have been replicated. Hypotheses that combine the replication of proteins and RNA seem promising. One such hypothesis is called **RNA world**. RNA world explains how the pathway of DNA to RNA to protein may have originated by proposing the reverse process. RNA world proposes that self-replicating RNA was the precursor to DNA. Scientists have shown that RNA can actually function both as a gene and as an enzyme and could therefore have carried genetic information in earlier life stages. Also, RNA can be transcribed into DNA using reverse transcription. In RNA world, RNA molecules self-replicated and evolved through recombination and mutations. RNA molecules developed the ability to act as enzymes.

Eventually, RNA began to synthesize proteins. Finally, DNA molecules were copied from the RNA in a process of reverse transcription.

Extinction of Species

Causes of Extinction of Species

Lack of Genetic Diversity

Genetic diversity provides a mechanism for populations to adapt to changing environments or even human impacts. With a diverse genome, individuals possessing genes making them better suited for the environment are more likely to exist. Without genetic diversity, populations cannot develop adaptations. Populations cannot resist diseases or adapt to changes in the habitat. As the populations of endangered species decrease, genetic diversity decreases even further. Normally, specific genes that resist disease or help the organism to adapt to changes in the habitat and therefore increase survivability are passed on to future generations. However, if those genes have drifted out of the population, the population cannot evolve with their changing environment and may become extinct. A small gene pool does not provide much variety for selection. For example, tigers in India are now in danger of extinction. Studies show that more than 90% of the genome has been lost largely due to a period when tigers were heavily killed by British officials and Indian royalty. With fewer than 2,000 tigers in the world and these in small populations, the genetic diversity can continue to decrease, possibly leading to extinction if much effort is not made to preserve the remaining genetic diversity.

Environmental Pressures

A changing environment may lead to the extinction of a species. If an animal has a small tolerance range to food sources and habitat needs or if a population is small, it is less likely to adapt to changes in the environment. For example, the giant panda feeds almost exclusively on bamboo. Bamboo is being threatened by global warming. Due to the dwindling of their food source, giant pandas are less able to adapt to a changing environment. **Climate change** and global warming can affect an ecosystem and some species may not be able to adapt to even seemingly minor temperature changes especially if their populations are small. If possible, animals needing cooler climates may need to move to cooler habitats. Melting ice caps and glaciers and rising sea levels can seriously disrupt many ecosystems and affect numerous species. For example, the polar bear may become extinct due to global warming as the polar bears' habitat is destroyed. Sea turtles may become extinct as the rising sea levels destroy the beaches needed for laying eggs. Even if the beaches are not destroyed, increasing temperatures affect the incubation process and the number of offspring being produced.

Human Impacts

Humans are responsible for impacting the environment in ways that endanger or harm species, which may even lead to those species' extinction. Humans destroy habitats directly through deforestation and clearing land for agriculture, logging, mining, and urbanization. Humans also threaten or endanger species through overfishing and overhunting. Pollution can destroy a habitat, and if a species is unable to relocate, this can eventually cause extinction if the effects cause drastic impacts. The intentional or unintentional introduction of an invasive species allows a new predator or competitor into the ecosystem, and it can threaten native species in that specific ecosystem if they cannot outcompete the invasive species. An example of human impacts leading to the extinction of a species is the case of the passenger pigeon. Millions of passenger pigeons were killed for meat from around 1850 to 1880. Because passenger pigeons only laid one egg at a time, huge flocks were destroyed. The last passenger pigeon died in 1914.

Interspecific Competition

Interspecific competition is competition between individuals of different species for the same limited resources such as food, water, sunlight, and living space. This is especially threatening if the two species share a limiting resource and that resource is not in abundant supply. Interspecific competition can limit the population size of a species. With reduced population size, there is less genetic variation. The species may not be able to adapt to environmental changes. For example, firs and spruces compete for resources in coniferous forests. Cheetahs and lions compete for prey in savannas.

Chapter Quiz

Ready to see how well you retained what you just read? Scan the QR code to go directly to the chapter quiz interface for this study guide. If you're using a computer, simply visit the online resources page at **mometrix.com/resources719/abctebio** and click the Chapter Quizzes link.

Comparative Physiology

Characteristics of Living Versus Nonliving Things

Importance and Structural Organization of Cells

Cells are the basic structural units of all organisms. All organisms have a highly organized cellular structure. In single-celled organisms, that single cell contains all of the components necessary for life. In multicellular organisms, cells can become specialized. Different types of cells can have different functions. Life begins as a single cell whether by asexual or sexual reproduction. All cells contain DNA and RNA and can synthesize proteins. Each cell consists of nucleic acids, cytoplasm, and a cell membrane. Specialized organelles such as mitochondria and chloroplasts have specific functions within the cell.

Energy

All cells must obtain and use energy in order to grow, make repairs, and reproduce. Cells obtain the energy they need by the breaking of bonds of molecules. Cellular respiration is the process of converting nutrient molecules into energy. Cells also use energy to take in food, process that food, and eliminate waste. Organisms differ in how they obtain food. Plants and other autotrophs can produce their own energy through processes such as photosynthesis or chemosynthesis. Animals and other heterotrophs obtain their energy from consuming autotrophs or other heterotrophs.

Growth and Reproduction

All organisms must be capable of growth and reproduction. Growth is necessary for multicellular organisms to develop and mature. While all cells eventually die, growth allows cells to be replaced or repaired. Without growth from cell division, tissues could not be maintained or repaired. Through mitosis, most cells routinely replace themselves with identical daughter cells. Reproduction is necessary to increase the number of individuals in a population, since all organisms eventually die. Reproduction is either sexual by the joining of gametes or asexual by binary fission or some other related method.

Adaptation to Environment

Organisms must be able to adapt to their environment in order to thrive or survive. Individuals must be able to recognize stimuli in their surroundings and adapt quickly. For example, an individual euglena can sense light and respond by moving toward the light. Individual organisms must also be able to adapt to changes in the environment on a larger scale. For example, plants must be able to respond to the change in the length of the day to flower at the correct time. Populations must also be able to adapt to a changing environment. Evolution by **natural selection** is the process by which populations change over many generations to become better adapted to their environment, thus surviving longer and reproducing more successfully. For example, wooly mammoths were unable to adapt to a warming climate and are now extinct, but many species of deer did adapt and are abundant today.

Historical and Current Biological Classifications of Organisms

Historical and Current Kingdom Systems

In 1735 Carolus Linnaeus devised a two-kingdom classification system. He placed all living things into either the *Animalia* kingdom or the *Plantae* kingdom. Fungi and algae were classified as plants. Also, Linnaeus developed the binomial nomenclature system that is still used today. In 1866, Ernst Haeckel introduced a three-kingdom classification system, adding the *Protista* kingdom to Linnaeus's animal and plant kingdoms. Bacteria were classified as protists and cyanobacteria were still classified as plants. In 1938, Herbert Copeland introduced a four-kingdom classification system in which bacteria and cyanobacteria were moved to the *Monera* kingdom. In 1969, Robert Whittaker introduced a five-kingdom system that moved fungi from the plant kingdom to the *Fungi* kingdom. Some algae were still classified as plants. In 1977, Carl Woese introduced a six-kingdom system in which in the *Monera* kingdom was replaced with the *Eubacteria* kingdom and the *Archaebacteria* kingdom.

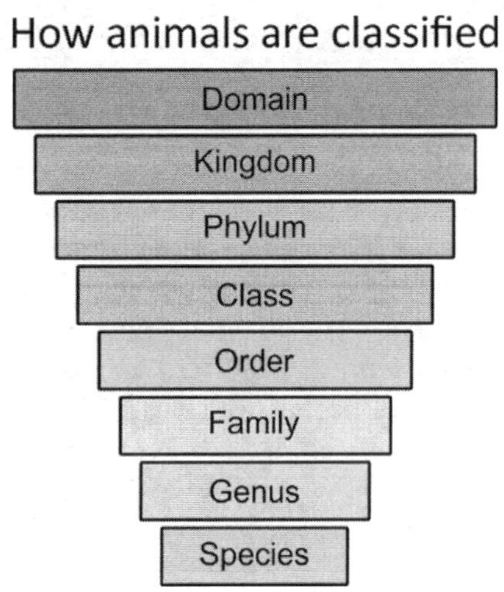

Domain Classification System

In 1990, Carl Woese introduced his domain classification system. **Domains** are broader groupings above the kingdom level. This system consists of three domains—*Archaea*, *Bacteria*, and *Eukarya*. All eukaryotes such as plants, animals, fungi, and protists are classified in the *Eukarya* domain. The *Bacteria* and *Archaea* domains consist of prokaryotes. Organisms previously classified in the *Monera* kingdom are now classified into either the *Bacteria* or *Archaea* domain based on their ribosomal RNA structure. Members of the *Archaea* domain often live in extremely harsh environments.

Review Video: Biological Classification Systems
Visit mometrix.com/academy and enter code: 736052

Viruses, Bacteria, Protists, Fungi, Plants, and Animals

VIRUSES

Viruses are nonliving, infectious particles that act as parasites in living organisms. Viruses are acellular, which means that they lack cell structure. Viruses cannot reproduce outside of living cells. The structure of a virus is a nucleic acid genome, which may be either DNA or RNA, surrounded by a protective protein coat or **capsid**. In some viruses, the capsid may be surrounded by a lipid membrane or envelope. Viruses can contain up to 500 genes and have various shapes. They usually are too small to be seen without the aid of an electron microscope. Viruses can infect plants, animals, fungi, protists, and bacteria. Viruses can attack only specific types of cells that have specific receptors on their surfaces. Viruses do not divide or reproduce like living cells. Instead, they use the host cell they infect by "reprogramming" it, using the nucleic acid genome, to make more copies of the virus. The host cell usually bursts to release these copies.

Review Video: Viruses and Antiviral Drugs
Visit mometrix.com/academy and enter code: 984455

BACTERIA

Bacteria are small, prokaryotic, single-celled organisms. Bacteria have a circular loop of DNA (plasmid) that is not contained within a nuclear membrane. Bacterial ribosomes are not bound to the endoplasmic reticulum, as in eukaryotes. A cell wall containing peptidoglycan surrounds the bacterial plasma membrane. Some bacteria such as pathogens are further encased in a gel-like, sticky layer called the **capsule**, which enhances their ability to cause disease. Bacteria can be autotrophs or heterotrophs. Some bacterial heterotrophs are saprophytes that function as decomposers in ecosystems. Many types of bacteria share commensal or mutualistic relationships with other organisms. Most bacteria reproduce asexually by binary fission. Two identical daughter cells are produced from one parent cell. Some bacteria can transfer genetic material to other bacteria through a process called conjugation, while some bacteria can incorporate DNA from the environment in a process called transformation.

PROTISTS

Protists are small, eukaryotic, single-celled organisms. Although protists are small, they are much larger than prokaryotic bacteria. Protists have three general forms, which include plantlike protists, animal-like protists, and fungus-like protists. **Plantlike protists** are algae that contain chlorophyll and perform photosynthesis. Animal-like protists are **protozoa** with no cell walls that typically lack chlorophyll and are grouped by their method of locomotion, which may use flagella, cilia, or a different structure. **Fungus-like protists**, which do not have chitin in their cell walls, are generally grouped as either slime molds or water molds. Protists may be autotrophic or heterotrophic. Autotrophic protists include many species of algae, while heterotrophic protists include parasitic, commensal, and mutualistic protozoa. Slime molds are heterotrophic fungus-like protists, which consume microorganisms. Some protists reproduce sexually, but most reproduce asexually by binary fission. Some reproduce asexually by spores while others reproduce by alternation of generations and require two hosts in their life cycle.

FUNGI

Fungi are nonmotile organisms with eukaryotic cells and contain chitin in their cell walls. Most fungi are multicellular, but a few including yeast are unicellular. Fungi have multicellular filaments called **hyphae** that are grouped together into the mycelium. Fungi do not perform photosynthesis and are considered heterotrophs. Fungi can be parasitic, mutualistic or free living. Free-living fungi include mushrooms and toadstools. Parasitic fungi include fungi responsible for ringworm and athlete's foot. Mycorrhizae are mutualistic fungi that live in or near plant roots increasing the roots' surface area of absorption. Almost all fungi reproduce asexually by spores, but most fungi also have a sexual phase in the production of spores. Some fungi reproduce by budding or fragmentation.

Review Video: Feeding Among Heterotrophs
Visit mometrix.com/academy and enter code: 836017

PLANTS

Plants are multicellular organisms with eukaryotic cells containing cellulose in their cell walls. Plant cells have chlorophyll and perform photosynthesis. Plants can be vascular or nonvascular. **Vascular plants** have true leaves, stems, and roots that contain xylem and phloem. **Nonvascular plants** lack true leaves, stems and roots and do not have any true vascular tissue but instead rely on diffusion and osmosis to transport most of materials or resources needed to survive. Almost all plants are autotrophic, relying on photosynthesis for food. A small number do not have chlorophyll and are parasitic, but these are extremely rare. Plants can reproduce sexually or asexually. Many plants reproduce by seeds produced in the fruits of the plants, while some plants reproduce by seeds on cones. One type of plant, ferns, reproduce by a different system that utilizes spores. Some plants can even reproduce asexually by vegetative reproduction.

Review Video: Kingdom Plantae
Visit mometrix.com/academy and enter code: 710084

STRUCTURE, ORGANIZATION, MODES OF NUTRITION, AND REPRODUCTION OF ANIMALS

Animals are multicellular organism with eukaryotic cells that do not have cell walls surrounding their plasma membranes. Animals have several possible structural body forms. Animals can be relatively simple in structure such as sponges, which do not have a nervous system. Other animals are more complex with cells organized into tissues, and tissues organized into organs, and organs even further organized into systems. Invertebrates such as arthropods, nematodes, and annelids have complex body systems. Vertebrates including fish, amphibians, reptiles, birds, and mammals are the most complex with detailed systems such as those with gills, air sacs, or lungs designed to exchange respiratory gases. All animals are heterotrophs and obtain their nutrition by consuming autotrophs or other heterotrophs. Most animals are motile, but some animals move their environment to bring food to them. All animals reproduce sexually at some point in their life cycle. Typically, this involves the union of a sperm and egg to produce a zygote.

Characteristics of the Major Animal Phyla

CHARACTERISTICS OF THE MAJOR ANIMAL PHYLA

BODY PLANES

Animals can exhibit bilateral symmetry, radial symmetry, or asymmetry. With **bilateral symmetry**, the organism can be cut in half along only one plane to produce two identical halves. Most animals, including all vertebrates such as mammals, birds, reptiles, amphibians, and fish, exhibit bilateral symmetry. Many invertebrates including arthropods and crustaceans also exhibit bilateral symmetry. With **radial symmetry**, the organism can be cut in half along several planes to produce two identical halves. Starfish, sea urchins, and jellyfish exhibit radial symmetry. With **asymmetry**, the organism exhibits no symmetry. Very few organisms in the animal phyla exhibit asymmetry, but a few species of sponges are asymmetrical.

BODY CAVITIES

Animals can be grouped based on their types of body cavities. A **coelom** is a fluid-filled body cavity between the alimentary canal and the body wall. The three body plans based on the formation of the coelom are coelomates, pseudocoelomates, and acoelomates. **Coelomates** have a true coelom located within the mesoderm. Most animals including arthropods, mollusks, annelids, echinoderms, and chordates are coelomates. **Pseudocoelomates** have a body cavity called a pseudocoelom. **Pseudocoeloms** are not considered true coeloms. Pseudocoeloms are located between mesoderm and endoderm instead of actually in the mesoderm as in a true coelom. Pseudocoelomates include roundworms and rotifers. **Acoelomates** do not have body cavities. Simple or primitive animals such as sponges, jellyfish, sea anemones, hydras, flatworms, and ribbon worms are acoelomates.

MODES OF REPRODUCTION

Animals can reproduce sexually or asexually. Most animals reproduce sexually. In **sexual reproduction**, males and females have different reproductive organs that produce **gametes**. Males have testes that produce sperm, and females have ovaries that produce eggs. During fertilization, a sperm cell unites with an egg cell, forming a **zygote**. Fertilization can occur internally such as in most mammals and birds or externally such as aquatic animals such as fish and frogs. The zygote undergoes cell division, which develops into an embryo and eventually develops into an adult organism. Some embryos develop in eggs such as in fish, amphibians, reptiles, and birds. Some mammals are **oviparous** meaning that they lay eggs, but most are **viviparous** meaning they have a uterus in which the embryo develops. One particular type of mammal called **marsupials** give birth to an immature fetus that finishes development in a pouch. However, there are some animals reproduce **asexually**. For example, hydras reproduce by budding, and starfish and planarians can reproduce by fragmentation and regeneration. Some fish, frogs, and insects can even reproduce by parthenogenesis, which is a type of self-reproduction without fertilization.

MODES OF TEMPERATURE REGULATION

Animals can be classified as either homeotherms or poikilotherms. **Homeotherms**, also called warm-blooded animals or **endotherms**, maintain a constant body temperature regardless of the temperature of the environment. Homeotherms such as mammals and birds have a high metabolic rate because a lot of energy is needed to maintain the constant temperature. **Poikilotherms**, also called cold-blooded animals or **ectotherms**, do not maintain a constant body temperature. Their body temperature fluctuates with the temperature of the environment. Poikilotherms such as arthropods, fish, amphibians, and reptiles have metabolic rates that fluctuate with their body temperature.

Hierarchy of Multicellular Organisms

ORGANIZATIONAL HIERARCHY WITHIN MULTICELLULAR ORGANISMS

Cells are the smallest living units of organisms. Tissues are groups of cells that work together to perform a specific function. Organs are groups of tissues that work together to perform a specific function. Organ systems are groups of organs that work together to perform a specific function. An organism is an individual that contains several body systems.

CELLS

Cells are the basic structural units of all living things. Cells are composed of various molecules including proteins, carbohydrates, lipids, and nucleic acids. All animal cells are eukaryotic and have a nucleus, cytoplasm, and a cell membrane. Organelles include mitochondria, ribosomes, endoplasmic reticulum, Golgi apparatuses, and vacuoles. Specialized cells are numerous, including but not limited to, muscle cells, nerve cells, epithelial cells, bone cells, blood cells, and cartilage cells. Cells can be grouped together in tissues to perform specific functions.

TISSUES

Tissues are groups of cells that work together to perform a specific function. Tissues can be grouped into four broad categories: muscle tissue, connective tissue, nerve tissue, and epithelial tissue. Muscle tissue is involved in body movement. **Muscle tissues** can be composed of skeletal muscle cells, cardiac muscle cells, or smooth muscle cells. Skeletal muscles include the muscles commonly called biceps, triceps, hamstrings, and quadriceps. Cardiac muscle tissue is found only in the heart. Smooth muscle tissue provides tension in the blood vessels, controls pupil dilation, and aids in peristalsis. **Connective tissues** include bone tissue, cartilage, tendons, ligaments, fat, blood, and lymph. **Nerve tissue** is located in the brain, spinal cord, and nerves.

Epithelial tissue makes up the layers of the skin and various membranes. Tissues are grouped together as organs to perform specific functions.

ORGANS AND ORGAN SYSTEMS

Organs are groups of tissues that work together to perform specific functions. **Organ systems** are groups of organs that work together to perform specific functions. Complex animals have several organs that are grouped together in multiple systems. In mammals, there are 11 major organ systems: integumentary system, respiratory system, cardiovascular system, endocrine system, nervous system, immune system, digestive system, excretory system, muscular system, skeletal system, and reproductive system.

Homeostasis

MAINTENANCE OF HOMEOSTASIS IN ORGANISMS

ROLE OF FEEDBACK MECHANISMS

Homeostasis is the regulation of internal chemistry to maintain a constant internal environment. This state is controlled through various feedback mechanisms that consist of receptors, an integrator, and effectors. **Receptors** such as mechanoreceptors or thermoreceptors in the skin detect the stimuli. Then, an **integrator**, such as the brain or spinal cord, receives the information concerning the stimuli and sends out signals to other parts of the body. Finally, **effectors**, such as muscles or glands, respond to the stimulus. Basically, the receptors receive the stimuli and notify an integrator, which signals the effectors to respond.

Feedback mechanisms can be negative or positive. **Negative-feedback** mechanisms are mechanisms that provide a decrease in response with an increase in stimulus that inhibits the stimulus, which in turn decreases the response. **Positive-feedback** mechanisms are mechanisms that provide an increase in response with an increase in stimulus, which actually increases the stimulus, which in turn increases the response.

ROLE OF HYPOTHALAMUS

The hypothalamus plays a major role in the homoeostasis of vertebrates. The **hypothalamus** is the central portion of the brain just above the brainstem and is linked to the endocrine system through the pituitary gland. The hypothalamus releases special hormones that influence the secretion of pituitary hormones. The hypothalamus regulates the fundamental physiological state by controlling body temperature, hunger, thirst, sleep, behaviors related to attachment, sexual development, fight-or-flight stress response, and circadian rhythms.

ROLE OF ENDOCRINE SYSTEM AND HORMONES

All vertebrates have an **endocrine system** that consists of numerous ductless glands that produce hormones to help coordinate many functions of the body. **Hormones** are signaling molecules that are received by receptors. Many hormones are secreted in response to signals from the pituitary gland and hypothalamus gland. Other hormones are secreted in response to signals from inside the body. Hormones can consist of amino acids, proteins, or lipid molecules such as steroid hormones. Hormones can affect target cells, which have the correct receptor that is able to bind to that particular hormone. Most cells have receptors for more than one type of hormone. Hormones are distributed to the target cells in the blood by the cardiovascular system. Hormones incorporate feedback mechanisms to help the body maintain homeostasis.

ROLE OF ANTIDIURETIC HORMONE

Antidiuretic hormone (ADH) helps maintain homeostasis in vertebrates. ADH is produced by the posterior pituitary gland, and it regulates the reabsorption of water in the kidneys and concentrates the urine. The stimulus in this feedback mechanism is a drop in blood volume due to water loss. This signal is picked up by the hypothalamus, which signals the pituitary gland to secrete ADH. ADH is carried by the cardiovascular system to the nephrons in the kidneys signaling them to reabsorb more water and send less out as waste. As more water is reabsorbed, the blood volume increases, which is monitored by the hypothalamus. As the blood volume reaches the set point, the hypothalamus signals for a decrease in the secretion of ADH, and the cycle continues.

Role of Insulin and Glucagon

Insulin and glucagon are hormones that help maintain the glucose concentration in the blood. Insulin and glucagon are secreted by the clumps of endocrine cells called the **pancreatic islets** that are located in the pancreas. Insulin and glucagon work together to maintain the blood glucose level. **Insulin** stimulates cells to remove glucose from the blood. **Glucagon** stimulates the liver to convert glycogen to glucose. After eating, glucose levels increase in the blood. This stimulus signals the pancreas to stop the secretion of glucagon and to start secreting insulin. Cells respond to the insulin and remove glucose from the blood, lowering the level of glucose in the blood. Later, after eating, the level of glucose in the blood decreases further. This stimulus signals the pancreas to secrete glucagon and decrease the secretion of insulin. In response to the stimulus, the liver converts glycogen to glucose, and the level of glucose in the blood rises. When the individual eats, the cycle begins again.

Thermoregulation

Animals exhibit many adaptations that help them achieve homeostasis, or a stable internal environment. Some of these adaptions are behavioral. Most organisms exhibit some type of behavioral thermoregulation. **Thermoregulation** is the ability to keep the body temperature within certain boundaries. The type of behavioral thermoregulation depends on whether the animal is an ectotherm or an endotherm. **Ectotherms** are "cold-blooded," and their body temperature changes with their external environment. **Endotherms** are "warm-blooded" and maintain a stable body temperature by internal means.

To regulate their temperature, ectotherms often move to an appropriate location. For example, fish move to warmer waters while animals will climb to higher grounds. **Diurnal ectotherms** such as reptiles often bask in the sun to increase their body temperatures. Butterflies are special ectotherms classified as **heliotherms** since they get nearly all of their heat from basking in the sun.

While they have internal systems that regulate temperature, many endotherms that live in hot environments have adapted to the nocturnal lifestyle. Desert animals are often nocturnal to escape high daytime temperatures. Other nocturnal animals sleep during the day in underground burrows or dens.

Reproduction, Development, and Growth in Animals

Gamete Formation

Gametogenesis is the formation of gametes, or reproductive cells. Gametes are produced by meiosis. **Meiosis** is a special type of cell division that consists of two consecutive mitotic divisions referred to as meiosis I and meiosis II. **Meiosis I** is a reduction division in which a diploid cell is reduced to two haploid daughter cells that contain only one of each pair of homologous chromosomes. During **meiosis II**, those haploid cells are further divided to form four haploid cells. **Spermatogenesis** in males produces four viable sperm cells from each complete cycle of meiosis. **Oogenesis** produces four daughter cells, but only one is a viable egg and the other three are polar bodies.

Fertilization

Fertilization is the union of a sperm cell and an egg cell to produce a zygote. Many sperm may bind to an egg, but only one joins with the egg and injects its nuclei into the egg. Fertilization can be external or internal. **External fertilization** takes place outside of the female's body. For example, many fish, amphibians, crustaceans, mollusks, and corals reproduce externally by **spawning** or releasing gametes into the water simultaneously or right after each other. Reptiles and birds reproduce by **internal fertilization**. All mammals except monotremes (e.g. platypus) reproduce by internal fertilization.

EMBRYONIC DEVELOPMENT

Embryonic development in animals is typically divided into four stages: cleavage, patterning, differentiation, and growth. **Cleavage** occurs immediately after fertilization when the large single-celled zygote immediately begins to divide into smaller and smaller cells without an increase in mass. A hollow ball of cells forms a blastula. Next, during patterning, gastrulation occurs. During gastrulation, the cells are organized into three primary germ layers: ectoderm, mesoderm, and endoderm. Then, the cells in these layers differentiate into special tissues and organs. For example, the nervous system develops from the ectoderm. The muscular system develops from the mesoderm. Much of the digestive system develops from the endoderm. The final stage of embryonic development is growth and further tissue specialization. The embryo continues to grow until ready for hatching or birth.

POSTNATAL GROWTH

Postnatal growth occurs from hatching or birth until death. The length of the postnatal growth depends on the species. Elephants can live 70 years, but mice only about 4 years. Right after animals are hatched or born, they go through a period of rapid growth and development. In vertebrates, bones lengthen, muscles grow in bulk, and fat is deposited. At maturity, bones stop growing in length, but bones can grow in width and repair themselves throughout the animal's lifetime, and muscle deposition slows down. Fat cells continue to increase and decrease in size throughout the animal's life. Growth is controlled by genetics but is also influenced by nutrition and disease. Most animals are sexually mature in less than two years and can produce offspring.

Chapter Quiz

Ready to see how well you retained what you just read? Scan the QR code to go directly to the chapter quiz interface for this study guide. If you're using a computer, simply visit the online resources page at **mometrix.com/resources719/abctebio** and click the Chapter Quizzes link.

Human Physiology

Human Anatomy and Physiology

Body Systems

Functions of the human body can be divided into the following body systems.

- **Cardiovascular**: Pumps blood throughout the body via the heart and blood vessels
- **Respiratory**: Regulates gas exchange (oxygen intake and carbon dioxide expulsion)
- **Digestive**: Transforms food into energy and eliminates solid waste
- **Urinary**: Removes waste and toxins from the blood and expels them from the body through urine
- **Endocrine**: Releases hormones into the bloodstream to control metabolism, growth, and reproduction
- **Immune and Lymphatic Systems**: Defends against all foreign substances
- **Integumentary**: Skin prevents moisture loss, regulates temperature, protects from sunburn, and senses pain, pressure, touch, hot and cold
- **Musculoskeletal**: Skeletal muscles move the body, smooth muscles control the physical functioning of internal organs, and cardiac muscle pumps blood. The skeleton supports and shapes, protects internal organs, stores minerals, and produces blood cells
- **Nervous**: Controls movement, memory, and senses and communicates with the outside world
- **Reproductive**: Allows continuation of the human species through reproduction and childbearing and differentiates the sexes

Note that different models may have overlapping approaches to the body systems. For instance, the excretory system is not listed above, but the functions of the excretory systems overlap and are covered by the urinary and digestive systems.

The Three Primary Body Planes

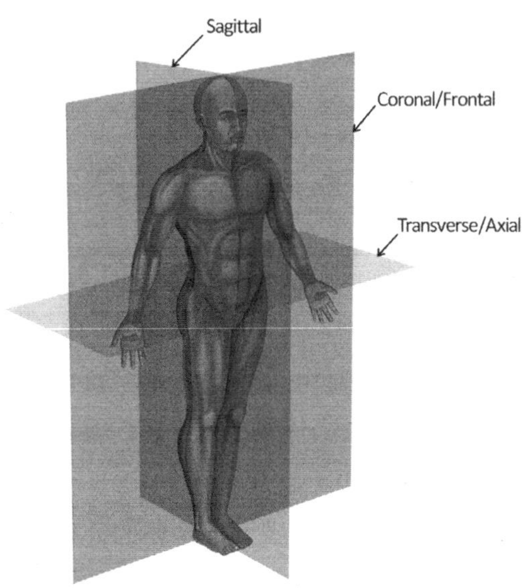

- The **transverse (or horizontal) plane** divides the patient's body into imaginary upper (*superior*) and lower (*inferior or caudal*) halves.

- The **sagittal plane** divides the body, or any body part, vertically into right and left sections. The sagittal plane runs parallel to the midline of the body.
- The **coronal (or frontal) plane** divides the body, or any body structure, vertically into front and back (*anterior* and *posterior*) sections. The coronal plane runs vertically through the body at right angles to the midline.

Terms of Direction

- **Medial** means *nearer to the midline* of the body. In anatomical position, the little finger is medial to the thumb.
- **Lateral** is the opposite of medial. It refers to structures *further away from the body's midline*, at the sides. In anatomical position, the thumb is lateral to the little finger.
- **Proximal** refers to structures *closer to the center* of the body. The hip is proximal to the knee.
- **Distal** refers to structures *further away from the center* of the body. The knee is distal to the hip.
- **Anterior** refers to structures in *front*.
- **Posterior** refers to structures *behind*.
- **Cephalad** and **cephalic** are adverbs meaning towards the *head*. **Cranial** is the adjective, meaning of the *skull*.
- **Caudad** is an adverb meaning towards the *tail* or posterior. **Caudal** is the adjective, meaning of the *hindquarters*.
- **Superior** means *above*, or closer to the head.
- **Inferior** means *below*, or closer to the feet.

CARDIOVASCULAR SYSTEM

The main functions of the **cardiovascular system** are gas exchange, the delivery of nutrients and hormones, and waste removal. The cardiovascular system consists primarily of the heart, blood, and blood vessels. The **heart** is a pump that pushes blood through the arteries. **Arteries** are blood vessels that carry blood away from the heart, and **veins** are blood vessels that carry blood back to the heart. The exchange of materials between blood and cells occur in the **capillaries**, which are the smallest of the blood vessels.

Review Video: Functions of the Circulatory System
Visit mometrix.com/academy and enter code: 376581

Review Video: Mnemonics for Heart Anatomy and Physiology
Visit mometrix.com/academy and enter code: 849489

Review Video: Electrical Conduction System of the Heart
Visit mometrix.com/academy and enter code: 624557

Review Video: How the Heart Functions
Visit mometrix.com/academy and enter code: 569724

HEART CHAMBERS AND VALVES

There are four chambers of the heart that have valves separating them and regulating a one-way flow of blood between the chambers.

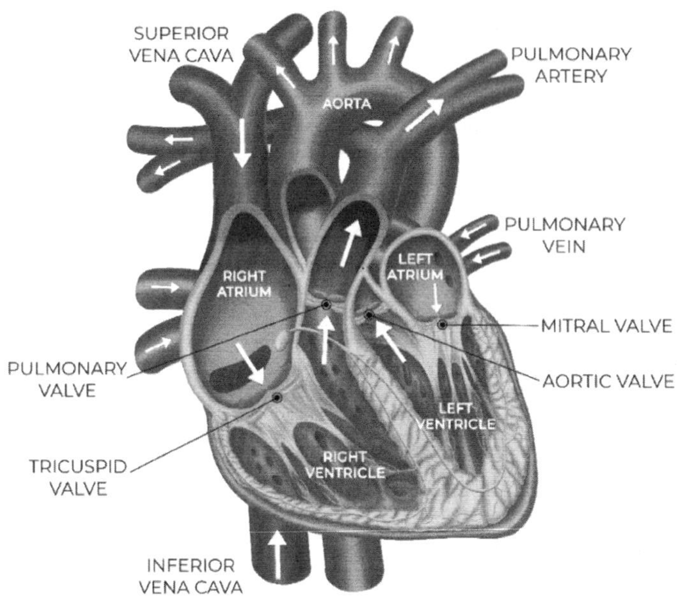

Respiratory System

The primary function of the **respiratory system** is to move air in and out of the body in order to facilitate the exchange of oxygen and carbon dioxide. The respiratory system consists of the nasal passages, pharynx, larynx, trachea, bronchial tubes, lungs, and diaphragm. **Bronchial tubes** branch into **bronchioles**, which end in clusters of alveoli. The **alveoli** are tiny sacs inside the lungs where gas exchange takes place. When the **diaphragm** contracts, the volume of the chest increases, which reduces the pressure in the **lungs**. Then, air is inhaled through the nose or mouth and passes through the pharynx, larynx, trachea, and bronchial tubes into the lungs. When the diaphragm relaxes, the volume in the chest cavity decreases, forcing the air out of the lungs. The respiratory system works jointly with the **cardiovascular system** by taking **oxygenated blood** (red blood cells) and distributing them through arteries and capillaries. **Deoxygenated blood** (carbon dioxide) is transported via the venous system back to the lungs to exhaled. The respiratory system also functions to enhance speech and smell.

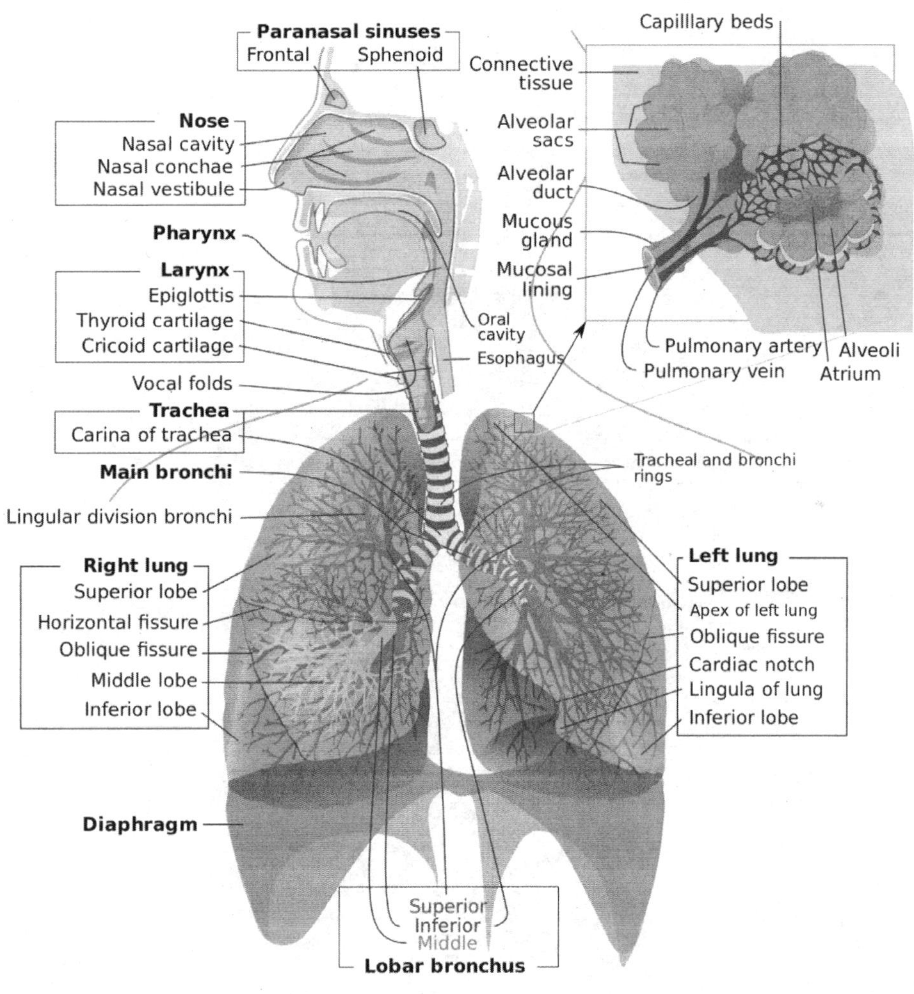

Review Video: Respiratory System
Visit mometrix.com/academy and enter code: 783075

Review Video: Pulmonary Circuit
Visit mometrix.com/academy and enter code: 955608

Digestive System

The main function of the **digestive system** is to process the food that is consumed by an organism. This includes mechanical and chemical processing. Depending on the organism, **mechanical processes**, or the physical process of breaking food into smaller pieces, can happen in various ways. Mammals have teeth to chew their food, while many animals such as birds, earthworms, crocodilians, and crustaceans have a gizzard or gizzard-like organ that grinds their food. **Chemical digestion** includes breaking food into simpler nutrients that the body can use for specific processes. While chewing, saliva (which contains special enzymes) is secreted to begin the breakdown of starches. Many animals such as mammals, birds, reptiles, amphibians, and fish have a stomach that stores and absorbs food. Gastric juice containing enzymes and hydrochloric acid is mixed with the food. The intestine or intestines absorb nutrients and reabsorb water from the undigested material. Additionally, many animals have a liver, gallbladder, and pancreas, which aid in digestion of proteins and fats. Undigested wasted are eliminated from the body through an anus or cloaca.

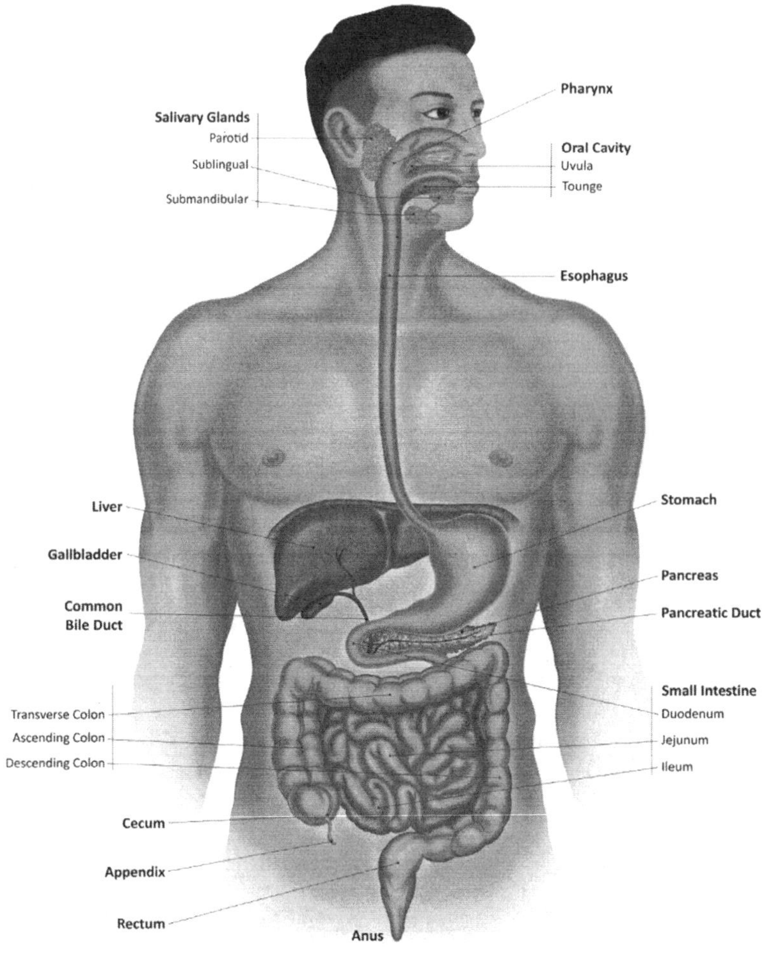

Review Video: Gastrointestinal System
Visit mometrix.com/academy and enter code: 378740

Urinary System

The **urinary system** consists of the bladder, kidneys, ureter, and urethra. Their main function is to eliminate waste products by expelling urine. This system also maintains homeostatic balance of water by excreting excess urine, maintaining electrolytes in the blood stream, and regulating blood Ph levels. This balance of water is crucial to body functioning as dehydration can lead to low blood pressure, which in turn can result in metabolic shock. **Metabolic shock** is characterized by low blood pressure that affects the kidneys, liver, and brain. **Dehydration** can also affect the muscular, system resulting in cramps from poor thermal regulation and altered fluid movement across tissue membranes.

Kidneys

The **kidneys** are involved in blood filtration, pH balance, and the reabsorption of nutrients to maintain proper blood volume and ion balance. The **nephron** is the working unit of the kidney. The parts of the nephron include the glomerulus, Bowman's capsule, and loop of Henle. Filtration takes place in the nephron's **glomerulus.** Water and dissolved materials such as glucose and amino acids pass on into the Bowman's capsule. Depending on concentration gradients, water and dissolved materials can pass back into the blood primarily through the proximal convoluted tubule. Reabsorption and water removal occurs in the **loop of Henle** and the conducting duct. Urine and other nitrogenous wastes pass from the kidneys to the bladders and are expelled.

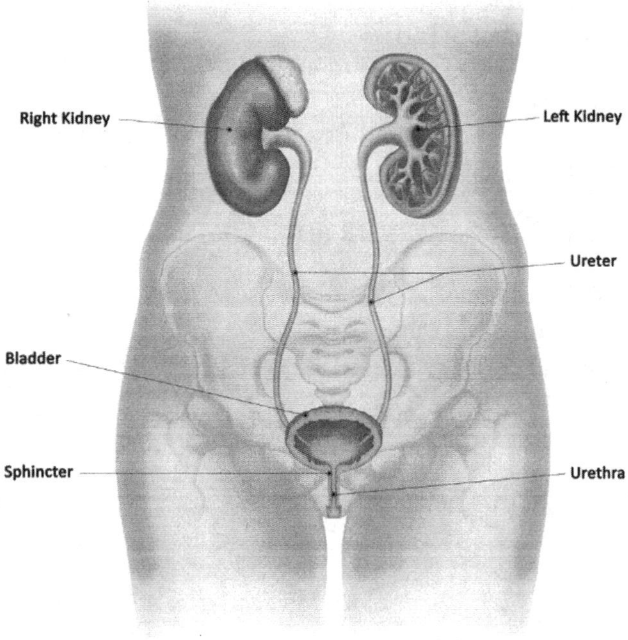

Review Video: Urinary System
Visit mometrix.com/academy and enter code: 601053

Endocrine System

The **endocrine system** consists of several ductless glands, which secrete hormones directly into the bloodstream. The **pituitary gland** controls the functions of the other glands in the system, regulates skeletal growth, and initiates the development of reproductive organs. The **pineal gland** regulates sleep cycles. The **thyroid gland** regulates metabolism and work with the **parathyroid glands** to help regulate the calcium level in the blood. The **adrenal glands** secrete the emergency hormone epinephrine, stimulate body repairs, and regulate sodium and potassium levels in the blood. The **islets of Langerhans**, located in the pancreas, secrete insulin and glucagon to regulate the level of blood sugar. In females, **ovaries** produce estrogen, which stimulates sexual development, and progesterone, which functions during pregnancy. In males, the **testes** secrete testosterone, which stimulates sexual development and sperm production.

Gland	Hormones	Disease
Adrenal Cortex	Aldosterone Cortisol Androgens	Addison's Disease Cushing's Disease
Adrenal Medulla	Epinephrine Norepinephrine	Anxiety Attacks Depression
Anterior Pituitary	Adrenocorticotropic hormone (ACTH) Follicle-stimulating hormone (FSH) Gonadotropic hormones Growth hormone (GH) Luteinizing hormone (LH) Prolactin Thyroid Stimulating Hormone (TSH)	Dwarfism Gigantism
Hypothalamus/ Posterior Pituitary	Inhibiting hormones (stop the release of other hormones) Antidiuretic hormone (ADH) Oxytocin Releasing hormones (trigger the release of other hormones)	Diabetes Insipidus
Kidneys	Calcitriol Erythropoietin	Hypertension
Ovaries	Estrogen Progesterone	Endometriosis Menometrorrhagia
Pancreas	Insulin Glucagon	Diabetes Mellitus
Parathyroid	Parathyroid hormone	Tetany Renal calculi
Pineal	Melatonin	Alzheimer's Disease
Testes	Testosterone	Gynecomastia Klinefelter Syndrome
Thymus	Thymic factor (TF) Thymosin Thymic humoral factor (THF) Thymopoietin	DiGeorge Syndrome

Gland	Hormones	Disease
Thyroid	Calcitonin Thyroxine (T4) Triiodothyronine (T3)	Cretinism Hypo/Hyperthyroidism Goiter Myxedema
Digestive tract	Gastrin Cholecystokinin Secretin Ghrelin Motilin	Gastritis Gastroesophageal reflux

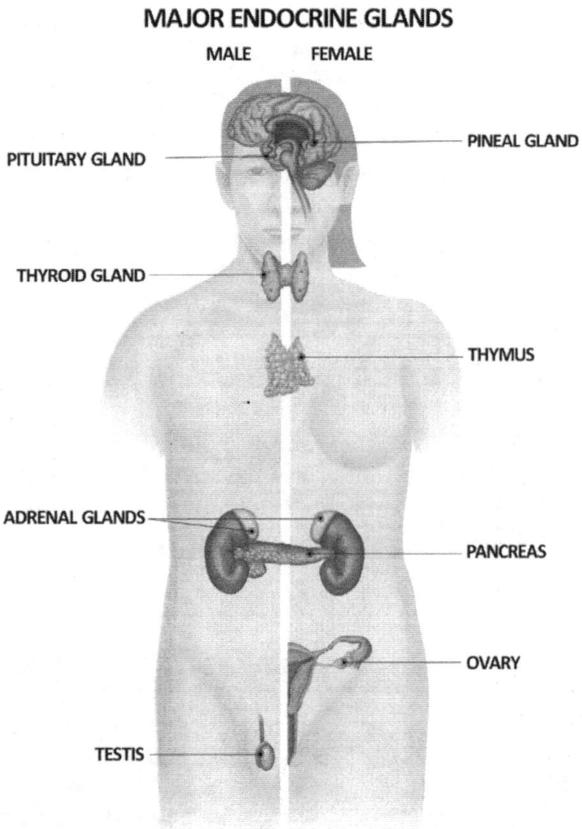

Review Video: Endocrine System
Visit mometrix.com/academy and enter code: 678939

Immune and Lymphatic Systems

Immune System

The **immune system** in animals defends the body against infection and disease. The immune system can be divided into two broad categories: innate immunity and adaptive immunity. **Innate immunity** includes the skin and mucous membranes, which provide a physical barrier to prevent pathogens from entering the body. Special chemicals including enzymes and proteins in mucus, tears, sweat, and stomach juices destroy pathogens. Numerous white blood cells such as neutrophils and macrophages protect the body from invading pathogens. **Adaptive immunity** involves the body responding to a specific antigen. Typically, B-lymphocytes or B cells produce antibodies against a specific antigen, and T-lymphocytes or T-cells take special roles as helpers, regulators, or killers. Some T-cells function as memory cells.

Review Video: Immune System
Visit mometrix.com/academy and enter code: 622899

Lymphatic System

The **lymphatic system** is connected to the cardiovascular system through a network of capillaries. The lymphatic system filters out organisms that cause disease, controls the production of disease-fighting antibodies, and produces white blood cells. The lymphatic system also prevents body tissues from swelling by draining fluids from them. Two of the most important areas in this system are the right lymphatic duct and the thoracic duct. The **right lymphatic duct** moves the immunity-bolstering lymph fluid through the top half of the body, while the **thoracic duct** moves lymph throughout the lower half. The spleen, thymus, and lymph nodes all generate and store the chemicals which form lymph and which are essential to protecting the body from disease.

The **lymphatic system** consists of the **thymus**, **lymph nodes**, **bone marrow**, and **spleen**. They primarily serve to distribute filtered fluids throughout the body and to remove excess fluid and debris. **White blood cells** are a key element of the lymphatic system which serve to prevent disease and repair the body after infection to prevent further illness.

Integumentary System

The integumentary system includes skin, hair, nails, sense receptors, sweat glands, and oil glands. The **skin** acts as a sensory organ, provides an exterior barrier against disease, regulates body temperature through perspiration, manufactures chemicals and hormones, and provides a place for nerves from the nervous system and parts of the circulation system to travel through. Skin has three layers: epidermis, dermis, and subcutaneous. The **epidermis** is the thin, outermost, waterproof layer. The **dermis** has the sweat glands, oil glands, and hair follicles. The **subcutaneous layer** has connective tissue. Also, this layer has **adipose** (i.e., fat) tissue, nerves, arteries, and veins.

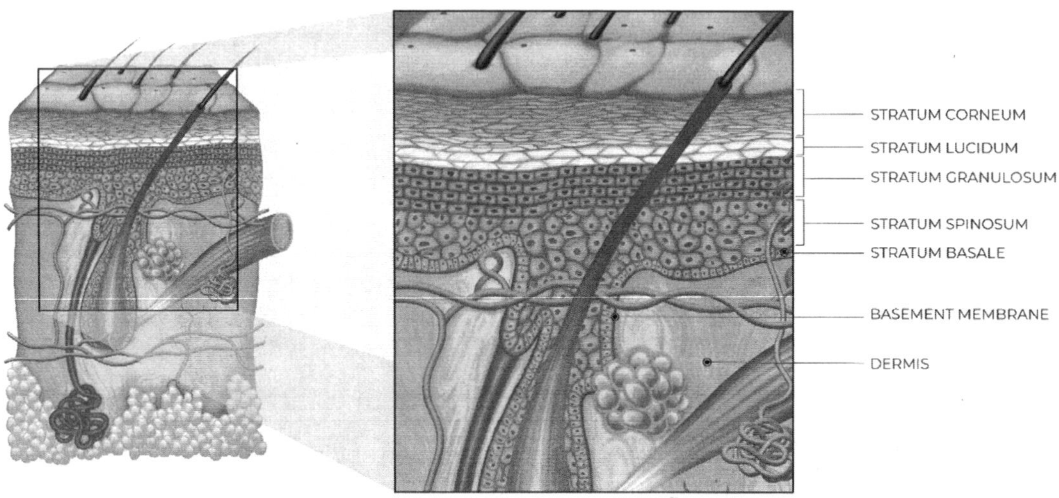

Review Video: Integumentary System
Visit mometrix.com/academy and enter code: 655980

Muscular System

The **muscular system** works in concert with the **skeletal system** to move the body and perform such core functions as cardiac activity. Key elements include:

- **Smooth muscle tissues** are involuntary muscles that are found in the walls of internal organs such as the stomach, intestines, and blood vessels. Smooth muscle tissues, or **visceral tissue,** is nonstriated. Smooth muscle cells are shorter and wider than skeletal muscle fibers. Smooth muscle tissue is also found in sphincters or valves that control the movement of material through openings throughout the body.
- **Cardiac muscle** tissue is involuntary muscle that is found only in the heart. Like skeletal muscle cells, cardiac muscle cells are also striated.
- **Skeletal muscles** are voluntary muscles that work in pairs to move parts of the skeleton. Skeletal muscles are composed of **muscle fibers** (cells) that are bound together in parallel bundles. Skeletal muscles are also known as **striated muscle** due to their striped histological appearance under a microscope.

Only skeletal muscle interacts with the skeleton to move the body. When they contract, the muscles transmit force to the attached bones. Working together, the muscles and bones act as a system of levers that move around the joints.

Review Video: Muscular System
Visit mometrix.com/academy and enter code: 967216

Major Muscles

The human body has more than 650 skeletal muscles than account for approximately half of a person's weight. Starting with the head and face, the temporalis and masseter move the mandible (lower jaw bone). The orbicularis oculi closes the eye. The orbicularis oris draws the lips together. The sternocleidomastoids move the head. The trapezius moves the shoulder, and the pectoralis major, deltoid, and latissimus dorsi move the upper arm. The biceps brachii and the triceps brachii move the lower arm. The rectus abdominis, external oblique, and erector spine move the trunk. The external and internal obliques elevate and depress the ribs. The gluteus maximus moves the upper leg. The quadriceps femoris, hamstrings, and sartorius move the lower leg. The gastrocnemius and the soleus extend the foot.

Skeletal Muscle Contraction

Skeletal muscles consist of numerous muscle fibers. Each muscle fiber contains a bundle of myofibrils, which are composed of multiple repeating contractile units called sarcomeres. **Myofibrils** contain two protein microfilaments: a thick filament and a thin filament. The **thick filament** is composed of the protein myosin. The **thin filament** is composed of the protein actin. The dark bands (striations) in skeletal muscles are formed when thick and thin filaments overlap. Light bands occur where the thin filament is overlapped. Skeletal muscle attraction occurs when the thin filaments slide over the thick filaments shortening the sarcomere. When an action potential (electrical signal) reaches a muscle fiber, calcium ions are released. According to the sliding filament model of muscle contraction, these calcium ions bind to the myosin and actin, which assists in the binding of the myosin heads of the thick filaments to the actin molecules of the thin filaments. Adenosine triphosphate released from glucose provides the energy necessary for the contraction.

SKELETAL SYSTEM

The skeletal system serves many functions including providing structural support, movement, and protection; producing blood cells; and storing substances such as fat and minerals. The **axial skeleton** transfers the weight from the upper body to the lower appendages. Bones provide attachment points for muscles. The cranium protects the brain. The vertebrae protect the spinal cord. The rib cage protects the heart and lungs. The pelvis protects the reproductive organs. **Joints** including hinge joints, ball-and-socket joints, pivot joints, ellipsoid joints, gliding joints, and saddle joints. The **red marrow** manufactures red and white blood cells. All bone marrow is red at birth, but adults have approximately one-half red bone marrow and one-half yellow bone marrow. Yellow bone marrow stores fat.

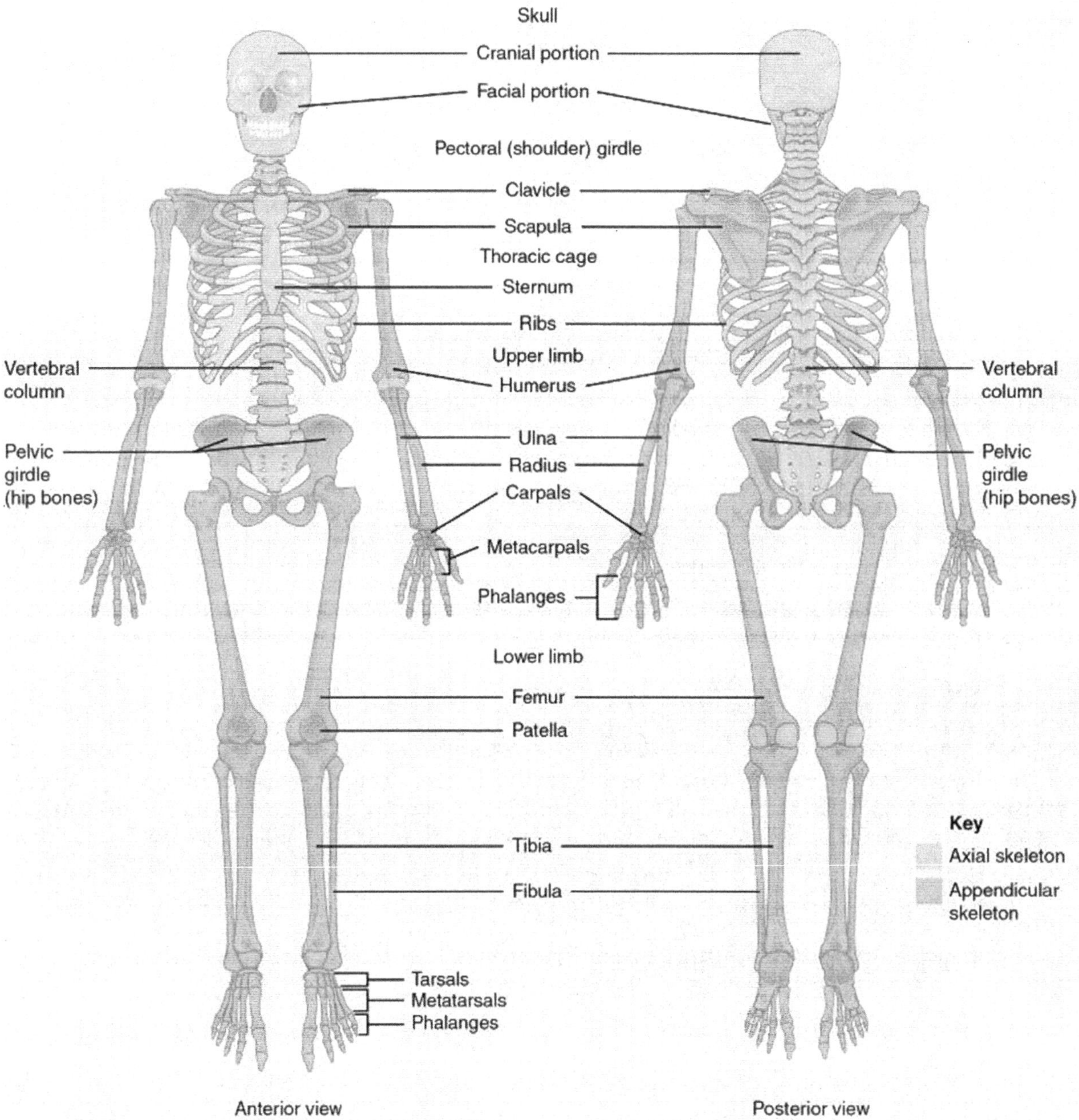

Structure of Axial Skeleton and Appendicular Skeleton

The **human skeletal system**, which consists of 206 bones along with numerous tendons, ligaments, and cartilage, is divided into the axial skeleton and the appendicular skeleton.

The **axial skeleton** consists of 80 bones and includes the vertebral column, rib cage, sternum, skull, and hyoid bone. The **vertebral column** consists of 33 vertebrae classified as cervical vertebrae, thoracic vertebrae, lumbar vertebrae, and sacral vertebrae. The **rib cage** includes 12 paired ribs, 10 pairs of true ribs and two pairs of floating ribs, and the **sternum**, which consists of the manubrium, corpus sterni, and xiphoid process. The **skull** includes the cranium and facial bones. The **ossicles** are bones in the middle ear. The **hyoid bone** provides an attachment point for the tongue muscles. The axial skeleton protects vital organs including the brain, heart, and lungs.

The **appendicular skeleton** consists of 126 bones including the pectoral girdle, pelvic girdle, and appendages. The **pectoral girdle** consists of the scapulae (shoulder blades) and clavicles (collarbones). The **pelvic girdle** attaches to the sacrum at the sacroiliac joint. The upper appendages (arms) include the humerus, radius, ulna, carpals, metacarpals, and phalanges. The lower appendages (legs) include the femur, patella, fibula, tibia, tarsals, metatarsals, and phalanges.

The axial skeleton and the appendicular skeleton:

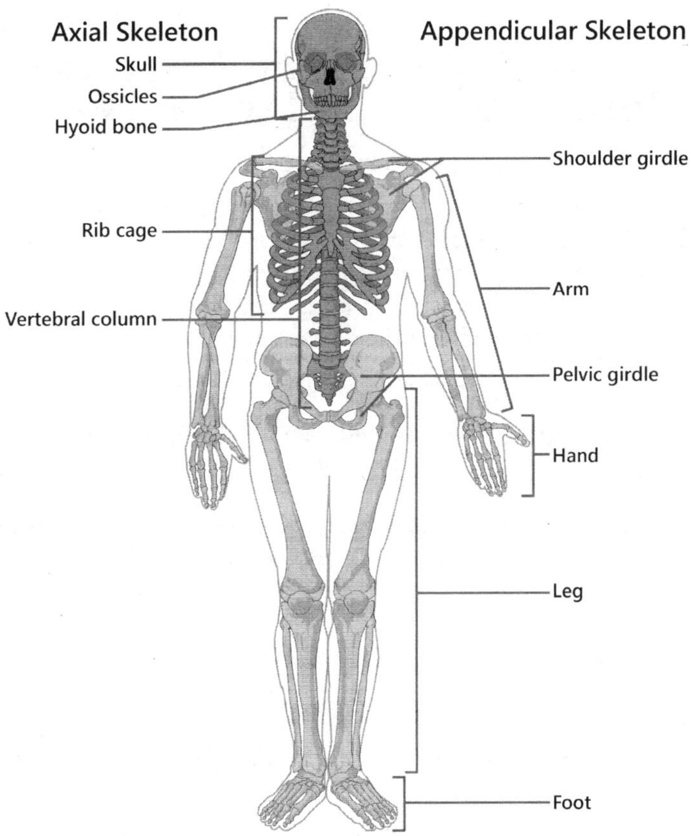

Review Video: Skeletal System
Visit mometrix.com/academy and enter code: 256447

Nervous System

The human **nervous system** consists of the **central nervous system** (i.e., brain and spinal cord) and the **peripheral nervous system** (i.e., nerves). They deliver voluntary and involuntary messages throughout the body. Core functions, such as digestion and respiration, are controlled by the brain via messages sent through the peripheral nervous system. The brain also receives external cues to regulate temperature and activate certain muscle groups.

Review Video: Function of the Nervous System
Visit mometrix.com/academy and enter code: 708428

The human nervous system senses, interprets, and issues commands as a response to conditions in the body's environment. This process is made possible by a complex communication system of cells called **neurons**.

Messages are sent across the plasma membrane of neurons through a process called **action potential**. These messages occur when a neuron is stimulated past a necessary threshold. These stimulations occur in a sequence from the stimulation point of one neuron to its contact with another neuron. At the point of contact, called a **chemical synapse**, a substance is released that stimulates or inhibits the action of the adjoining cell. A network of nerves composed of neurons fans out across the body and forms the framework for the nervous system. The direction the information flows depends on the specific organizations of nerve circuits and pathways.

Review Video: What is the Function of the Nervous System
Visit mometrix.com/academy and enter code: 708428

The Somatic Nervous system and the Reflex Arc

The somatic nervous system (**SNS**) controls the five senses and the voluntary movement of skeletal muscle. So, this system has all of the neurons that are connected to sense organs. Efferent (motor) and afferent (sensory) nerves help the somatic nervous system operate the senses and the movement of skeletal muscle. **Efferent nerves** bring signals from the central nervous system to the sensory organs and the muscles. **Afferent nerves** bring signals from the sensory organs and the muscles to the central nervous system. The somatic nervous system also performs involuntary movements which are known as reflex arcs.

A **reflex**, the simplest act of the nervous system, is an automatic response without any conscious thought to a stimulus via the reflex arc. The **reflex arc** is the simplest nerve pathway, which bypasses the brain and is controlled by the spinal cord. For example, in the classic knee-jerk response (patellar tendon reflex), the stimulus is the reflex hammer hitting the tendon, and the response is the muscle contracting, which jerks the foot upward. The stimulus is detected by sensory receptors, and a message is sent along a **sensory** (afferent) neuron to one or more **interneurons** in the spinal cord. The interneuron(s) transmit this message to a **motor** (efferent) neuron, which carries the message to the correct **effector** (muscle).

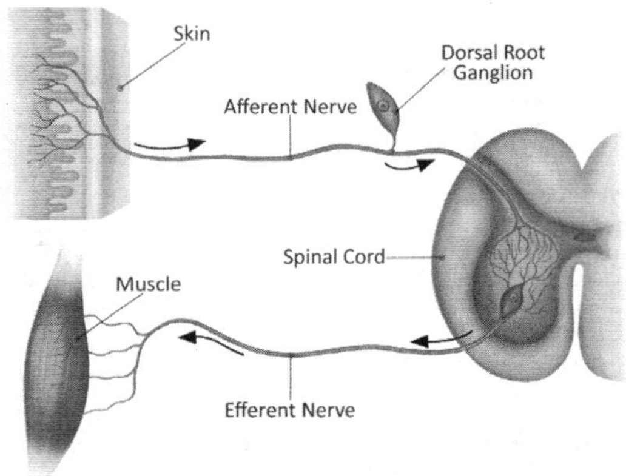

THE EYES

The eyes are a sensory organ, and therefore, belong to the nervous system. The main **parts of the eye** and their functions are as follows:

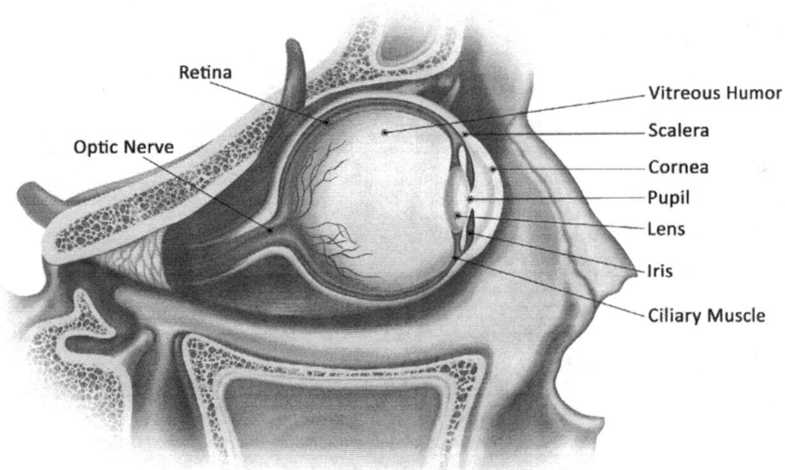

- **Aqueous humor** is watery fluid that maintains eye pressure.
- The **bony orbit** is the socket protecting the eye.
- **Cranial nerves** that help with the function of the eye such as movement or vision include:
    - the optic nerve (cranial nerve II)
    - oculomotor (III)
    - trochlear (IV)
    - trigeminal (V)
    - abducens (VI)
    - vagus (X) nerves
- **Eyelashes and lids** protect the eye and sweep out particles.

- **Extrinsic muscles** focus the eye.
- The **lacrimal glands** are tear ducts to moisten the eye.
- The **lens** refracts light.
- The **optic disc** is the blind spot.
- The **pupil** regulates light entry.
- The **retina** has rods for black and white imaging and cones for color imaging, and helps trigger the optic nerve to send impulses to the brain.
- The **macula** is at the retinal center that is very sensitive to light. The black spot in the center is called the fovea which provides the sharpest vision.
- The **choroid** is a black layer behind the retina that absorbs light and nourishes the retina.
- The **cornea** is the window at the front of the eye that helps with focus.
- The **iris** regulates light entry.
- The **sclera** is tough, white fibrous connective tissue holding nerves and vessels that acts as protection for the eye.
- The **suspensory ligament** connects the lens to the ciliary muscles of the iris.
- The **vitreous humor** is jelly that maintains the eye's shape and refracts images.

Reproductive System

The **reproductive system** consists of the prostate, testicle, penis, and scrotum in males and ovaries, uterus, vagina, fallopian tubes, and mammary glands in females. The primary function is the creation of human life. **Sperm** is produced by the testes and is delivered to the ovary-produced **eggs** in the fallopian tubes for fertilization. The uterus then serves as the home for the developing fetus. **Mammary glands** secrete nutrients for the newborn child.

Male Reproductive System

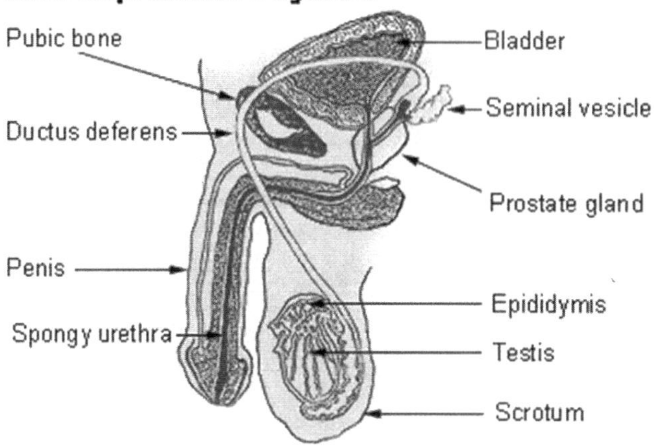

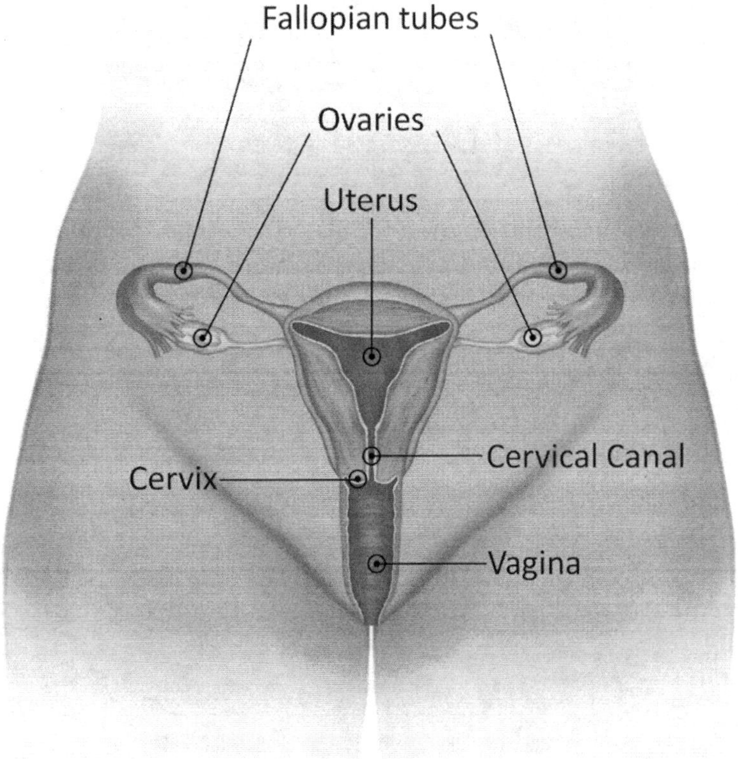

Review Video: Reproductive Systems
Visit mometrix.com/academy and enter code: 505450

Interconnectedness of Body Systems

Respiratory and Circulatory Systems Working Together

Body systems work in concert with each other to respond to increasing and decreasing demands on the body and regulate **homeostasis**, the manner in which the human body regulates itself based on internal and external conditions in order to maintain a physiological balance. For example, the heart pumps blood through the **circulatory system** to distribute oxygenated blood throughout the body to meet physiological demands at any given time. Blood becomes oxygenated in the lungs (**respiratory system**) after excess **carbon dioxide** is released from the body through respiration. Inspiration of **oxygen** into the lungs allows the blood to become oxygen-rich so as to be distributed throughout the body. When physiological demands of the body increase (i.e., quickly climbing stairs), inspiration of oxygen increases and the heart pumps faster in order to more efficiently increase the delivery of oxygenated blood throughout the body. When the intense physical activity subsides, breathing slows and the heart returns to a normal resting heart rate.

Impact of Diet and Exercise on the Circulatory System

The delivery of **oxygenated blood** throughout the body can be accomplished more efficiently with a pattern of consistent exercise and good dietary habits. **Aerobic** activity strengthens the heart by increasing the oxygen carrying capacity of the red blood cells (**hemoglobin**) while also lowering resting blood pressure. In addition, aerobic exercise helps increase high density lipoproteins (HDL) (i.e., "good cholesterol") and decreasing low density lipoproteins (i.e., "bad cholesterol") which helps keep the arteries (**circulatory system**) clear. Consistent and adequate physical activity also helps regulate blood sugars, which can reduce the likelihood of developing Type II diabetes. A high fiber, low fat diet also directly contributes to lower blood sugar levels, cholesterol management, and helps maintain healthy bowels (**digestive system**). Combining regular aerobic physical activity with a high fiber, low fat diet is one of the most effective methods to improve one's cardiovascular health, maintain a healthy weight, and increase personal longevity.

Chapter Quiz

Ready to see how well you retained what you just read? Scan the QR code to go directly to the chapter quiz interface for this study guide. If you're using a computer, simply visit the online resources page at **mometrix.com/resources719/abctebio** and click the Chapter Quizzes link.

Plant Biology and Physiology

Characteristics of Major Plant Divisions

Vascular and Nonvascular Plants

Vascular plants, also referred to as **tracheophytes**, have dermal tissue, meristematic tissue, ground tissues, and vascular tissues. Nonvascular plants, also referred to as **bryophytes**, do not have the vascular tissue xylem and phloem. Vascular plants can grow very tall, whereas nonvascular plants are short and close to the ground. Vascular plants can be found in dry regions, but nonvascular plants typically grow near or in moist areas. Vascular plants have leaves, roots, and stems, but nonvascular plants have leaf-like, root-like, and stem-like structures that do not have true vascular tissue. Nonvascular plants have hair-like **rhizoids**, that act like roots by anchoring them to the ground and absorbing water. Vascular plants include angiosperms, gymnosperms, and ferns. Nonvascular plants include mosses and liverworts.

Flowering Versus Nonflowering Plants

Angiosperms and gymnosperms are both vascular plants. **Angiosperms** are flowering plants, and **gymnosperms** are non-flowering plants. Angiosperms reproduce by seeds that are enclosed in an ovary, usually in a fruit, while gymnosperms reproduce by unenclosed or "naked" seeds on scales, leaves, or cones. Angiosperms can be further classified as either monocots or dicots, depending on if they have one or two cotyledons, respectively. Angiosperms include grasses, garden flowers, vegetables, and broadleaf trees such as maples, birches, elms, and oaks. Gymnosperms include conifers such as pines, spruces, cedars, and redwoods.

Review Video: Kingdom Plantae Characteristics
Visit mometrix.com/academy and enter code: 710084

Monocots and Dicots

Angiosperms can be classified as either monocots or dicots. The seeds of **monocots** have one cotyledon, and the seeds of **dicots** have two cotyledons. The flowers of monocots have petals in multiples of three, and the flowers of dicots have petals in multiples of four or five. The leaves of monocots are slender with parallel veins, while the leaves of dicots are broad and flat with branching veins. The vascular bundles in monocots are distributed throughout the stem, whereas the vascular bundles in dicots are arranged in rings. Monocots have a **fibrous root system**, and dicots have a **taproot system**.

Major Plant Tissues and Organs

Plant Dermal Tissue

Plant dermal tissue is called the epidermis, and is usually a single layer of closely-packed cells that covers leaves and young stems. The epidermis protects the plant by secreting the cuticle, which is a waxy substance that helps prevent water loss and infections. The epidermis in leaves has tiny pores called **stomata**. Guard cells in the epidermis control the opening and closing of the stomata. The epidermis usually does not have chloroplasts. The epidermis may be replaced by periderm in older plants. The **periderm** is also referred to as bark. The layers of the periderm are cork cells or phellem, phelloderm, and cork cambium or phellogen. Cork is the outer layer of the periderm and consists of nonliving cells. The periderm protects the plant and provides insulation.

Plant Vascular Tissue

The two major types of plant vascular tissue are xylem and phloem. Xylem and phloem are bound together in vascular bundles. A meristem called vascular cambium is located between the xylem and phloem and produces new xylem and phloem. **Xylem** is made up of tracheids and vessel elements. All vascular plants contain tracheids, but only angiosperms contain vessel elements. Xylem provides support and transports water and dissolved minerals unidirectionally from the roots upward using processes like transpiration pull and root pressure. Phloem is made up of companion cells and sieve-tube cells. **Phloem** transports dissolved sugars produced during photosynthesis and other nutrients bidirectionally to non-photosynthetic areas of the plant. By active transport, the companion vessels move glucose in and out of the sieve-tube cells.

Plant Ground Tissue

The three major types of ground tissue are parenchyma tissue, collenchyma tissue, and sclerenchyma tissue. Most ground tissue is made up of parenchyma. **Parenchyma** is formed by parenchyma cells, and it function in photosynthesis, food storage, and tissue repair. The inner tissue of a leaf, mesophyll, is an example of parenchyma tissue. **Collenchyma** is made of collenchyma cells and provides support in roots, stems, and petioles. **Sclerenchyma** tissue is made of sclereid cells, which are more rigid than the collenchyma cells, and provides rigid support and protection. Plant sclerenchyma tissue may contain cellulose or lignin. Fabrics such as jute, hemp, and flax are made of sclerenchyma tissue.

Plant Meristematic Tissue

Meristems or meristematic tissues are regions of plant growth. The cells in meristems are undifferentiated and always remain **totipotent**, which means they can always develop into any type of special tissue. Meristem cells can divide and produce new cells, which can aid in the process of regenerating damaged parts. Cells of meristems reproduce asexually through mitosis or cell division that is regulated by hormones. The two types of meristems are lateral meristems and apical meristems. **Primary growth** occurs at **apical meristems**, located at the tip of roots and shoots, and increases the length of the plant. Primary meristems include the protoderm, which produces epidermis; the procambium, which produces cambium, or lateral meristems; xylem and phloem; and the ground meristem, which produces ground tissue including parenchyma. **Secondary growth** occurs at the lateral or secondary meristems and causes an increase in diameter or thickness.

Flowers

The primary function of flowers is to produce seeds for reproduction of the plant. Flowers have a **pedicel**, a stalk with a receptacle or enlarged upper portion, which holds the developing seeds. Flowers also can have sepals and petals. **Sepals** are leaflike structures that protect the bud. **Petals**, which are collectively called the corolla, help to attract pollinators. Plants can have stamens, pistils, or both depending on the type of plant. The **stamen** consists of the anther and filament. The end of the stamen is called the **anther** and is where pollen is produced. Pollen also contains sperm, which is needed in order for a proper plant zygot to form. The **pistil** consists of the stigma, style, and ovary. The ovary contains the ovules, which house the egg cells.

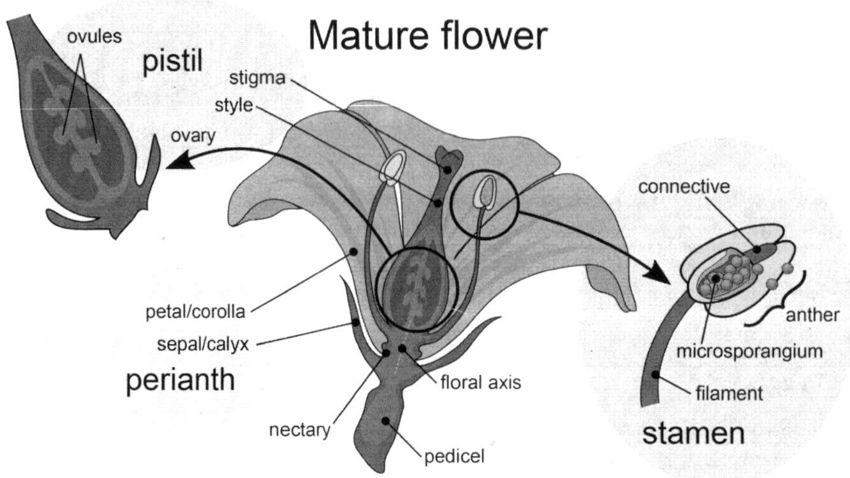

STEMS

Plants can have either woody or nonwoody (herbaceous) stems. **Woody** stems consist of wood, or bark, as a structural tissue, while **herbaceous** stems are very flexible. The stem is divided into nodes and internodes. Buds are located at the nodes and may develop into leaves, roots, flowers, cones, or more stems. Stems consist of dermal tissue, ground tissue, and vascular tissue. **Monocot stems have vascular bundles distributed through the stem. Dicots have rings of vascular bundles**. Stems have four main functions: (1) they provide support to leaves, flowers, and fruits; (2) they transport materials in the xylem and phloem; (3) they store food; and (4) they have meristems, which provide all of the new cells for the plant.

MONOCOT	DICOT
Single Cotyledon 	Two Cotyledon 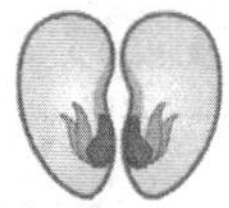
Long Narrow Leaf Parallel Veins 	Broad Leaf Network of Veins 
Vascular Bundles Scattered 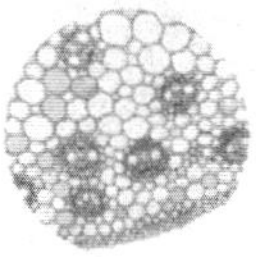	Vascular Bundles in a Ring 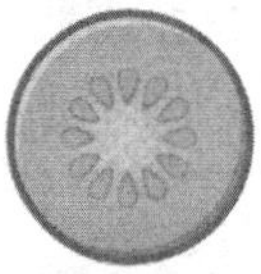
Floral Parts in Multiples of 3 	Floral Parts in Multiples of 4 or 5 

LEAVES

The primary function of a **leaf** is to manufacture food through photosynthesis. The leaf consists of a flat portion called the **blade** and a stalk called the **petiole**. The edge of the leaf is called the margin and can be entire, toothed, or lobed. Veins transport food and water and make up the skeleton of the leaf. The large central vein is called the **midrib**. The blade has an upper and lower epidermis. The epidermis is covered by a protective cuticle. The lower epidermis contains many stomata, which are pores that allow air to enter and leave the leaf. Stomata also regulate transpiration. The middle portion of the leaf is called the **mesophyll**. The mesophyll consists of the palisade mesophyll and the spongy mesophyll. Most photosynthesis occurs in chloroplasts located in the palisade mesophyll.

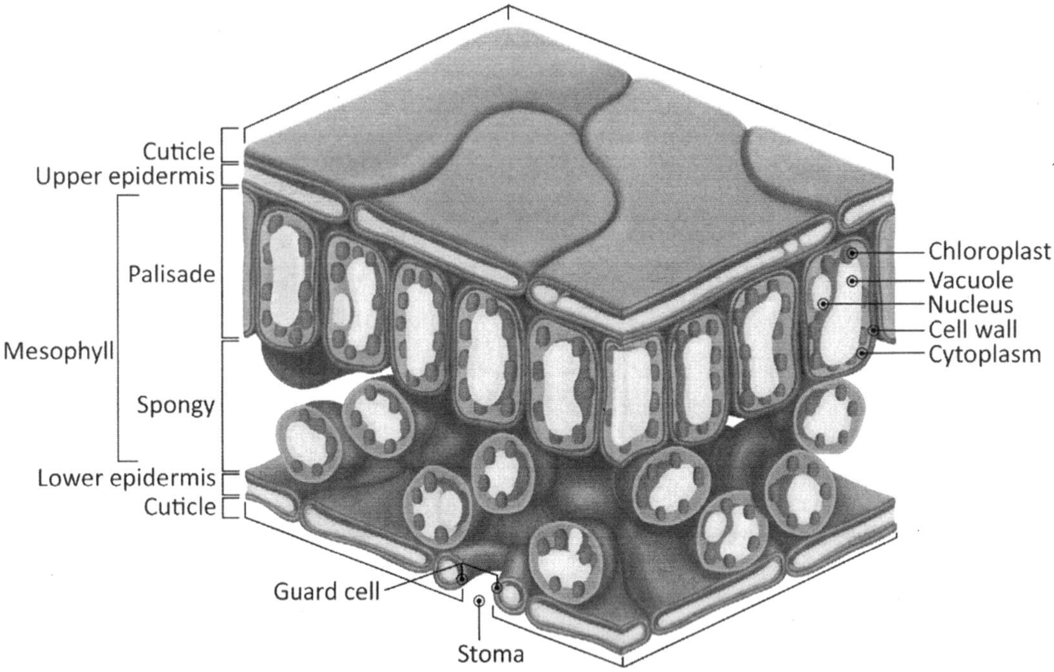

Roots

The primary functions of roots are to anchor the plant, absorb materials, and store food. The two basic types of root systems are taproot systems and fibrous root systems. **Taproot systems** have a primary root with many smaller secondary roots. **Fibrous root systems**, which lack a primary root, consist of a mass of many small secondary roots. The root has three main regions: the area of maturation, the area of elongation, and the area of cell division or the meristematic region. The root is covered by an epidermal cell, some of which develops into root hairs. **Root hairs** absorb water and minerals by osmosis, and capillary action helps move the water upward through the roots to the rest of the plant. The center of the root is the **vascular cylinder**, which contains the xylem and phloem. The vascular cylinder is surrounded by the cortex where the food is stored. Primary growth occurs at the root tip. Secondary growth occurs at the vascular cambium located between the xylem and phloem.

Plant Life Cycles and Reproductive Strategies

Pollination Strategies

Pollination is the transfer of pollen from the anther of the stamen to the stigma of the pistil on the same plant or on a different plant. Pollinators can be either **abiotic** (not derived from a living organism) or **biotic** (derived from a living organism). Abiotic pollinators include wind and water. Approximately 20% of pollination occurs by abiotic pollinators. For example, grasses are typically pollinated by wind, and aquatic plants are typically pollinated by water. Biotic pollinators include insects, birds, mammals, and occasionally reptiles. Most biotic pollinators are insects. Many plants have colored petals and strong scents, which attract insects. Pollen rubs off on the insects and is transferred as they move from plant to plant.

Seed Dispersal Methods

Methods of **seed dispersal** can be abiotic or biotic. Methods of seed dispersal include gravity, wind, water, and animals. Some plants produce seeds in fruits that get eaten by animals and then are distributed to new locations in the animals' waste. Some seeds (e.g. dandelions) have structures to aid in dispersal by wind. Some seeds have barbs that get caught in animal hair or bird feathers and are then carried to new locations by the animals. Interestingly, some animals bury seeds for food storage but do not return for the seeds. The seeds of aquatic plants can be dispersed by water, while the seeds of plants near rivers, streams, lakes, and beaches (e.g. coconuts) are also often dispersed by water. Some plants, in a method called **mechanical dispersal**, can propel or shoot their seeds away from them even up to several feet. For example, touch-me-nots and violets utilize mechanical dispersal.

Alternation of Generations

Alternation of generations, also referred to as **metagenesis**, contains both a sexual phase and an asexual phase in the life cycle of the plant. Mosses and ferns reproduce by alternation of generations: the sexual phase is called the **gametophyte**, and the asexual phase is called the **sporophyte**. During the sexual phase, a sperm fertilizes an egg to form a zygote. By mitosis, the zygote develops into the sporophyte. The sporangia in the sori of the sporophyte produce the spores through meiosis. The spores germinate and by mitosis produce the gametophyte.

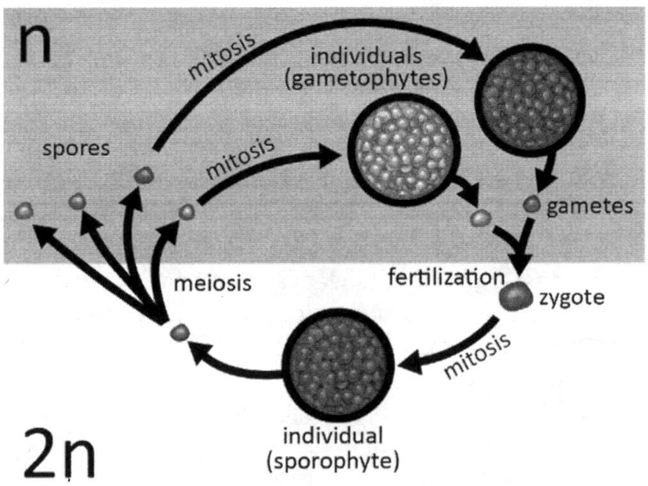

Plant Transportation of Water and Nutrients

Obtaining and Transporting Water and Inorganic Nutrients

Inorganic nutrients and water enter plants through the root hair and travel to the xylem. Once the water, minerals, and salts have crossed the endodermis, they must be moved upward through the xylem by water uptake. Most of a plant's water is lost through the stomata by transpiration. This loss is necessary to provide the tension needed to pull the water and nutrients up through the xylem. In order to maintain the remaining water that is necessary for the functioning of the plant, guard cells control the stomata. Whether an individual stoma is closed or open is controlled by two guard cells. When the guard cells lose water and become flaccid, they collapse together, closing the stoma. When the guard cells swell with water and become turgid, they move apart, opening the stoma.

Use of Roots

Plant roots have numerous root hairs that absorb water and inorganic nutrients such as minerals and salts. Root hairs are thin, hair-like outgrowths of the root's epidermal cells that exponentially increase the root's surface area. Water molecules cross the cell membranes of the root hairs by **osmosis** and then travel on to the vascular cylinder. Inorganic nutrients are transported across the cell membranes of the root endodermis by **active transport**. The endodermis is a single layer of cells that the water and nutrients must pass through by osmosis or active transport. To control mineral uptake by the roots, Casparian strips act as an extracellular diffusion barrier, and forces nutrients to be pulled into the plant. While water passes through by osmosis, mineral uptake is controlled by transport proteins.

Use of Xylem

The xylem contains dead, water-conducting cells called tracheids and vessels. The movement of water upward through the tracheids and vessels is explained by the **cohesion-tension theory**. First, water is lost through evaporation of the plant's surface through transpiration. This can occur at any surface exposed to air but is mainly through the stomata in the epidermis. This transpiration puts the water inside the xylem in a state of tension. Because water is cohesive due to the strong hydrogen bonds between molecules, the water is pulled up the xylem as long as the water is transpiring.

Products of Photosynthesis

Glucose Produced During Photosynthesis

Plants produce glucose, a simple carbohydrate or monosaccharide, during photosynthesis. Plants do not transport glucose molecules directly, but instead glucose undergoes reactions to form sucrose, starch, and cellulose which are then used in different ways. Glucose is joined to a fructose molecule to form **sucrose**, a disaccharide, which is transported in sap. Like glucose, sucrose is also considered a simple carbohydrate. Starches and cellulose are complex carbohydrates consisting of long chains of glucose molecules called polysaccharides. Plants use **starch** to store glucose, and **cellulose** for rigidity in cell walls.

Use of Phloem to Transport Products of Photosynthesis

The movement of sugars and other materials from the leaves to other tissues throughout the plants is called **translocation**. Nutrients are translocated from **sources**, or areas with excess sugars such as mature leaves, to **sinks**, areas where sugars are needed (i.e. roots or developing seeds). Phloem vessels are found in the vascular bundles along with the xylem. Phloem contains conducting cells called sieve elements, which are connected end to end in sieve tubes. **Sieve tubes** carry sap from sugar sources to sugar sinks. Phloem sap contains mostly sucrose dissolved in water. The sap can also contain proteins, amino acids, and hormones. Some plants transport sugar alcohols. Loading the sugar into the sieve tubes causes water to enter the tubes by osmosis, creating a higher hydrostatic pressure at the source end of the tube. This pressure is what causes nutrients to move upward towards the sink areas. Sugar is removed from the sieve tube at the sink end and the solute potential is increased, thus causing water to leave the phloem. This process is referred to as the **pressure-flow mechanism**.

Chapter Quiz

Ready to see how well you retained what you just read? Scan the QR code to go directly to the chapter quiz interface for this study guide. If you're using a computer, simply visit the online resources page at **mometrix.com/resources719/abctebio** and click the Chapter Quizzes link.

Ecology

Hierarchical Structure of the Biosphere

Biosphere

Components

The **biosphere** is the region of the earth inhabited by living things. The components of the biosphere from smallest to largest are organisms, populations, communities, ecosystems, and biomes. Organisms of the same species make up a **population**. All of the populations in an area make up the **community**. The community combined with the physical environment for a region forms an **ecosystem**. Several ecosystems are grouped together to form large geographic regions called **biomes**.

Population

A **population** is a group of all the individuals of one species in a specific area or region at a certain time. A **species** is a group of organisms that can breed and produce fertile offspring. There may be many populations of a specific species in a large geographic region. **Ecologists** study the size, density, and growth rate of populations to determine their stability. Population size continuously changes with births, deaths, and migrations. The population density is the number of individuals per unit of area. Growth rates for a population may be exponential or logistic. Ecologists also study how the individuals are dispersed within a population. Some species form clusters, while others are evenly or randomly spaced. However, every population has limiting factors. Changes in the environment or geography can reduce or limit population size. The individuals of a population interact with each other and with other organisms in the community in various ways, including competition and predation, which have direct impacts population size.

Community Interactions

A **community** is all of the populations of different species that live in an area and interact with each other. Community interaction can be intraspecific or interspecific. **Intraspecific interactions** occur between members of the same species. **Interspecific interactions** occur between members of different species. Different types of interactions include competition, predation, and symbiosis. Communities with high diversity are more complex and more stable than communities with low diversity. The level of diversity can be seen in a food web of the community, which shows all the feeding relationships within the community.

Ecosystems

An **ecosystem** is the basic unit of ecology. An ecosystem is the sum of all the biotic and abiotic factors in an area. **Biotic factors** are all living things such as plants, animals, fungi, and microorganisms. **Abiotic factors** include the light, water, air, temperature, and soil in an area. Ecosystems obtain the energy they need from sunlight. Ecosystems also contain biogeochemical cycles such as the hydrologic cycle and the nitrogen cycle. Ecosystems are generally classified as either terrestrial or aquatic. All of the living things within an ecosystem are called its community. The number and variety of living things within a community describes the ecosystem's **biodiversity**. However, each ecosystem can only support a limited number of organisms known as the **carrying capacity**.

Influences on Population Size

Biotic and Abiotic Factors in an Ecosystem

Every ecosystem consists of multiple abiotic and biotic factors. **Abiotic factors** are the nonbiological physical and chemical factors that affect the ecosystem. Abiotic factors include soil type, atmospheric conditions, sunlight, water, wind, chemical elements, and natural disturbances. In aquatic ecosystems, abiotic factors include salinity, turbidity, water depth, current, temperature, and light. **Biotic factors** are all of the living organisms in the ecosystem. Biotic factors include plants, algae, fungi, bacteria, archaea, animals, and protozoa.

Influence of Resource Availability and Abiotic Factors on Population Size

Population size is affected by resource availability and abiotic factors. As the population density increases, intraspecific competition for available resources intensifies. If the availability of resources decreases, death rates may increase and birth rates may decrease. For example, territoriality for mating or nesting may limit available resources for individuals in a population and limit the population size. Abiotic factors such as temperature, rainfall, wind, and light intensity all influence the population size. For example, temperatures near a species' tolerance limit may decrease the population. Natural disasters such as fire or flood can destroy resources and greatly decrease a population's size. In general, any abiotic factor that reduces or limits resources will also reduce or limit population size.

Significance of Habitat and Niche to Populations

The **habitat** of an organism is the type of place where that organism usually lives. A habitat is a piece of an environmental area, which may be a geographic area or even the body of another organism. The habitat describes an organism's natural living environment. A habitat includes biotic and abiotic factors such as temperature, light, food resources, and predators. Whereas a habitat describes an organism's "home," a niche can be thought of as an organism's "occupation." A **niche** describes an organism's functional role in the community and how the organism uses its habitat. A niche can be quite complex because it should include the impacts that the organism has on the biotic and abiotic surroundings. Niches can be broad or narrow.

Influence of Competition and Predation on Population Size

Feeding relationships between organisms can affect population size. Competition and predation both tend to limit population size. **Competition** occurs when two individuals need the same resource. This competition can be **intraspecific**, which is between members of the same species, or **interspecific**, which is between members of different species. Intraspecific competition reduces resources as that species' own population increases, which limits population growth. Interspecific competition reduces resources as a different species uses those same resources. **Predation** occurs when one individual is a food resource for another individual. Predator and prey populations can cycle over a range of years. If prey resources increase, predator numbers increase. An example of the predator-prey population cycle is the Canadian lynx and snowshoe hare.

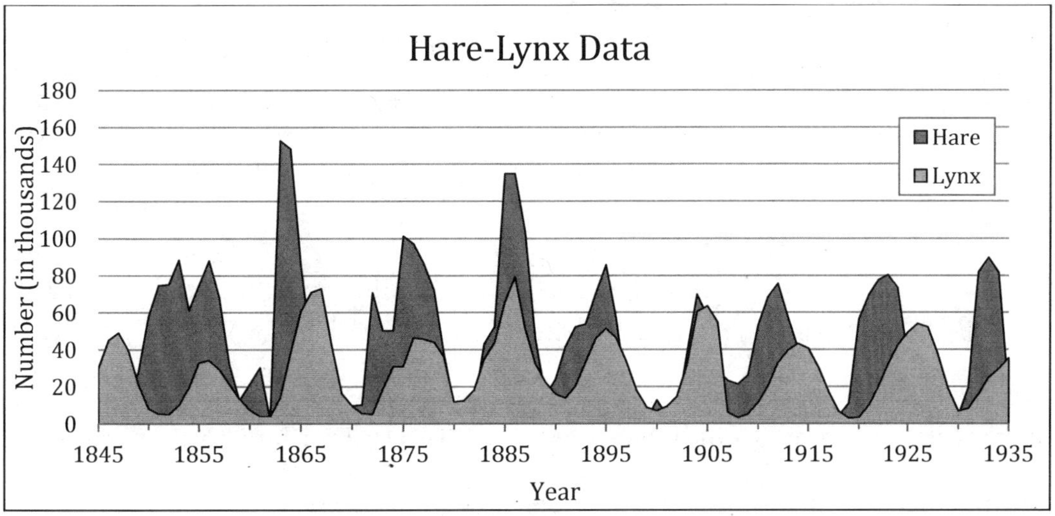

Models of Population Growth

Logistic Population Growth Model

Populations vary over time due to deaths, births, immigration, and emigration. In most situations, resources such as food, water, and shelter are limited. Each environment or habitat can only support a limited number of individuals, which is known as the **carrying capacity**. Population growth models that factor in the carrying capacity are called **logistic growth models**. With logistic population growth models, the rate of population growth decreases as the population size increases. Logistic growth graphs as an S-shaped curve. Comparing logistic growth and exponential growth shows that the graph for exponential growth continues to become steeper, but the graph for logistics growth levels off once the population reaches the carrying capacity. As the population increases, fewer resources are available per individual. This limits the number of individuals that can occupy that environment or habitat.

Exponential Population Growth Model

While populations change over time due to births, deaths, and migrations, sometimes conditions are near ideal and populations can increase at their maximum rate, exhibiting exponential growth. **Exponential growth** is growth in which the rate of change is proportional to the increasing size in an exponential progression. Exponential growth graphs as a J-shaped curve. Exponential growth is often observed in single-celled organisms such as bacteria or protozoa in which the population or number of cells increases by a factor of two per unit of time. One cell divides into two cells, which divide into four cells, and so forth. The exponential growth model describes population growth under ideal conditions and does not take limiting factors or carrying capacity into account. Realistically, exponential growth cannot occur indefinitely, but it may occur for a period of time. It does show a species' capacity for increase and may be helpful when studying a particular species or ecosystem. For example, if a species with no natural predator is introduced into a new habitat, that species may experience exponential growth. If this growth is allowed to go unchecked, the population may overshoot the carrying capacity and then starve. Efforts may need to be taken to reduce the population before this occurs.

Reproduction and Mortality in Populations

Advantages and Disadvantages of Asexual Reproduction in Animals

Very few species of animals reproduce by asexual reproduction, and nearly all of those species also have the ability to reproduce sexually. While not common, asexual reproduction is useful for animals that tend to stay in one place and may not find mates. Asexual reproduction takes considerably less effort and energy than sexual reproduction. In asexual reproduction, all of the offspring are genetically identical to the parent. This can be a disadvantage because of the lack of genetic variation. Although asexual reproduction is advantageous in a stable environment, if the environment changes, the organisms may lack the genetic variability to survive or selectively adapt.

Review Video: Asexual Reproduction
Visit mometrix.com/academy and enter code: 565616

Life Histories

The **life history** of a species describes the typical organism's life cycle from birth through reproduction to death. Life histories can typically be classified as opportunistic life histories or equilibrial life histories. Species exhibiting **opportunistic life histories** are typically small, short-lived organisms that have a high reproductive capacity but invest little time and care into their offspring. Their population sizes tend to oscillate significantly over periods of several years. Species exhibiting **equilibrial life histories** are typically large, long-lived organisms that have a low reproductive capacity but invest much time and care into their offspring. Their populations tend to fluctuate within a smaller range. A general observation is that species that tend to produce numerous offspring typically tend to invest little care into that offspring, resulting in a high mortality rate of that offspring. Organisms of species that tend to produce few offspring typically invest much more care into that offspring, resulting in a lower mortality rate.

Relationships between Species

Symbiosis

Many species share a special nutritional relationship with another species, called **symbiosis**. The term symbiosis means "living together." In symbiosis, two organisms share a close physical relationship that can be helpful, harmful, or neutral for each organism. Three forms of symbiotic relationships are parasitism, commensalism, and mutualism. **Parasitism** is a relationship between two organisms in which one organism is the parasite, and the other organism is the host. The parasite benefits from the relationship because the parasite obtains its nutrition from the host. The host is harmed from the relationship because the parasite is using the host's energy and giving nothing in return. For example, a tick and a dog share a parasitic relationship in which the tick is the parasite, and the dog is the host. **Commensalism** is a relationship between two organisms in which one benefits, and the other is not affected. For example, a small fish called a remora can attach to the belly of a shark and ride along. The remora is safe under the shark, and the shark is not affected. **Mutualism** is a relationship between two organisms in which both organisms benefit. For example, a rhinoceros usually can be seen with a few tick birds perched on its back. The tick birds are helped by the easy food source of ticks, and the rhino benefits from the tick removal.

Predation

Predation is a special nutritional relationship in which one organism is the predator, and the other organism is the prey. The predator benefits from the relationship, but the prey is harmed. The predator hunts and kills the prey for food. The predator is specially adapted to hunt its prey, and the prey is specially adapted to escape its predator. While predators harm (kill) their individual prey, predation usually helps the prey species. Predation keeps the population of the prey species under control and prevents them from overshooting the carrying capacity, which often leads to starvation. Also, predation usually helps to remove weak or slow members of the prey species leaving the healthier, stronger, and better adapted individuals to reproduce. Examples of predator-prey relationships include lions and zebras, snakes and rats, and hawks and rabbits.

Competition and Territoriality

Competition is a relationship between two organisms in which the organisms compete for the same vital resource that is in short supply. Typically, both organisms are harmed, but one is usually harmed more than the other, which provides an avenue for natural selection. Organisms compete for resources such as food, water, mates, and space. **Interspecific competition** is between members of different species, while **intraspecific competition** is between members of the same species. **Territoriality** can be considered to be a type of interspecific competition for space. Many animals including mammals, birds, reptiles, fish, spiders, and insects have exhibited territorial behavior. Once territories are established, there are fewer conflicts between organisms. For example, a male redwing blackbird can establish a large territory. By singing and flashing his red patches, he is able to warn other males to avoid his territory, and they can avoid fighting.

Altruistic Behaviors Between Animals

Altruism is a self-sacrificing behavior in which an individual animal may serve or protect another animal. For example, in a honey bee colony there is one queen with many workers (females). There are also drones (males), but only during the mating seasons. Adult workers do all the work of the hive and will die defending it. Another example of altruism is seen in a naked mole rat colony. Each colony has one queen that mates with a few males, and the rest of the colony is nonbreeding and lives to service the queen, her mates, and her offspring.

Review Video: Mutualism, Commensalism, and Parasitism
Visit mometrix.com/academy and enter code: 757249

Ecological Succession

Changes During Primary and Secondary Succession

Ecological succession is the process by which a community changes over time. The final stage of this succession is a climax community, which remains relatively unchanged unless a major event causes it to change or become destroyed. The two types of ecological succession are primary succession and secondary succession. **Primary succession** occurs in a region where there is no soil and also has never been populated, such as a new volcanic island or a region where a glacier has retreated. During the pioneer stage, the progression of species is typically lichen and algae, followed by small annual plants, then perennial herbs and grasses. During the intermediate stage, shrubs, grasses, and shade-intolerant trees are dominant. Finally, after hundreds of years, a climax community is reached with shade-tolerant trees. **Secondary succession** occurs when a climax community is destroyed or nearly destroyed, such as after a forest fire or in an abandoned field. With secondary succession, the area starts with soil and seeds from the original climax community. Typically, weeds and annuals are dominant in the first two years. This is followed by grasses and biennials. In a few years, shrubs and perennials are dominant, followed by pine trees, which are eventually replaced by deciduous trees. Secondary succession takes place in less than 100 years.

Review Video: Ecological Succession
Visit mometrix.com/academy and enter code: 466994

Types of Biomes

Biomes

The biosphere consists of numerous biomes. A **biome** is a large region that supports a specific community. Each biome has a characteristic climate and geography. Differences in latitude, altitude, and worldwide patterns affect temperature, precipitation, and humidity. Biomes can be classified as terrestrial or aquatic biomes. **Terrestrial biomes** include ecosystems with land environments, such as tundra, coniferous forest, temperate broadleaf forest, temperate grassland, chaparral, desert, savannas, and tropical forests. Terrestrial biomes tend to grade into each other in regions called ecotones. **Aquatic biomes** are water-dwelling ecosystems. Aquatic biomes include areas such as lakes, rivers, estuaries, coral reefs, oceanic pelagic zone, intertidal zone, and the abyssal zone.

Aquatic Biomes

Aquatic biomes are characterized by multiple factors including the temperature of the water, the amount of dissolved solids in the water, the availability of light, the depth of the water, and the material at the bottom of the biome. Aquatic biomes are classified as marine or freshwater biomes based on the amount of dissolved salt in the water. **Marine biomes** include the intertidal zone, the pelagic zone, the benthic zone, the abyssal zone, coral reefs, and estuaries. Marine biomes have a salinity of at least 35 parts per thousand. **Freshwater biomes** include lakes, ponds, rivers, and streams. Freshwater biomes have a salinity that is less than 0.5 parts per thousand. Lakes and ponds, which are relatively stationary, consist of two zones: the littoral zone and the limnetic zone. The **littoral zone** is closest to the shore and is home to many plants (floating and rooted), invertebrates, crustaceans, amphibians, and fish. The **limnetic zone** is further from the shore and has no rooted plants. Rivers and streams typically originate in the mountains and make their way to the oceans. Because this water is running and colder, it contains different plants and animals than lakes and ponds. For example, salmon, trout, crayfish, plants, and algae are found in rivers and streams.

Marine Regions

Marine regions are located in three broad areas: the ocean, estuaries, and coral reefs. The ocean consists of two general regions: the pelagic zone and the benthic zone. The **pelagic zone** is in the open ocean. Organisms in the pelagic zone include phytoplankton such as algae and bacteria; zooplankton such as protozoa and crustaceans; and larger animals such as squid, sharks, and whales. The **benthic zone** consists of the ocean floor. Organisms in the benthic zone can include sponges, clams, oysters, starfish, sea anemones, sea urchins, worms, and fish. The deepest part of the benthic zone is called the **abyssal plain** and is usually very cold and dark. This is the deep ocean floor, which is home to numerous scavengers, many of which have light-generating capability. **Estuaries** are somewhat-enclosed coastal regions where water from rivers and streams is mixed with seawater. **Coral reefs** are located in warm, shallow water. Corals are small colonial animals that share a mutualistic relationship with algae.

Terrestrial Biomes

Terrestrial biomes are classified predominantly by their vegetation, which is primarily determined by precipitation and temperature. **Tropical rainforests** experience the highest annual precipitation and relatively high temperatures. The dominant vegetation in tropical forests is tall evergreen trees. **Temperate deciduous forests** experience moderate precipitation and temperatures. The dominant vegetation is deciduous trees. **Boreal forests** experience moderate precipitation and lower temperatures. The dominant vegetation is coniferous trees. The **tundra** experiences lower precipitation and cold temperatures. The dominant vegetation is shrubs. The **savanna** experiences lower precipitation and high temperatures. The dominant vegetation is grasses. **Deserts** experience the lowest precipitation and the hottest temperatures. The dominant vegetation is scattered thorny plants.

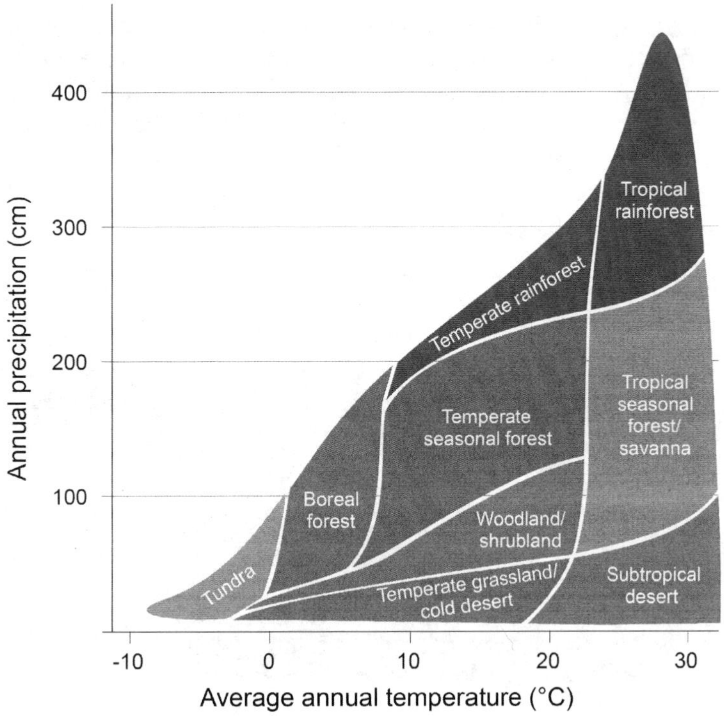

Energy Flow in the Environment

Using Trophic Levels with an Energy Pyramid

Energy flow through an ecosystem can be tracked through an energy pyramid. An **energy pyramid** shows how energy is transferred from one trophic level to another. **Producers** always form the base of an energy pyramid, and the consumers form successive levels above the producers. Producers only store about 1% of the solar energy they receive. Then, each successive level only uses about 10% of the energy of the previous level. That means that **primary consumers** use about 10% of the energy used by primary producers, such as grasses and trees. Next, **secondary consumers** use 10% of primary consumers' 10%, or 1% overall. This continues up for as many trophic levels as exist in a particular ecosystem.

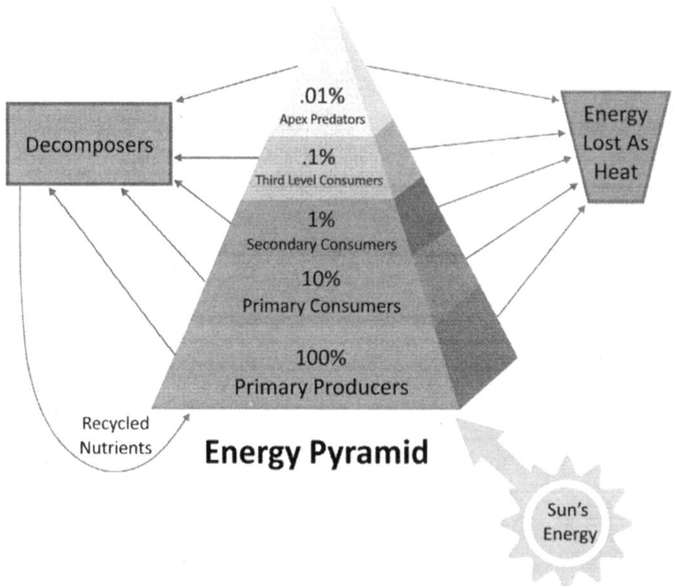

FOOD WEB

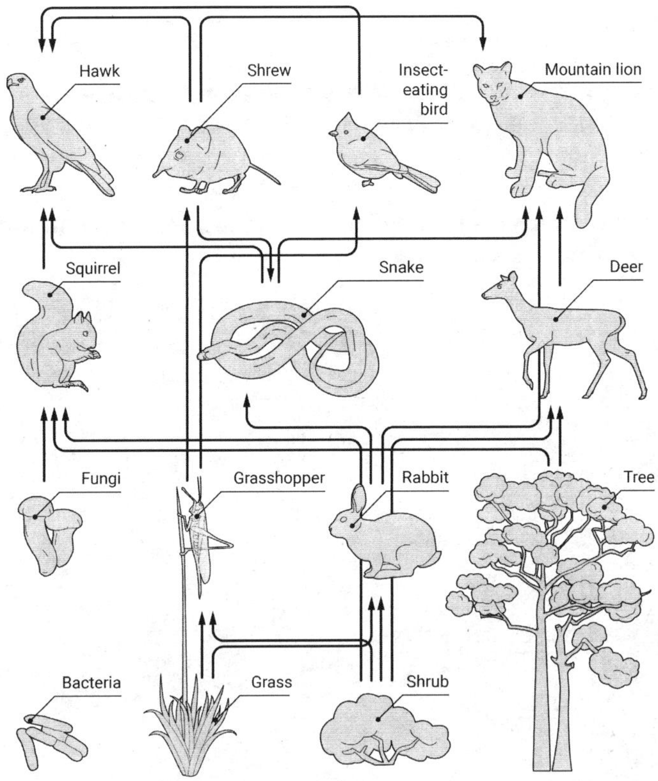

Energy flow through an ecosystem can be illustrated by a **food web**. Energy moves through the food web in the direction of the arrows. In the food web, producers such as grass, trees, and shrubs use energy from the sun to produce food through photosynthesis. Herbivores or primary consumers such as squirrels, grasshoppers, and rabbits obtain energy by eating the producers. Secondary consumers, which are carnivores such as snakes and shrews, obtain energy by eating the primary consumers. Tertiary consumers, which are carnivores such as hawks and mountain lions, obtain energy by eating the secondary consumers. Note that the hawk and the mountain lion can also be considered quaternary consumers in this food web if a different food chain within the web is followed.

Review Video: Food Webs
Visit mometrix.com/academy and enter code: 853254

Biogeochemical Cycles

WATER CYCLE

The water cycle, also referred to as the **hydrologic cycle**, is a biogeochemical cycle that describes the continuous movement of the Earth's water. Water in the form of **precipitation** such as rain or snow moves from the atmosphere to the ground. The water is collected in oceans, lakes, rivers, and other bodies of water. Heat from the sun then causes water to **evaporate** from those oceans, lakes, rivers, and other bodies of water. As plants transpire, this water also undergoes evaporation. This water vapor collects in the sky and forms clouds. As the water vapor in the clouds cools, the water vapor **condenses** or sublimes depending on the conditions. Then, water moves back to the ground in the form of precipitation.

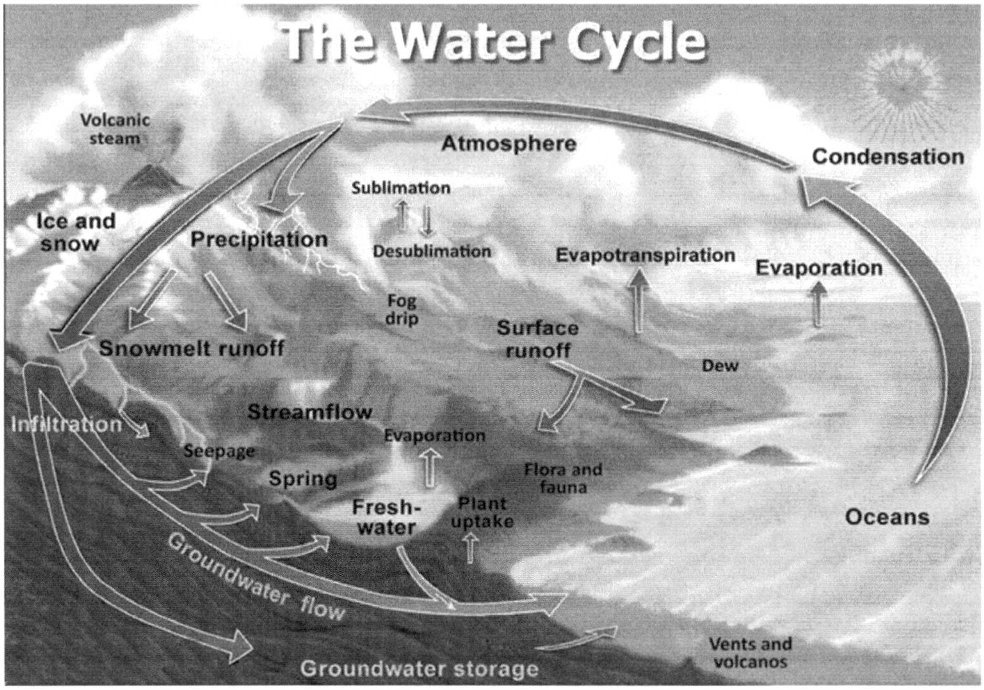

CARBON CYCLE

The **carbon cycle** is a biogeochemical cycle that describes the continuous movement of the Earth's carbon. Carbon is in the atmosphere, the soil, living organisms, fossil fuels, oceans, and freshwater systems. These areas are referred to as **carbon reservoirs**. Carbon flows between these reservoirs in an exchange called the carbon cycle. In the atmosphere, carbon is in the form of carbon dioxide. Carbon moves from the atmosphere to plants through the process of photosynthesis. Carbon moves from plants to animals through food chains, and then moves from living organisms to the soil when these organisms die. Carbon moves from living organisms to the atmosphere through cellular respiration. Carbon moves from fossil fuels to the atmosphere when fossil fuels are burned. Carbon moves from the atmosphere to the oceans and freshwater systems through absorption.

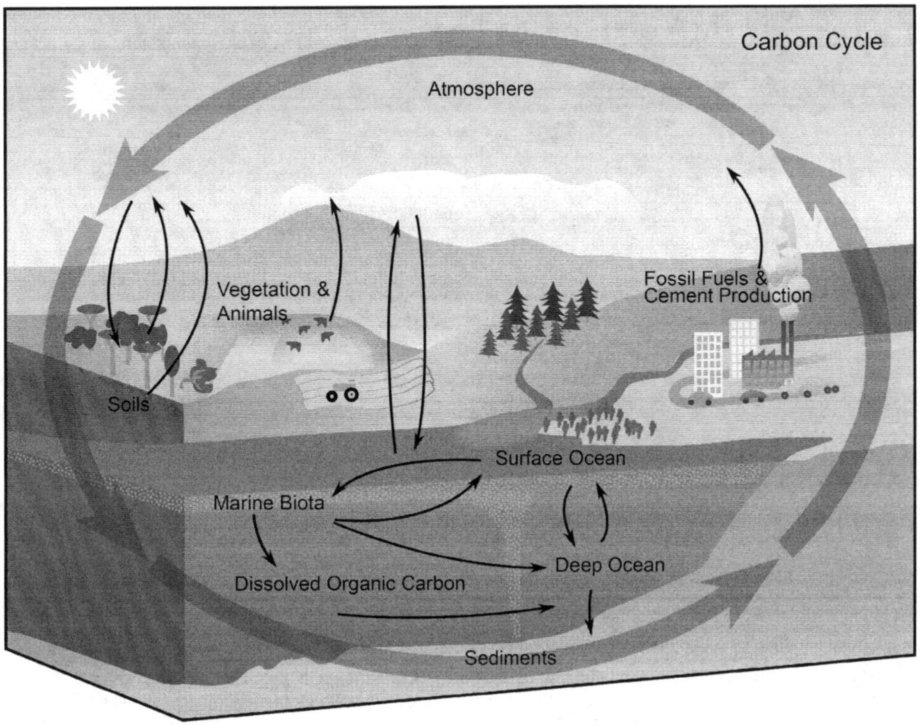

NITROGEN CYCLE

The **nitrogen cycle** is a biogeochemical cycle that describes the continuous movement of the Earth's nitrogen. Approximately 78% of the Earth's atmosphere consists of nitrogen in its elemental form N_2. Nitrogen is essential to the formation of proteins, but most organisms cannot use nitrogen in this form and require the nitrogen to be converted into some form of **nitrates**. Lightning can cause nitrates to form in the atmosphere, which can be carried to the soil by rain to be used by plants. Legumes have nitrogen-fixing bacteria in their roots, which can convert the N_2 to ammonia (NH_3). Nitrifying bacteria in the soil can also convert ammonia into nitrates. Plants absorb nitrates from the soil, and animals can consume the plants and other animals for protein. Denitrifying bacteria can convert unused nitrates back to nitrogen to be returned to the atmosphere.

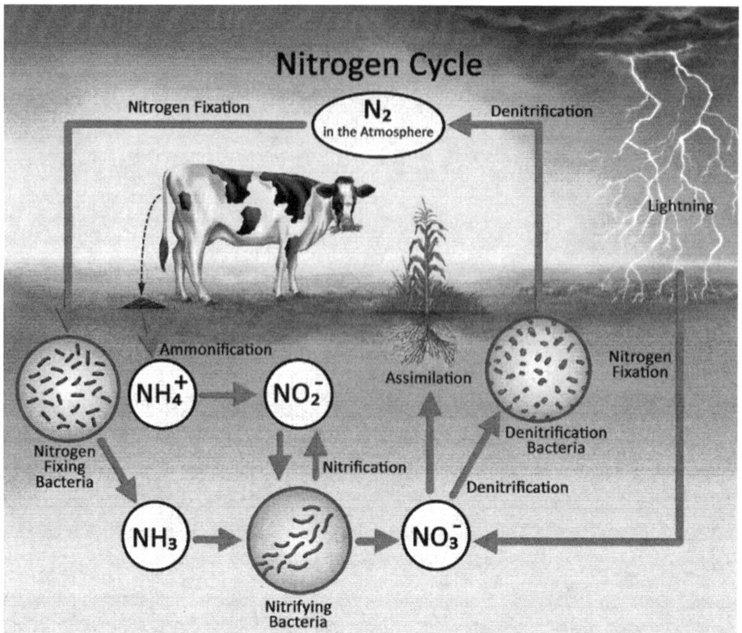

Phosphorus Cycle

The **phosphorus cycle** is a biogeochemical cycle that describes the continuous movement of the Earth's phosphorus. Phosphorus is found in rocks. When these rocks weather and erode, the phosphorus moves into the soil. The phosphorus found in the soil and rocks is in the form of phosphates or compounds with the PO_4^{3-} ion. When it rains, phosphates can be dissolved into the water. Plants are able to use phosphates from the soil. Plants need phosphorus for growth and development. Phosphorus is also a component of DNA, RNA, ATP, cell membranes, and bones. Plants and algae can absorb phosphate ions from the water and convert them into many organic compounds. Animals can get phosphorus by eating food or drinking water. When organisms die, the phosphorus is returned to the soil. This is the slowest of all biogeochemical cycles.

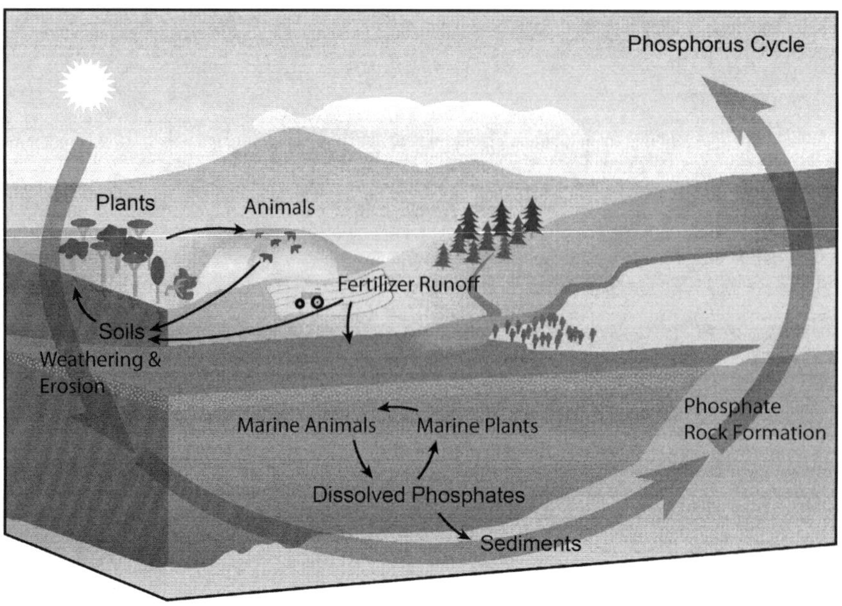

Effects of Natural Disturbances

Natural Disturbances That Affect Ecosystems

A **natural disturbance** is an event caused by nature, not human activity. Natural disturbances can be brought on by weather such as droughts, storms, wind, freezing, and fires from lightning. Other natural disturbances include earthquakes, volcanic eruptions, and diseases. Natural disturbances can disrupt or disturb the ecosystem in many ways, such as altering resources or removing individuals from the community. Natural disturbances can cover small regions, or they can affect an entire ecosystem. The effect may be long lasting and take several years to recover, or the effect may be minor and take only a few months to recover.

Effect of Fragmentation of Ecosystems on Biodiversity

Habitats can become fragmented due to natural disturbances such as fire, volcanic activity, and climate change. Some of the original habitat is destroyed during **fragmentation**, reducing the total area of the habitat. As a result, there may be insufficient food or other resources to support a species. The resulting habitats may also be reproductively isolated from each other, thus limiting genetic variation and biodiversity. Small fluctuations in resources or climate can be catastrophic in small populations. Larger populations may be able to overcome these fluctuations in variation.

Human Effect on Ecological Systems

Effects of Human Population on Ecological Systems and Biodiversity

Human population has been increasing at a near-exponential rate for the past 50 years. As the human population increases, the demand for resources such as food, water, land, and energy also increases. As the human population increases, the number of other species decreases due to habitat destruction, introduced species, and overhunting. The increased greenhouse gases and resulting climate changes have also significantly affected many ecosystems as temperatures rise and habitats are slowly changed or even destroyed. Increasing human population means increasing pollution, which harms habitats. Many animals have become extinct due to the effects of an exponentially increasing human population. High rates of extinction greatly reduce biodiversity.

Habitat Destruction by Humans on Ecological Systems and Biodiversity

Many habitats have been altered or destroyed by humans. In fact, habitat destruction brought about by human endeavors has been the most significant cause of species extinctions, which has resulted in the decrease in biodiversity throughout the world. As the human population has increased exponentially, the extinction rate has also increased exponentially. This is largely due to habitat destruction by humans. Humans use many resources in their agriculture, industry, mining, logging, and recreation. For example, humans have cleared much land for agriculture and urban development. As habitats are destroyed, species are either destroyed or displaced. Often, habitats are fragmented into smaller areas, which only allow for small populations that are under threat by predators, diseases, weather, and limited resources. Areas near the coastline are especially affected, including estuaries, coral reefs, wetlands, and mangrove forests. Nearly half of all mangrove ecosystems have been destroyed by human activity. Coral reefs have nearly been decimated from pollution such as oil spills and exploitation from the aquarium fish market and coral market.

Effects of Introduced Species on Ecological Systems and Biodiversity

Introduced species are species that are moved into new geographic regions by humans. They are also called invasive or nonnative species. Introduction can be intentional, such as the introduction of livestock, or unintentional, such as the introduction of Dutch elm disease. Introduced species can disrupt their new communities by using the limited resources and preying on other members of the community. Introduced species are often free from predators and can reproduce exponentially. This typically causes a decrease in biodiversity. Introduced species are contributors or even responsible for numerous extinctions. For example, zebra mussels, which are native to the Black Sea and the Caspian Sea, were accidentally introduced to the Great

Lakes. The zebra mussels greatly reduced the amount of plankton available for the native mussel species, many of which are now endangered.

Impact of Nonpoint Sources of Pollution on the Environment

Nonpoint-source pollution is the leading cause of water pollution in the United States. Nonpoint-source pollution is pollution that does not flow through a pipe, channel, or container. Most nonpoint-source pollution is due to agricultural runoff. Urban runoff from lawns, streets, and parking lots is also treated as nonpoint-source pollution because much of that storm water does not go into a storm drain before entering streams, rivers, lakes, or other bodies of water. Urban runoff contains chemicals such as lawn fertilizers, motor oils, grease, pesticides, soaps, and detergents, each of which is harmful to the environment.

Effects of Remediation on Ecological Systems and Biodiversity

In **remediation**, or land rehabilitation, environmental damages are reversed or stopped by attempting to restore land to its prior condition. Examples of remediation are reforestation and mine reclamation. Mining reclamation includes the backfilling of open-pit mines and covering ores containing sulfides to prevent rain from mixing with them to produce sulfuric acid. **Reforestation** is the restocking of forests and wetlands. This can at least partially offset the damaging effects brought about by the deforestation. Reforestation can help reduce global warming due to an increase in the absorption of light by the trees. Restoration can also help to restore the carbon cycle and counter erosion. Reforestation can help maintain or preserve the biodiversity of the region and possibly increase biodiversity if new organisms immigrate into the region.

Pollution Mitigation and the Clean Air Act

Pollution mitigation has greatly reduced pollution and its effects during the past 40 years. The **Clean Air Act** has reduced pollution by requiring that new industrial sites contain pollution-control technology. These technologies avoid or minimize the negative effects on the environment. For example, new coal-fired power plants are fitted with pollution-control devices that greatly reduce and nearly eliminate sulfur dioxide and nitrogen oxide emissions. This greatly reduces acid rain, improves water quality, and improves the overall health of ecosystems. Reducing acid rain improves soil quality, which in turn improves the health of producers, which consequently improves the health of consumers, essentially strengthening the entire ecosystem. Reduced greenhouse gas emissions have lessened the impact of global warming such as rising sea levels due to melting glaciers and the resulting loss of habitats and biodiversity. Reduced smog and haze improves the intensity of sunlight required for photosynthesis.

Resource Management

Resource management such as waste management and recycling greatly impacts the environment. **Waste management** is the monitoring, collection, transportation, and recycling of waste products. Well-managed landfills include using clay or another lining material to prevent liquid leachate and layers of soil on top to reduce odors and vermin. Wastes, including hazardous biomedical waste, can also be incinerated to reduce waste volume. However, incineration does emit pollutants and greenhouse gases. Proper waste management always includes recycling. **Recycling** is a method to recover resources. Recycled materials can be reprocessed into new products. Metals such as aluminum, copper, and steel are recycled. Plastics, glass, and paper products can also be recycled. In addition, organic materials such as plant materials and food scraps can be composted. The current trend is to shift from waste management to resource recovery. Wastes should be minimized and reduced to minimize the need for disposal. Unavoidable nonrecyclable wastes should be converted to energy by combustion if at all possible.

Impact of Global Warming, Rising Sea Levels, and Flooding on Society

Global warming caused largely by greenhouse gas emission will greatly affect society in the next several years. The increase in global temperature leads to more extreme levels of otherwise normal weather events such hurricanes, tornadoes, floods, and droughts. Rising temperatures cause weather patterns to shift, leading to even more floods and droughts. Rising temperatures mean a decrease in glaciers, sea ice, ice sheets, and snow cover, which contributes to rising sea levels. Rising sea levels lead to habitat change or loss, which greatly affects numerous species, but could also mean higher storm surges and related issues. Some motile species are already moving north to cooler climates. Earlier annual snowmelt and runoff may overwhelm water management systems.

Endangered Species Act

The **Endangered Species Act** (ESA) of 1973 has had a positive impact on many species. The law was designed to protect "imperiled species" from extinction due to factors such as loss of habitat, overhunting, and lack of conservation. The ESA also protects the species' ecosystems and removes threats to those ecosystems. If an animal is placed on the endangered or threatened list, it is prohibited to "harass, harm, pursue, hunt, shoot, wound, kill, trap, capture, or collect, or to attempt to engage in any such conduct" with the endangered animal. The populations of many imperiled species have increased significantly, including the whooping crane, the gray wolf, the red wolf, and the Hawaiian goose. Some species have even been removed from the endangered species list, including the bald eagle, the peregrine falcon, the gray whale, and the grizzly bear. The ESA has protected numerous species while balancing human economic needs and rights to private property.

National Park System

The purpose of the **National Park System** is to "conserve the scenery and the natural and historic objects and the wildlife therein and to provide for the enjoyment of the same in such manner and by such means as will leave them unimpaired for the enjoyment of future generations." The National Park System protects complete ecosystems and houses great biodiversity. National parks are an integral part of the survival of many species. National parks provide a home to hundreds of endangered or threatened species. Studies show that preserved habitats near national parks help many species better survive with the resources they need. This will prevent fragmentation and further habitat loss. Nevertheless, National parks may be threatened by invasion species or pressure for use of land along park boundaries. Biodiversity is threatened even within national parks. Even though many are vast, they are often not large enough to support a species population on their own.

Effects of Extraction of Minerals and Oil Drilling

The extraction of mineral and energy resources by mining and drilling has harmful effects on the environment including pollution and alterations to ecosystems. **Mining** often requires large amounts of deforestation, which harms habitats and affects biodiversity. Mining also causes water pollution. Toxic chemicals such as mercury and sulfuric acid are used in the mining process and are released into bodies of water, harming the aquatic life. If these toxic chemicals are leaked, the ground water is polluted. Rainwater mixes with the heavy metals in mines and produces an acid runoff that harms aquatic life, birds, and mammals. The pollution is especially bad in countries without proper mining regulations. Open-pit mines and mountaintop removal techniques are especially harsh to the environment, and reclamation is often not regulated in developing countries. Oil drilling is controversial due to habitat disruption or loss as well as the potential of an oil spill occurring. Oil spills are toxic to wildlife and difficult to clean up. Offshore drilling uses seismic waves to locate oil, which disturbs whales and dolphins and has been tied to hundreds of beached whales.

Sustainable Agriculture

The management of natural resources and the renewability or **sustainability** of those natural resources greatly impact society. Sustainable agriculture involves growing foods in economical ways that do not harm resources. If left unchecked, farming can deplete the soil of valuable nutrients. Crops grown in these depleted soils are less healthy and more susceptible to disease. Sustainable agriculture uses more effective pest control such as insect-resistant corn, which reduces runoff and water pollution in the surrounding area. Sustainable forestry involves replenishing trees as trees are being harvested, which maintains the environment.

Renewable and Nonrenewable Energy Resources

Energy sources such as wind, solar power, and biomass energy are all **renewable**. Wind power is clean with no pollution and no greenhouse gas emissions. Disadvantages of wind power include the use of land for wind farms, threats to birds, and the expense to build. Solar power has no greenhouse gas emissions, but some toxic metal wastes result in the production of photovoltaic cells, and solar power requires large areas of land.

Biomass energy is sustainable, but its combustion produces greenhouse emissions. Farming biomass requires large areas of land. Fossil fuels, which are **nonrenewable**, cause substantially more air pollution and greenhouse gas emissions, contributing to habitat loss and global warming.

Review Video: Renewable and Nonrenewable Resources
Visit mometrix.com/academy and enter code: 840194

Global and Local Ecology

Flow of Biotic Material Between Ecosystems

Various events can cause the **flow of materials and energy** from one ecosystem to another. In this sense, the local ecosystem is related to the global ecosystem. Both biotic and abiotic elements of an ecosystem can flow into another environment. **Abiotic factors** move through natural processes, such as erosion and deposition of sediment and transportation of those materials by rivers and weather systems. Harvesting of materials such as water, natural gas, and trees also plays a large role, as many materials used for building and survival and may be transported from one ecosystem to another. Plants are often moved through similar processes, whether by harvesting and planting by humans, or by passive systems of seed dispersal through rivers and animals. Animal movement is usually referred to as **migration**, and it is primarily driven by the pursuit of food, safety from predators and harsh environmental conditions, and reproductive opportunity. Ecosystems function through the interaction and balance of biotic and abiotic factors, such as competition and predation and reliance on water supply. As biotic and abiotic factors constantly flow from one local ecosystem to another, the balance has to shift constantly to accommodate ecological change on a global scale.

Chapter Quiz

Ready to see how well you retained what you just read? Scan the QR code to go directly to the chapter quiz interface for this study guide. If you're using a computer, simply visit the online resources page at **mometrix.com/resources719/abctebio** and click the Chapter Quizzes link.

ABCTE Biology Practice Test

Want to take this practice test in an online interactive format?
Check out the online resources page, which includes interactive practice questions and much more: **mometrix.com/resources719/abctebio**

Molecular and Cellular Biology

1. How do the hydrogen bonds in water affect its characteristics?

a. Hydrogen bonds are so polar that they can attract non-polar molecules.
b. Hydrogen bonds cause water to be denser when it is a solid than when it is a liquid.
c. Hydrogen bonds cause water to have a high enough surface tension that some organisms can move across it.
d. Hydrogen bonds cause water to be a poor solvent.
e. Hydrogen bonds make water an excellent buffer.

2. The breakdown of a disaccharide releases energy, which is stored as ATP. This is an example of a(n):

a. Combination reaction
b. Replacement reaction
c. Endothermic reaction
d. Exothermic reaction
e. Thermodynamic reaction

3. Which of the following metabolic compounds is composed of only carbon, oxygen, and hydrogen?

a. Phospholipids
b. Glycogen
c. Peptides
d. RNA
e. Amino acids

4. When an animal takes in more energy than it uses over an extended time, the extra chemical energy is stored as:

a. Fat
b. Starch
c. Protein
d. Enzymes
e. Cholesterol

5. Which of the following molecules is thought to have acted as the first enzyme in early life on earth?

a. Protein
b. RNA
c. DNA
d. Triglycerides
e. Phospholipids

6. Which of the following are formed when the plasma membrane surrounds a particle outside of the cell?

a. Golgi bodies
b. Rough endoplasmic reticulum
c. Lysosomes
d. Endocytic vesicles

7. Which of the following plant organelles contain the pigment that gives green leaves their color?

a. Centrioles
b. Cell walls
c. Chloroplasts
d. Central vacuole
e. Golgi apparatus

8. All but which of the following processes are ways of moving solutes across a plasma membrane?

a. Osmosis
b. Passive transport
c. Active transport
d. Facilitated diffusion
e. Endocytosis

9. Prokaryotic and eukaryotic cells are similar in having which of the following?

a. Membrane-bound organelles
b. Protein-studded DNA
c. Presence of a nucleus
d. Integral membrane proteins in the plasma membrane
e. Flagella composed of microtubules

10. Which of the following cell types has a peptidoglycan cell wall?

a. Algae
b. Bacteria
c. Fungi
d. Land plants
e. Protists

11. Enzymes catalyze biochemical reactions by

a. Lowering the potential energy of the products
b. Separating inhibitors from products
c. Forming a complex with the products
d. Lowering the activation energy of the reaction
e. Providing energy to the reaction

12. Which of the following is an example of a cofactor?

a. Zinc
b. Actin
c. Cholesterol
d. GTP
e. Chlorophyll

13. Cyanide is a poison that binds to the active site of the enzyme cytochrome c oxidase and prevents its activity. Cyanide is a(n)

a. Prosthetic group
b. Cofactor
c. Coenzyme
d. Inhibitor
e. Reverse regulator

14. The graph below shows the potential energy of molecules during the process of a chemical reaction. All of the following may be true EXCEPT

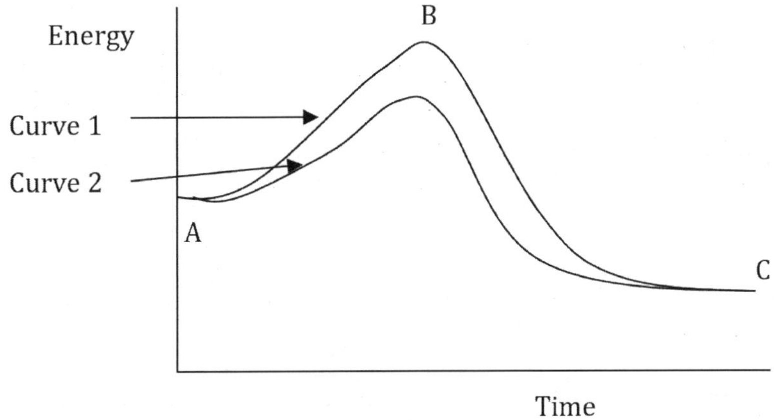

a. This is an endergonic reaction
b. The activation energy in curve 2 is less than the activation energy in curve 1
c. The energy of the products is less than the energy of the substrate
d. Curve 2 shows the reaction in the presence of an enzyme
e. The reaction required ATP

15. Which of the following is NOT a characteristic of enzymes?

a. They change shape when they bind their substrates.
b. They can catalyze reactions in both forward and reverse directions.
c. Their activity is sensitive to changes in temperature.
d. They are always active on more than one kind of substrate.
e. They may have more than one binding site.

16. In a strenuously exercising muscle, NADH begins to accumulate in high concentration. Which of the following metabolic processes will be activated to reduce the concentration of NADH?

a. Glycolysis
b. The Krebs cycle
c. Lactic acid fermentation
d. Oxidative phosphorylation
e. Acetyl CoA synthesis

17. Which of the following statements regarding chemiosmosis in mitochondria is NOT correct?

a. ATP synthase is powered by protons flowing through membrane channels.
b. Energy from ATP is used to transport protons to the intermembrane space.
c. Energy from the electron transport chain is used to transport protons to the intermembrane space.
d. An electrical gradient and a pH gradient both exist across the inner membrane.
e. The waste product of chemiosmosis is water.

18. In photosynthesis, high-energy electrons move through electron transport chains to produce ATP and NADPH. Which of the following provides the energy to create high energy electrons?

a. NADH
b. $NADP^+$
c. O_2
d. Water
e. Light

19. Which of the following kinds of plants is most likely to perform CAM photosynthesis?

a. Mosses
b. Grasses
c. Deciduous trees
d. Cacti
e. Legumes

20. The combination of DNA with histones is called

a. A centromere
b. Chromatin
c. A chromatid
d. Nucleoli
e. A plasmid

21. How many chromosomes does a human cell have after meiosis I?

a. 92
b. 46
c. 23
d. 22
e. 12

22. In plants and animals, genetic variation is introduced during

a. Crossing over in mitosis
b. Chromosome segregation in mitosis
c. Cytokinesis of meiosis
d. Prophase I of meiosis
e. Anaphase II of meiosis

23. DNA replication occurs during which of the following phases?

a. Prophase I
b. Prophase II
c. Interphase I
d. Interphase II
e. Telophase I

24. The synaptonemal complex is present in which of the following phases of the cell cycle?

a. Metaphase of mitosis
b. Prophase of meiosis I
c. Metaphase of meiosis I
d. Prophase of meiosis II
e. Anaphase of meiosis II

25. A length of DNA coding for a particular protein is called a(n)

a. Allele
b. Genome
c. Gene
d. Transcript
e. Codon

26. In DNA replication, which of the following enzymes is required for separating the DNA molecule into two strands?

a. DNA polymerase
b. Single-strand binding protein
c. DNA gyrase
d. Helicase
e. Primase

27. Which of the following chemical moieties forms the backbone of DNA?

a. Nitrogenous bases
b. Glycerol
c. Amino groups
d. Pentose and phosphate
e. Glucose and phosphate

28. Which of the following is required for the activity of DNA polymerase?

a. Okazaki fragments
b. RNA primer
c. Single-strand binding protein
d. Leading strand
e. Replication fork

29. Which of the following is the substrate for DNA ligase?

a. Okazaki fragments
b. RNA primer
c. Single-strand binding protein
d. Leading strand
e. Replication fork

30. Which of the following is true of the enzyme telomerase?

a. It is active on the leading strand during DNA synthesis
b. It requires a chromosomal DNA template
c. It acts in the $3' \rightarrow 5'$ direction
d. It adds a repetitive DNA sequence to the end of chromosomes
e. It takes the place of primase at the ends of chromosomes

31. Which enzyme in DNA replication is a potential source of new mutations?

a. DNA ligase
b. Primase
c. DNA gyrase
d. DNA polymerase
e. Topoisomerase

32. Which of the following mutations is most likely to have a dramatic effect on the sequence of a protein?

a. A point mutation
b. A missense mutation
c. A deletion
d. A silent mutation
e. A proofreading mutation

33. Which of the following could be an end product of transcription?

a. rRNA
b. DNA
c. Protein
d. snRNP
e. Amino acids

34. The *lac* operon controls

a. Conjugation between bacteria
b. Chromatin organization
c. Gene transcription
d. Excision repair
e. Termination of translation

35. All of the following are common ways of controlling eukaryotic gene expression EXCEPT

a. Regulatory proteins
b. Nucleosome packing
c. Methylation of DNA
d. RNA interference
e. Operons

36. Transfer of DNA between bacteria using a narrow tube called a pilus is known as:

a. Transformation
b. Transduction
c. Operation
d. Conjugation
e. Conformation

37. A virus that has incorporated into the DNA of its host

a. Lysogenic cycle
b. Lytic cycle
c. Retrovirus
d. Provirus
e. Bacteriophage

38. A virus is actively replicating DNA in what stage?

a. Lysogenic cycle
b. Lytic cycle
c. Retrovirus
d. Provirus
e. Bacteriophage

39. A bacterial mini-chromosome used in recombinant DNA technology is called a

a. Centromere
b. Telomere
c. Plasmid
d. Transposon
e. cDNA

Organismal Biology

40. Which of the following parts of an angiosperm gives rise to the fruit?

a. Pedicel
b. Filament
c. Sepal
d. Ovary
e. Meristem

41. Which of the following structures is NOT present in gymnosperms?

a. Leaves
b. Pollen
c. Flowers
d. Stomata
e. Roots

42. Which of the following plant structures allows for gas exchange?

a. Xylem
b. Phloem
c. Cuticle
d. Meristem
e. Stomata

43. Which type of plant has leaves with parallel veins?

a. Monocots
b. Dicots
c. Angiosperms
d. Gymnosperms
e. Nonvascular plants

44. Which type of plant does NOT produce seeds?

a. Monocots
b. Dicots
c. Angiosperms
d. Gymnosperms
e. Nonvascular plants

45. Which type of plant produces seeds that are housed inside a fruit?

a. Monocots
b. Dicots
c. Angiosperms
d. Gymnosperms
e. Nonvascular plants

46. Which structure of a tree contains tissue that is dead at maturity?

a. Heartwood
b. Sapwood
c. Cork cambium
d. Phloem (inner bark)
e. Roots

Refer to the following for question 47:

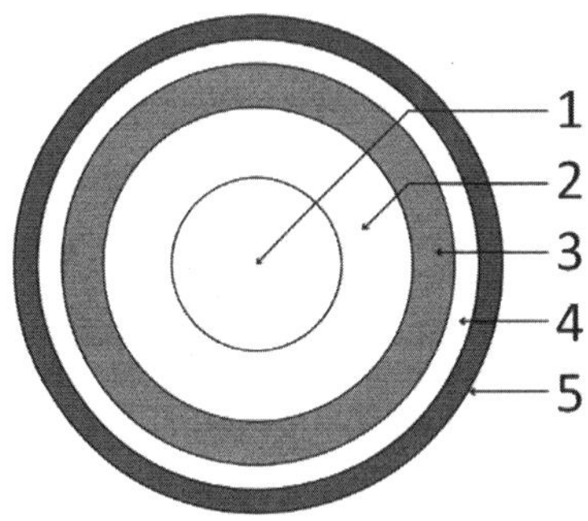

47. Which structure transports carbohydrates to the roots?

a. 1
b. 2
c. 3
d. 4
e. 5

48. In ferns, the joining of egg and sperm produces a zygote, which will grow into the

a. Gametophyte
b. Sporophyte
c. Spore
d. Sporangium
e. Seedling

49. Which of the following is an example of the alternation of generations life cycle?

a. Asexual reproduction of strawberries by runners
b. Annual plants that live through a single growing season
c. Ferns that have a large diploid and a diminutive haploid stage
d. Insects that have distinct larval and adult stages
e. Reptiles that have long periods of dormancy and metabolic inactivity

Refer to the following for questions 50–51:

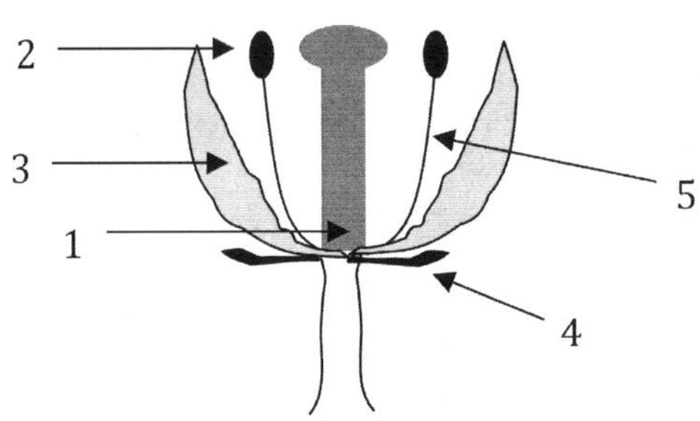

50. The structure in which microspores are produced is:

a. 1
b. 2
c. 3
d. 4
e. 5

51. The structures composed solely of diploid cells are:

a. 1, 2, and 3
b. 2, 3, and 4
c. 3, 4, and 5
d. 1, 4, and 5
e. 1, 2, and 4

52. Auxins are plant hormones that are involved in all but which of the following processes?

a. Fruit ripening
b. Gravitropism
c. Growth
d. Phototropism
e. Seed germination

53. Which of the following plant hormones is most likely to delay aging when sprayed on cut flowers and fruit?

a. Ethylene
b. Gibberellins
c. Cytokinins
d. Abscisic acid
e. Jasmonic acid

54. Which of the following would most likely be disruptive to the flowering time of a day-neutral plant?

a. Daylight interrupted by a brief dark period
b. Daylight interrupted by a long dark period
c. High daytime temperatures
d. Night interrupted by a brief exposure to red light
e. Night interrupted by a long exposure to red light

55. Animals exchange gases with the environment in all of the following ways EXCEPT

a. Direct exchange through the skin
b. Exchange through gills
c. Stomata
d. Tracheae
e. Lungs

56. Which of the following blood components is involved in blood clotting?

a. Red blood cells
b. Platelets
c. White blood cells
d. Leukocytes
e. Plasma

57. Which section of the digestive system is responsible for water reabsorption?

a. The large intestine
b. The duodenum
c. The small intestine
d. The gallbladder
e. The stomach

58. When Ca^{2+} channels open in a presynaptic cell

a. The cell depolarizes
b. The cell hyperpolarizes
c. An action potential is propagated
d. Synaptic vesicles release neurotransmitter
e. The nerve signal is propagated by salutatory conduction

59. Which of the following processes is an example of positive feedback?

a. High CO_2 blood levels stimulate respiration which decreases blood CO_2 levels
b. High blood glucose levels stimulate insulin release, which makes muscle and liver cells take in glucose
c. Increased nursing stimulates increased milk production in mammary glands
d. Low blood oxygen levels stimulate erythropoietin production which increases red blood cell production by bone marrow
e. Low blood calcium levels stimulate parathyroid hormone release from the parathyroid gland. Parathyroid hormone stimulates calcium release from bones.

60. Which of the following would be the most likely means of thermoregulation for a mammal in a cold environment?

a. Adjusting body surface area
b. Sweating
c. Countercurrent exchange
d. Muscle contractions
e. Increased blood flow to extremities

61. Which hormone is *not* secreted by a gland in the brain?

a. Human chorionic gonadotropin (hCG)
b. Gonadotropin-releasing hormone (GnRH)
c. Luteinizing hormone (LH)
d. Follicle-stimulating hormone (FSH)
e. None of these

62. Which hormone is secreted consistently by the placenta throughout pregnancy once established?

a. Human chorionic gonadotropin (hCG)
b. Gonadotropin-releasing hormone (GnRH)
c. Luteinizing hormone (LH)
d. Follicle-stimulating hormone (FSH)
e. Progesterone

63. Polar bodies are a by-product of

a. Meiosis I
b. Meiosis II
c. Both meiosis I and II
d. Zygote formation
e. Mitosis of the morula

64. Which of the following hormones triggers ovulation in females?

a. Estrogen
b. Progesterone
c. Serotonin
d. Luteinizing hormone
e. Testosterone

65. Spermatogenesis occurs in the

a. Prostate gland
b. Vas deferens
c. Seminal vesicles
d. Penis
e. Seminiferous tubules

66. In which of the following stages of embryo development are the three primary germ layers first present?

a. Zygote
b. Gastrula
c. Morula
d. Blastula
e. Coelomate

67. Which of the following extraembryonic membranes is an important source of nutrition in many nonhuman animal species but NOT in humans?

a. Amnion
b. Allantois
c. Yolk sac
d. Chorion
e. Placenta

68. Which of the following is NOT a mechanism that contributes to cell differentiation and development in embryos?

a. Asymmetrical cell division
b. Asymmetrical cytoplasm distribution
c. Organizer cells
d. Location of cells on the lineage map
e. Homeotic genes

69. Which of the following is true of the gastrula?

a. It is a solid ball of cells.
b. It has three germ layers.
c. It is an extraembryonic membrane.
d. It gives rise to the blastula.
e. It derives from the zona pellucida.

70. In birds, gastrulation occurs along the

a. Dorsal lip of the embryo
b. Embryonic disc
c. Primitive streak
d. Circular blastopore
e. Inner cell mass

71. In snapdragons, the red (R) allele is incompletely dominant to the white (r) allele. If you saw a pink snapdragon, you would know:

a. Its phenotypes for both parents
b. Its genotypes for both parents
c. Its genotype for one parent
d. Its genotype
e. Its phenotype but not its genotype

72. In peas, purple flower color (P) is dominant to white (p) and tall stature (T) is dominant to dwarf (t). If the genes are unlinked, how many tall plants will be purple in the progeny of a $PpTt \times PpTT$ cross?

a. 0
b. $\frac{1}{4}$
c. $\frac{1}{2}$
d. $\frac{3}{4}$
e. 1

73. Which of the following does NOT obey the law of independent assortment?

a. Two genes on opposite ends of a chromosome
b. Flower color and height in snapdragons
c. Two genes on separate chromosomes
d. Seed color and flower color in peas
e. Two genes next to each other on a chromosome

74. In a dihybrid cross between bean plants with red (R) wrinkled (w) seeds and white (r) smooth (W) seeds, the F1 progeny is all red and smooth. If the F1 plants are selfed, what proportion of the F2 will also be red and smooth if the genes are linked?

a. All of them
b. $\frac{1}{4}$
c. $\frac{1}{2}$
d. $\frac{9}{16}$
e. None of them

75. Red-green color blindness is an X-linked trait. If a mother is heterozygous for this trait and a father has this trait, what is the probability that their child will have this trait?

a. 0
b. $\frac{1}{4}$
c. $\frac{1}{2}$
d. $\frac{3}{4}$
e. 1

76. An individual with an AB blood type needs a blood transfusion. Which of the following types could NOT be a donor?

a. O
b. AB
c. A
d. B
e. All of the above types can be donors

77. In humans, more than one gene contributes to the trait of hair color. What is this an example of?

a. Pleiotropy
b. Polygenic inheritance
c. Codominance
d. Linkage
e. Epistasis

78. A child is born with type A blood and his mother has type A. Which of the following is a possible combination of genotypes for the mother and father?

a. I^AI^B and ii
b. I^Ai and ii
c. I^AI^A and I^BI^B
d. I^Ai and I^BI^B
e. I^AI^B and I^Bi

Population Biology

79. Which of the following ecosystems is most likely to have an inverted biomass pyramid?

a. Forest ecosystem
b. Tundra ecosystem
c. Desert ecosystem
d. Aquatic ecosystem
e. Grassland ecosystem

80. In the food chain below, what do vultures represent?

$$grass \rightarrow cow \rightarrow wolf \rightarrow vulture$$

a. Scavengers
b. Detritivores
c. Primary carnivores
d. Herbivores
e. Secondary consumers

81. Which of the following is the major way in which carbon is released into the environment?

a. Transpiration
b. Respiration
c. Fixation
d. Sedimentation
e. Absorption

82. What is the largest reservoir of nitrogen on the planet?

a. The ocean
b. Plants
c. Soil
d. The atmosphere
e. Sediments, including fossil fuels

83. The diagram below represents the three types of survivorship curves, describing how mortality varies as species age. Which of the following species is most likely to exhibit Type I survivorship?

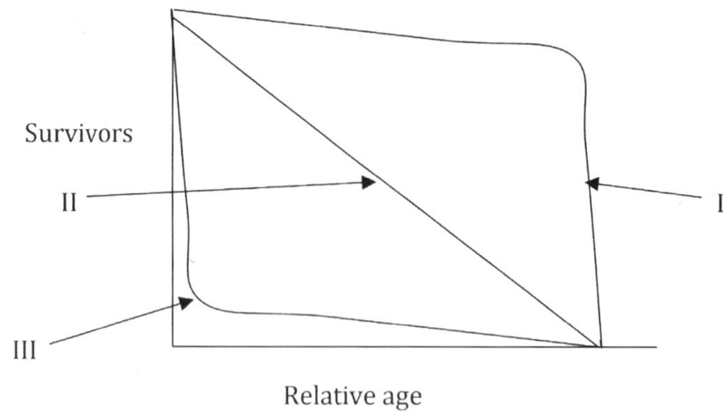

a. Frogs
b. Oysters
c. Salmon
d. Dolphins
e. Shrimp

84. A population of 1,000 individuals has 110 births and 10 deaths in a year. Its growth rate (r) is equal to

a. 0.01 per year
b. 0.1 per year
c. 0.09 per year
d. 0.11 per year
e. 0.009 per year

85. During primary succession, which species would most likely be a pioneer species?

a. Lichens
b. Fir trees
c. Mosquitoes
d. Dragonflies
e. Mushrooms

86. Which of the following habitats would provide an opportunity for secondary succession?

a. A retreating glacier
b. Burned cropland
c. A newly formed volcanic island
d. A 500-year-old forest
e. A sand dune

87. Which biome is most likely to support the growth of epiphytes?

a. Deserts
b. Tropical rain forests
c. Temperate deciduous forests
d. Taigas
e. Savannas

88. Which of the following is NOT a natural dispersal process that would lead to species colonization on an island?

a. Mussels carried into a lake on the hull of a ship
b. Drought connecting an island to other land
c. Floating seeds
d. Animals swimming long distances
e. Birds adapted to flying long distances

89. When a population reaches its carrying capacity:

a. Other populations will be forced out of the habitat
b. Density-dependent factors no longer play a role
c. Density-independent factors no longer play a role
d. The population growth rate approaches zero
e. The population size begins to decrease

90. Which of the following is an example of a density-dependent limiting factor?

a. Air pollution by a factory
b. The toxic effect of waste products
c. Nearby volcanic eruptions
d. Frosts
e. Fires

91. Two species of finches are able to utilize the same food supply, but their beaks are different. They are able to coexist on an island because of

a. Niche overlap
b. Character displacement
c. Resource partitioning
d. Competitive exclusion
e. Realized niches

92. Lichens consist of fungi and algae. The algae supply sugars through performing photosynthesis while the fungi provide minerals and a place to attach. This is an example of

a. Mutualism
b. Commensalism
c. Parasitism
d. Coevolution
e. Resource partitioning

93. Which of the following of Lamarck's evolutionary ideas turned out to be true?

a. Natural selection
b. Organisms naturally transform into increasingly complex organisms
c. Inheritance of acquired characters
d. Body parts develop with increased usage and weaken with disuse
e. Genes are the basic units of inheritance

94. The weight of adult wolves is within a fairly narrow range, even if they are well-fed in zoos. This is an example of

a. Stabilizing selection
b. Directional selection
c. Disruptive selection
d. Sexual selection
e. Artificial selection

95. Which of the following is a trait that results from disruptive selection?

a. Insecticide resistance
b. Only male peacocks having colorful plumage
c. Some birds having significantly large bills than others within the same species
d. Human height
e. Different varieties of wheat

96. Which of the following conditions would promote evolutionary change?

a. Gene flow
b. No selection
c. Random mating
d. A large population

97. Which of the following would create the greatest amount of genetic variation for a diploid species in a single generation?

a. Crossing over
b. Mutation
c. Hybridization
d. Independent assortment of homologs
e. Random joining of gametes

98. A population of pea plants has 25% dwarf plants and 75% tall plants. The tall allele, T is dominant to the dwarf allele, t. What is the frequency of the T allele?

a. 0.75
b. 0.67
c. 0.5
d. 0.25
e. 0.16

99. Darwin's idea that evolution occurs by the gradual accumulation of small changes can be described as:

a. Punctuated equilibrium
b. Phyletic gradualism
c. Convergent evolution
d. Adaptive radiation
e. Sympatric speciation

100. Which of the following processes of speciation would most likely occur if a species of bird were introduced into a group of islands that were previously uninhabited by animals?

a. Allopatric speciation
b. Adaptive radiation
c. Sympatric speciation
d. Artificial speciation
e. Hybridizing speciation

101. Hummingbirds drink nectar from *Ipomopsis* flowers. *Ipomopsis* are trumpet-shaped, and hummingbirds have long narrow beaks to access the nectar. These adaptations could best be described as

a. Divergent evolution
b. Convergent evolution
c. Parallel evolution
d. Coevolution
e. Macroevolution

102. All of the following are homologous structures EXCEPT

a. Bird feathers
b. Elephant eyelashes
c. Human fingernails
d. Dog fur
e. Insect exoskeleton

103. Human predation has cause the population of cheetahs to decline dramatically. Changes in allele frequencies in the remaining population of cheetahs would most likely be due to

a. Mutation
b. The bottleneck effect
c. The founder effect
d. Gene flow
e. Natural selection

104. The first living cells on earth were most likely

a. Heterotrophs
b. Autotrophs
c. Aerobic
d. Eukaryotes
e. Photosynthetic

105. Evidence that humans share a common ancestor with other primates includes all of the following EXCEPT

a. DNA sequence
b. Fossil evidence of intermediate species
c. Analogous structures
d. Homologous structures
e. Radiometric dating of fossils

106. Sea anemones pull food into their mouths by withdrawing their tentacles. If the tentacles are stimulated with a non-food item, they will ignore the stimulus after a few futile attempts to capture the food. This is known as which of the following?

a. Associative learning
b. Imprinting
c. Habituation
d. Chemical communication
e. Territoriality

107. Queen bees secrete pheromones that are eaten by workers and prevent the workers from being able to reproduce. This is known as which of the following?

a. Associative learning
b. Imprinting
c. Habituation
d. Chemical communication
e. Territoriality

108. Salmon hatch in freshwater streams and then migrate to the ocean to mature. When they are mature, they swim upstream to their birthplace to spawn. This is known as which of the following?

a. Associative learning
b. Imprinting
c. Habituation
d. Chemical communication
e. Territoriality

109. The species *Homo sapiens* first appeared in the fossil record approximately

a. 10 million years ago
b. 1 million years ago
c. 100,000 years ago
d. 10,000 years ago
e. 6,000 years ago

110. Which of the following demographic changes would lead to a population with an older age composition?

a. Increased birth rate
b. Environmental pollution
c. Increased availability of food
d. Medical advancements that increase life expectancy
e. Introduction of contraceptives

111. Which of the following factors has the greatest impact on birth rate in humans?

a. The carrying capacity of the earth
b. Age at reproductive maturity
c. Reproductive lifetime
d. Survivorship of offspring to reproductive maturity
e. Socioeconomic factors

112. Which of the following organisms is likely to have the greatest quantity of mercury in its body?

a. Mosquitoes
b. Carnivorous insects
c. Frogs
d. Filter-feeding fish
e. Fish-eating birds

113. Which of the following consequences is NOT a direct result of clear-cutting rain forests?

a. Climate change
b. Erosion
c. Reduction in species diversity
d. Air pollution
e. Desertification

114. Burning fossil fuels releases sulfur dioxide and nitrogen dioxide. These pollutants lead to which environmental problem?

a. Denitrification
b. Acid rain
c. Global climate change
d. Ozone depletion
e. Eutrophication

115. Genetic engineering:

a. Is a form of human reproduction
b. Always involves using restriction enzymes to cut DNA
c. Often involves transient expression of genes
d. Always involves introducing new proteins to a cell
e. Often involves using nucleases to cut DNA

Answer Key and Explanations

Molecular and Cellular Biology

1. C: Hydrogen bonds are a special type of dipole-dipole interaction between molecules that causes a strong attraction (negative dipole to positive dipole). This interaction gives water such a high surface tension that some small organisms, such as water striders, can move across its surface. Although water molecules are polar, they do not attract non-polar molecules, such as fats or oils. Thus, choice A is incorrect. Solid water is less dense than liquid water, which is why ice floats in water and why choice B is incorrect. Choice D is incorrect because water is generally a very good solvent, especially for substances whose molecules have polar or ionic bonds. Choice E is incorrect because water cannot produce more of either H^+ or OH^-, since both would be made in equal amounts from H_2O, making it a terrible buffer.

2. D: An exothermic reaction releases energy, whereas an endothermic reaction requires energy. The breakdown of a chemical compound is an example of a decomposition reaction ($AB \rightarrow A + B$). A combination reaction ($A + B \rightarrow AB$) is the reverse of a decomposition reaction, and a replacement (displacement) reaction is one where a compound breaks apart and forms a new compound plus a free reactant ($AB + C \rightarrow AC + B$ or $AB + CD \rightarrow AD + CB$).

3. B: Glycogen is a polysaccharide, a molecule composed of many bonded glucose molecules. Glucose is a carbohydrate, and most simple carbohydrates are composed of only carbon, oxygen, and hydrogen. Most other metabolic compounds contain other atoms, particularly nitrogen, phosphorus, and sulfur.

4. A: Long-term energy storage in animals takes the form of fat. Animals also store energy as glycogen, and plants store energy as starch, but these substances are for shorter-term use. Fats are a good storage form for chemical energy because fatty acids bond to glycerol in a condensation reaction to form fats (triglycerides). This reaction, which releases water, allows for the compacting of high-energy fatty acids in a concentrated form.

5. B: Some RNA molecules in extant organisms have enzymatic activity; for example, the formation of peptide bonds on ribosomes is catalyzed by an RNA molecule. This and other information have led scientists to believe that the most likely molecules to first demonstrate enzymatic activity were RNA molecules.

6. D: Endocytosis is a process by which cells absorb larger molecules (or even tiny organisms, such as bacteria) than would be able to pass through the plasma membrane. Endocytic vesicles containing molecules from the extracellular environment often undergo further processing once they enter the cell.

7. C: Chloroplasts contain the light-absorbing compound chlorophyll, which is essential in photosynthesis. This gives leaves their green color. Chloroplasts also contain yellow and red carotenoid pigments, which give leaves red and yellow colors in the fall as chloroplasts lose their chlorophyll.

8. A: Osmosis is the movement of water molecules (not solutes) across a semi-permeable membrane. Water moves from a region of higher concentration to a region of lower concentration. Osmosis occurs when the concentrations of a solute differ on either side of a semi-permeable membrane. For example, a cell (containing a higher concentration of water) in a salty solution (containing a lower concentration of water) will lose water as water leaves the cell. This continues until the solution outside the cell has the same salt concentration as the cytoplasm.

9. D: Both prokaryotes and eukaryotes interact with the extracellular environment and use membrane-bound or membrane-associated proteins to achieve this. They both use diffusion and active transport to move materials in and out of their cells. Prokaryotes have very few proteins associated with their DNA, whereas eukaryotes' DNA is richly studded with proteins. Both types of living things can have flagella, although with different structural characteristics in the two groups. The most important differences between prokaryotes and eukaryotes are the lack of a nucleus and membrane-bound organelles in prokaryotes.

10. B: Bacteria and cyanobacteria have cell walls constructed from peptidoglycans—a polysaccharide and protein molecule. Other types of organisms with cell walls, for instance, plants and fungi, have cell walls composed of different polysaccharides. Plant cell walls are composed of cellulose, and fungal cell walls are composed of chitin.

11. D: Enzymes act as catalysts for biochemical reactions. A catalyst is not consumed in a reaction, but rather lowers the activation energy for that reaction. The potential energy of the substrate and the product remain the same, but the activation energy—the energy needed to make the reaction progress—can be lowered with the help of an enzyme.

12. A: A cofactor is an inorganic substance that is required for an enzymatic reaction to occur. Cofactors bind to the active site of the enzyme and enable the substrate to fit properly. Many cofactors are metal ions, such as zinc, iron, and copper.

13. D: Enzyme inhibitors attach to an enzyme and block substrates from entering the active site, thereby preventing enzyme activity. Cyanide irreversibly binds to the enzyme cytochrome c oxidase and blocks its active site. Cyanide therefore fits the definition of an enzyme inhibitor.

14. A: Because the energy of the products is less than the energy of the substrate, the reaction releases energy and is an exergonic reaction.

15. D: Enzymes are substrate-specific. Most enzymes catalyze only one biochemical reaction. Their active sites are specific for a certain type of substrate and do not bind to other substrates and catalyze other reactions.

16. C: Lactic acid fermentation converts pyruvate into lactate using high-energy electrons from NADH. This process allows ATP production to continue in anaerobic conditions by providing NAD^+ so that ATP can be made in glycolysis.

17. B: Proteins in the inner membrane of the mitochondrion accept high-energy electrons from NAD and $FADH_2$, and in turn transport protons from the matrix to the intermembrane space. The high proton concentration in the intermembrane space creates a gradient, which is harnessed by ATP synthase to produce ATP.

18. E: Electrons trapped by the chlorophyll P680 molecule in photosystem II are energized by light. They are then transferred to electron acceptors in an electron transport chain.

19. D: Crassulacean acid metabolism (CAM) photosynthesis occurs in plants that grow where water loss must be minimized, such as cacti. These plants open their stomata and fix CO_2 at night. During the day, stomata are closed, reducing water loss. Thus, photosynthesis can proceed without water loss.

20. B: DNA wrapped around histone proteins is called chromatin. In a eukaryotic cell, DNA is always associated with protein; it is not "naked" as with prokaryotic cells.

21. C: The diploid chromosome number for humans is 46. After DNA duplication but before the first cell division of meiosis, there are 92 chromatids (46 chromosomes). After meiosis I is completed, the chromosome number is halved and equals 23. Each daughter cell is haploid, but the chromosomes are still paired (sister chromatids). During meiosis II, the two sister chromatids of each chromosome separate, resulting in 23 haploid chromosomes per germ cell.

22. D: In prophase I, homologous chromosomes pair up and form tetrads. The arms of the chromosomes can break and recombine to create new genetic variations, a process called crossing over. At the end of meiosis, in telophase I and cytokinesis, the tetrads split up. The cell divides into two daughter cells that each contain one chromosome from each pair. Each daughter cell contains a unique combination of chromosomes that is different from both the mother cell and its cognate daughter cell.

23. C: Although there are two cell divisions in meiosis, DNA replication occurs only once. It occurs in interphase I, before M phase begins.

24. B: The synaptonemal complex is a protein-based structure that is required for synapsis and recombination of homologous chromosomes. It provides a framework that aligns and stabilizes the chromosomes during synapsis. It is also required for the formation of chiasmata, where crossing over occurs. It is formed in the zygotene phase of prophase I (the second of five phases of prophase I) and disassembled during the diplotene stage (the fourth phase of prophase I). Therefore, it only exists during prophase I, which can also be referred to as prophase of meiosis I.

25. C: Genes code for proteins, and genes are discrete lengths of DNA on chromosomes. An allele is a variant of a gene (different DNA sequence). In diploid organisms, there may be two versions of each gene.

26. D: The enzyme helicase unwinds DNA. It depends on several other proteins to make the unwinding run smoothly, however. Single-strand binding protein holds the single-stranded DNA in place, and topoisomerase helps relieve tension at the replication fork.

27. D: DNA is composed of nucleotides joined together in long chains. Nucleotides are composed of a pentose sugar, a phosphate group, and a nitrogenous base. The bases form the "rungs" of the ladder at the core of the DNA helix, and the pentose-phosphates are on its outside, or backbone.

28. B: DNA replication begins with a short segment of RNA (not DNA). DNA polymerase cannot begin adding nucleotides without an existing piece of RNA (a primer).

29. A: DNA synthesis on the lagging strand forms short segments called Okazaki fragments. Because DNA polymerase can only add nucleotides in the $5' \rightarrow 3'$ direction, lagging strand synthesis is discontinuous. The final product is formed when DNA ligase joins Okazaki fragments together.

30. D: Each time a cell divides, a few base pairs of DNA at the end of each chromosome are lost. Telomerase is an enzyme that uses a built-in template to add a short sequence of DNA over and over at the end of chromosomes—a sort of protective "cap". This prevents the loss of genetic material with each round of DNA replication.

31. D: DNA polymerase does not match base pairs with 100% fidelity. Some level of mismatching is present for all DNA polymerases, and this is a source of mutation in nature. Cells have mechanisms of correcting base pair mismatches, but they do not fix all of them.

32. C: Insertions and deletions cause frameshift mutations. These mutations cause all subsequent nucleotides to be displaced by one position, and thereby cause all the amino acids to be different than they would have been if the mutation had not occurred.

33. A: Transcription is the process of creating an RNA strand from a DNA template. All forms of RNA—for example, mRNA, tRNA, and rRNA—are products of transcription.

34. C: The *lac* operon controls transcription of the gene that allows bacteria to metabolize lactose. It codes for both structural and regulatory proteins and includes promoter and operator sequences.

35. E: Operons are common in prokaryotes. They are units of DNA that control the transcription of DNA and code for their own regulatory proteins as well as structural proteins.

36. D: Conjugation is direct transfer of plasmid DNA between bacteria through a pilus. The F plasmid contains genes that enable bacteria to produce pili and is often the DNA that is transferred between bacteria.

37. D: In the lysogenic cycle, viral DNA gets incorporated into the DNA of the host. A virus in this dormant stage is called a provirus. Eventually, an external cue may trigger the virus to excise itself and begin the lytic cycle.

38. B: In the lytic cycle, viruses use host resources to produce viral DNA and proteins in order to create new viruses. In the process, they destroy the host cell by lysing it. For this reason, actively replicating viruses are said to be in the lytic cycle.

39. C: Plasmids are small circular pieces of DNA found in bacteria. Plasmids are widely used in recombinant DNA technology. They are cut with restriction enzymes and DNA of interest is ligated to them. They can then easily be used to transform bacteria.

Organismal Biology

40. D: The ovary houses the ovules in a flower. Pollen grains fertilize ovules to create seeds, and the ovary matures into a fruit.

41. C: Gymnosperms reproduce by producing pollen and ovules, but they do not have flowers. Instead, their reproductive structures are cones or cone-like structures.

42. E: Stomata are openings on leaves that allow for gas exchange, which is essential for photosynthesis. Stomata are surrounded by guard cells, which open and close based on their turgidity.

43. A: Monocots differ from dicots in that they have one cotyledon, or embryonic leaf in their embryos. They also have parallel veination, fibrous roots, petals in multiples of three, and a random arrangement of vascular bundles in their stems.

44. E: Nonvascular plants do not produce seeds like angiosperms and gymnosperms do. They generally reproduce sexually, but produce spores instead of seeds.

45. C: Angiosperms produce flowers, with ovules inside of ovaries. The ovaries become a fruit, with seeds inside. Gymnosperms have naked seeds that are produced in cones or cone like structures. Monocots and dicots/eudicots are subgroups within angiosperms. While they are technically a correct answer, the best answer is angiosperms.

46. A: The central, supporting pillar of the tree is known as heartwood. Heartwood does not function in the transport of water, and even though it is dead, it will not decay or lose strength as long as the outer layers remain intact.

47. D: The phloem is the pipeline through which carbohydrates are transported to the roots. It is located outside of the xylem and lives for only a short time before becoming part of the outer bark.

48. B: In ferns, the mature diploid plant is called a sporophyte. Sporophytes undergo meiosis to produce spores, which develop into gametophytes, which produce gametes.

49. C: Alternation of generations means the alternation between the diploid and haploid phases in plants.

50. B: Anthers produce microspores (the male gametophytes of flowering plants), which undergo meiosis to produce pollen grains.

51. C: In flowering plants, the anthers house the male gametophytes (which produce sperm) and the pistils house the female gametophytes (which produce eggs). Eggs and sperm are haploid. All other tissues are solely diploid.

52. A: The plant hormone ethylene is responsible for fruit ripening. Auxins are involved in a range of processes involving growth and development.

53. C: Cytokinins stimulate cell division (cytokinesis) and have been found to delay senescence (aging). They are often sprayed on cut flowers and fruit to prolong their shelf life.

54. C: Day-neutral plants are not affected by day length in their flowering times. Rather, they respond to other environmental cues, like temperature and water.

55. C: Plants exchange gases with the environment through pores in their leaves called stomata. Animals exchange gases with the environment in many different ways: small animals like flatworms exchange gases through their skin; insects use tracheae; and many species use lungs.

56. B: Platelets are cell fragments that are involved in blood clotting. Platelets are the site for the blood coagulation cascade. Its final steps are the formation of fibrinogen, which, when cleaved, forms fibrin, the "skeleton" of the blood clot.

57. A: The large intestine's main function is the reabsorption of water into the body to form solid waste. It also allows for the absorption of vitamin K produced by microbes living inside the large intestine.

58. D: When Ca^{2+} channels open, calcium enters the axon terminal and causes synaptic vesicles to release neurotransmitter into the synaptic cleft.

59. C: In a positive feedback loop, an action intensifies a chain of events that, in turn, intensify the conditions that caused the action beyond normal limits. Nursing stimulates lactation, which promotes nursing. Contractions during childbirth and sexual orgasm are examples of positive feedback.

60. D: Mammals often warm themselves by altering their metabolism. Shivering warms animals due to the heat generated by contractions in trunk muscles.

61. A: HCG (human chorionic gonadotropin) is secreted by the trophoblast, part of the early embryo, following implantation in the uterus. GnRH (gonadotropin-releasing hormone) is secreted by the hypothalamus, while LH (luteinizing hormone) and FSH (follicle-stimulating hormone) are secreted by the pituitary gland. GnRH stimulates the production of LH and FSH. LH stimulates ovulation and the production of estrogen and progesterone by the ovary in females, and testosterone production in males. FSH stimulates maturation of the ovarian follicle and estrogen production in females and sperm production in males.

62. E: The placenta secretes progesterone and estrogen once a pregnancy is established. The placenta secretes hCG early in pregnancy and in small doses throughout the pregnancy.

63. C: In oogenesis, meiosis I produces a secondary oocyte and a polar body. Both the first polar body and the secondary oocyte undergo meiosis II. The secondary oocyte divides to produce the ovum and the second polar body.

64. D: Positive feedback from rising levels of estrogen in the menstrual cycle produces a sudden surge of luteinizing hormone (LH). This high level triggers ovulation.

65. E: The testes contain hundreds of seminiferous tubules for the production of sperm, or spermatogenesis. This requires 64-72 days. Leydig cells surround the seminiferous tubules and produce male sex hormones called androgens, the most important of which is testosterone. Semen is made in the seminal vesicles, prostate gland, and other glands. Sperm are transferred to the penis via the epididymis, where they become motile, and thence through the vas deferens.

66. B: The gastrula is formed from the blastocyst, which contains a bilayered embryonic disc. One layer of this disc's inner cell mass further subdivides into the epiblast and the hypoblast, resulting in the three primary germ layers (endoderm, mesoderm, ectoderm).

67. C: In birds and reptiles, the yolk sac contains the yolk, the main source of nutrients for the embryo. In humans, the yolk sac is empty and embryos receive nutrition through the placenta. However, the yolk sac forms part of the digestive system and is where the earliest blood cells and blood vessels are formed.

68. D: A lineage map describes the fates of cells in the early embryo; in other words, it tells which germ layer different cells will occupy. In some small organisms such as the nematode *Caenorhabditis elegans*, all of the adult cells can be traced back to the egg. A lineage map is not a mechanism of embryo development, but rather a tool for describing it.

69. B: The gastrula is the first three-layered stage of the embryo, containing the ectoderm, mesoderm, and endoderm.

70. C: In birds, the invagination of gastrulation occurs along a line called the primitive streak. Cells migrate to the primitive streak, and the embryo becomes elongated. .

71. D: You would know the snapdragon has an Rr genotype, but you would not know whether its parents had an Rr genotype or a combination of Rr and rr or RR and rr.

72. D: All the plants will be tall, and flower color will assort independently of stature. In a $Pp \times Pp$ cross, $\frac{3}{4}$ of the progeny will be purple.

73. E: Two genes next to each other (or within a specified distance) are said to be linked. Linked genes do not follow the law of independent assortment because they are too close together to be segregated from each other in meiosis.

74. C: If the genes are linked, there would be only two kinds of alleles produced by the F1 plants: Rw and rW. A Punnett square with these alleles reveals that half the progeny will have both an R and a W allele.

75. C: Half of the boys will receive the color-blind allele from the mother, and the other half will receive the normal one. All the girls will receive the color-blind allele from the father; half of them will also get one from the mother, while the other half will get the normal one. Therefore, half the children will be colorblind.

76. E: An individual with AB blood is tolerant to both the A carbohydrate on red blood cells and the B carbohydrate as "self" and can therefore accept any of the 4 different blood types.

77. B: When more than one gene contributes to a trait, inheritance of that trait is said to be polygenic. This type of inheritance does not follow the rules of Mendelian genetics.

78. B: For this situation, one of the parental genotypes must be either I^Ai or I^AI^A. This rules out options A and E. Of the remaining options, the only one that would work is the one where the type A parent is paired with a parent with at least one i in their genotype. This leaves option B as the only possible combination from this selection.

Population Biology

79. D: Biomass pyramids are graphical representations of the total amount of organic matter present within an ecosystem. Most terrestrial ecosystems have the traditional pyramid presentation with the smallest point at the top. In aquatic ecosystems however, the pyramid is often inverted with the major producer within the system having a smaller biomass than the consumers above it. This is generally because the producers, often phytoplankton in these cases, produce multiple generations quickly while having shorter individual lives. These are then quickly devoured by the substantially larger mass of zooplankton.

80. A: Vultures eat carrion, or dead animals, so they are considered scavengers. Detritivores are heterotrophs that eat decomposing organic matter such as leaf litter. They are usually small.

81. B: Carbon is released in the form of CO_2 through respiration, burning, and decomposition.

82. D: Most nitrogen is in the atmosphere in the form of N_2. In order for it to be used by living things, it must be fixed by nitrogen-fixing bacteria. These microorganisms convert N_2 to ammonia, which then forms NH_4^+ (ammonium).

83. D: Type I curves describe species in which most individuals survive to middle age, after which deaths increase. Dolphins have few offspring, provide extended care to the young, and live a long time.

84. B: The growth rate is equal to the difference between births and deaths divided by population size. In this case, $r = \frac{110-10}{1,000} = 0.1$.

85. A: Pioneer species colonize vacant habitats, and the first such species in a habitat demonstrate primary succession. Succession on rock or lava often begins with lichens. Lichens need very little organic material and can erode rock into soil to provide a growth substrate for other organisms.

86. B: Secondary succession occurs when a habitat has been entirely or partially disturbed or destroyed by abandonment, burning, storms, etc.

87. B: Epiphytes are plants that grow in the canopy of trees, and the tropical rain forest has a rich canopy because of its density and extensive moisture.

88. A: Transportation by humans or human-associated means is not considered a natural dispersal process.

89. D: Within a habitat, there is a maximum number of individuals that can continue to thrive, known as the habitat's carrying capacity. When the population size approaches this number, population growth will stop.

90. B: Density-dependent limiting factors on population growth are factors that vary with population density. Pollution from a factory, volcanic eruptions, frosts, and fires do not vary as a function of population size. Waste products, however, increase with population density and could limit further population increases.

91. B: Character displacement means that, although similar, species in the same habitat have evolved characteristics that reduce competition between them. It occurs as a result of resource partitioning.

92. A: Because both species benefit, lichens constitute an example of mutualism.

93. D: Natural selection was Darwin's idea, not Lamarck's. Mendel discovered that genes are the basic units of inheritance. Lamarck's observation about use and disuse is true, although he did not connect it with the underlying mechanism of natural selection.

94. A: Stabilizing selection is a form of selection in which a particular trait, such as weight, becomes stable within a population. It results in reduced genetic variability, and the disappearance of alleles for extreme traits. Over time, the most common phenotypes survive.

95. C: Disruptive selection occurs when the environment favors alleles for extreme traits. In the example, seasonal changes can make different types of food available at different times of the year, favoring the large or small bills.

96. A: Gene flow, which is the movement of alleles between populations through migration and interbreeding, can change allele frequencies and promote evolutionary change. Options B-D all describe conditions that would lead to genetic equilibrium, where no evolution would occur.

97. C: Hybridization between two different species would result in more genetic variation than sexual reproduction within a species.

98. C: According to Hardy-Weinberg equilibrium, $p + q = 1$ and $p^2 + 2pq + q^2 = 1$. In this scenario, $q^2 = 0.25$, so $q = 0.5$. p must also be 0.5.

99. B: Phyletic gradualism is the view that evolution occurs at a more or less constant rate. Contrary to this view, punctuated equilibrium holds that evolutionary history consists of long periods of stasis punctuated by geologically short periods of evolution. This theory predicts that there will be few fossils revealing intermediate stages of evolution, whereas phyletic gradualism views the lack of intermediate-stage fossils as a deficit in the fossil record that will resolve when enough specimens are collected.

100. B: Adaptive radiation is the evolution of several species from a single ancestor. It occurs when a species colonizes a new area and members diverge geographically as they adapt to somewhat different conditions.

101. D: In coevolution, one species responds to new adaptations in another. Coevolution occurs between predator and prey, pathogens and the immune systems of animals, and plants and their pollinators.

102. E: Structures are homologous because they derive from a common ancestor. Insects do not share a common ancestor with birds and mammals. Birds and mammals share a reptile ancestor.

103. B: The bottleneck effect occurs when populations undergo a dramatic decrease in size. It could be due to natural or artificial causes.

104. A: The first living organisms probably had not yet evolved the ability to synthesize their own organic molecules for food. They were probably heterotrophs that consumed nutrition from the "organic soup."

105. C: Analogous structures do not reveal anything about common ancestors between species. They are simply features that arise due to adapting to similar ecological conditions.

106. C: Habituation is a learned behavior that teaches an animal to ignore meaningless or neutral stimuli.

107. D: Pheromones are chemicals used by animals for communication. They are released by certain individuals and elicit behavioral changes in other individuals.

108. B: Imprinting is a program for acquiring a behavior if an appropriate stimulus is given during a critical time period early in life. Salmon are imprinted with the odors of their birthplace after hatching.

109. C: *Homo sapiens* are thought to have evolved in Africa approximately 100,000 years ago.

110. D: Prolonging the life of individuals in a current population will lead to an older age composition. An increased birth rate will cause population growth, but a greater proportion will be younger, not older.

111. E: With many species, factors like food, space, and predation have large effects on reproduction. Humans are able to control or at least affect many of these challenges, as well as the reproductive process itself, so other factors like education, religion, wealth, and access to health care are more significant factors in birth rates.

112. E: Mercury is a fat-soluble pollutant and can be stored in body tissues. Animals higher up the food chain, which eat other animals, are most likely to accumulate mercury in their bodies.

113. D: Air pollution would not be a direct result of clear-cutting forests. Air pollution would be an indirect consequence, because the CO_2 contained in the wood is released when the wood is either burnt or decomposed. Deforestation contributes to an estimated ten percent of all emissions. With less trees to reduce CO_2 already present in the air, clear-cutting results in increased atmospheric CO_2, as well as localized climate change. Due to deforestation roots lose strength and cause the soil to become loose, this combined with the lack of trees and shrubs to absorb water during heavy rainfall, rapid runoff occurs causing flooding and erosion. This can develop into mudslides such as the 2017 Sierra Leone mudslide disaster which resulted in the death of 1,141 people and left 3,000 homeless. Transpiration from trees in the tropical rain forest contributes largely to cloud formation and rain, so rainfall decreases because of clear-cutting, resulting in desertification.

114. B: When sulfur dioxide and nitrogen dioxide mix with water and other substances in the atmosphere, they produce sulfuric acid and nitric acid. These acids kill plants and animals when they reach the surface of the earth.

115. E: *Genetic engineering* is a general term to describe altering DNA sequences through adding or removing pieces of DNA from a native sequence. In the earliest genetic engineering processes, restriction enzymes were used to perform this "clipping" function, but other methods have been devised and are in use today. Current technologies include those using nucleases (such as CRISPR-Cas9, zinc-finger nucleases, or TALENs) or site-specific recombinases.

Online Resources

Due to our efforts to try to keep this book to a manageable length, we've created a link that will give you access to all of your online resources:

mometrix.com/resources719/abctebio

It's Your Moment, Let's Celebrate It!

Share your story @mometrixtestpreparation